ADAPTIVE PREFERENCES
AND WOMEN'S EMPOWERMENT

Studies in Feminist Philosophy is designed to showcase cutting-edge monographs and collections that display the full range of feminist approaches to philosophy, that push feminist thought in important new directions, and that display the outstanding quality of feminist philosophical thought.

STUDIES IN FEMINIST PHILOSOPHY
Cheshire Calhoun, Series Editor

ADAPTIVE PREFERENCES AND WOMEN'S EMPOWERMENT

Serene J. Khader

OXFORD
UNIVERSITY PRESS

OXFORD
UNIVERSITY PRESS

Oxford University Press, Inc., publishes works that further
Oxford University's objective of excellence
in research, scholarship, and education.

Oxford   New York
Auckland   Cape Town   Dar es Salaam   Hong Kong   Karachi
Kuala Lumpur   Madrid   Melbourne   Mexico City   Nairobi
New Delhi   Shanghai   Taipei   Toronto

With offices in
Argentina   Austria   Brazil   Chile   Czech Republic   France   Greece
Guatemala   Hungary   Italy   Japan   Poland   Portugal   Singapore
South Korea   Switzerland   Thailand   Turkey   Ukraine   Vietnam

Published by Oxford University Press, Inc.
198 Madison Avenue, New York, New York 10016

www.oup.com

Oxford is a registered trademark of Oxford University Press

Library of Congress Cataloging-in-Publication Data
Khader, Serene J.
Adaptive preferences and women's empowerment/Serene J. Khader.
p.   cm.—(Studies in feminist philosophy)
Includes bibliographical references.
ISBN 978-0-19-977787-7 (pbk. : alk. paper)—ISBN 978-0-19-977788-4 (hbk. : alk. paper)
1. Well-being—Social aspects.   2. Well-being—Psychological aspects.
3. Preferences (Philosophy)   4. Oppression (Psychology)
5. Choice (Psychology)   6. Women—Developing countries—Social conditions.
7. Feminism.   I. Title.
HN25.K52 2011
179.7—dc22   2010048488

1 3 5 7 9 8 6 4 2
Printed in the United States of America

For my dear friend, Anna Tverskoy

1978–2009

CONTENTS

ACKNOWLEDGMENTS

I owe an enormous intellectual and personal debt to Eva Feder Kittay, who has nurtured and challenged the ideas in this book since I was a first-year graduate student. Uma Narayan's thought and mentorship have also contributed significantly to the formulation of the ideas in these pages. The kernel of this book was a dissertation at Stony Brook University, and I am grateful to the other members of my dissertation committee, Mary C. Rawlinson, Clyde Lee Miller, and Eduardo Mendieta, for their criticism as well as their support. I also thank Alison Jaggar for her encouragement at a couple of key moments in the development of this book.

My work has benefited from the comments of audiences at the Human Development and Capability Association and the Association for Feminist Ethics and Social Theory, as well as from the anonymous reviewers of this manuscript.

Thanks to my colleagues at Wheaton College for offering me such a collegial work environment in which to write this book and to my undergraduate research assistant, Alyssa Colby, for her assistance in the preparation of the manuscript.

Finally, I am especially indebted to my parents for their support, and for teaching me what it was to love knowledge. My sincere gratitude goes also to my sister and brother and a number of wonderful friends. They have nourished this project through invaluable conversation and companionship.

ADAPTIVE PREFERENCES
AND WOMEN'S EMPOWERMENT

INTRODUCTION: ADAPTIVE PREFERENCES AND GLOBAL JUSTICE

As a woman who is organized you feel...stronger with more courage to be able to speak, because before, when you had never been organized, you don't know what organization is, you are scared to speak. How were you going to speak to someone you respect? You can't. But now...I've seen the change that I've made. Before I was very timid and now I'm not; I was too shy to talk with other women, but now I feel different. I have changed.

(SONIA, *Quoted in Rowlands* 1997, 78)

A woman on her own, without anyone to help her understand the situation she is living in, she couldn't do anything....If we met here, just feeling things we feel inside without expressing it outside...but no, through training, you start to talk about what you feel, about what you see, with the other women. I haven't forgotten when she [activist Maria Esther Ruiz] told us in a meeting that she had some friends...."I have some friends that can help me to study...". That was to encourage us to get organized, so that we would realize that getting together and talking about problems would help us.

(ANONYMOUS WOMAN, *Quoted in Rowlands* 1997, 78)

Above are the words of two participants in a women's empowerment project initiated by the Programa Educativo de La Mujer (Women's Educational Project, PAEM) in rural Honduras in the 1980s and '90s. The general life situation the women describe having endured before coming to PAEM is common to many of the world's women—in both rich and poor countries. Before PAEM, the women lived with very limited senses of what they were capable of and faced limited opportunities for flourishing.[1] The particular women in the epigraph lived in the poor but beautiful village of El Pital, where they faced daily struggles for basic well-being (Rowlands 1997, 74). In addition to poverty, these women lived with a "clear sexual division of labor and scanty social services" (Rowlands 1997, 67). Many of them had husbands who severely restricted their mobility and expected them to live in isolation from one another. Sonia, the PAEM participant who is the voice of the first epigraph, had a husband who left her locked in the house for most of the day while he was gone (Rowlands 1997, 68). Another PAEM participant describes herself as encountering "serious problems" in learning "how to leave the house" (Rowlands 1997, 81), and still another says that women "never used to get out of the house" (Rowlands 1997, 79) before PAEM. The limits on these women's opportunities for flourishing were significant and persistent.

Many of the women also seem to have internalized limiting views about what they were capable of. By some of the women of El Pital's own accounts, they acquiesced to their own deprivation before they became involved in PAEM programs. Some of them described themselves as previously having been "timid" and "afraid to speak" (Rowlands 1997, 77–78). One described herself as having felt as though she were "hardly worth anything" (Rowlands 1997, 77). The village's priest described the typical woman as not believing "she is entitled to certain rights and to defend them" (Rowlands 1997, 79). Maria Esther Ruiz, the Honduran activist who founded PAEM, describes the initial problem for PAEM participants as "the way they are devalued by themselves and society" (Rowlands 1997, 97). Jo Rowlands, an Oxfam researcher who interviewed these women and others from nearby communities described them as frequently seeing "poverty as their lot and hav[ing] a fatalistic attitude toward things that ha[d] to be overcome every time they act[ed]" (Rowlands 1997, 104).

This book is about what public institutions owe to people like the women of El Pital—people who seem to acquiesce to their own deprivation. Amartya Sen writes that "there is much evidence in history that acute inequalities often survive precisely by making allies out of the deprived" (Sen 1990, 126). The story of the women of El Pital suggests that Sen is right; oppressed and deprived people sometimes become complicit in perpetuating their own deprivation. In contemporary feminist philosophy and development ethics, self-depriving desires people form under unjust conditions are typically referred to as "adaptive preferences." People with adaptive preferences experience deprivation partly as a result of their own behaviors or desires—behaviors and desires that have been shaped by unjust social conditions.

We know that not all oppressed and deprived people resist their deprivation. This fact raises a number of questions for political philosophy. Should public institutions uncritically accept deprived people's existing desires in the name of respecting those people's capacities for choice or promoting cultural diversity? Was PAEM wrong to question the women of El Pital's self-subordinating beliefs and behaviors? Should PAEM have instead have refused to question the women's existing preferences on the grounds that the women were adults whose choices should be respected? At the other extreme, should public institutions simply override beliefs and behaviors that are deprivation-perpetuating? That is, should PAEM have forced women to leave their homes and participate in public life because that would have made their lives better? In this book, I suggest that we can answer all these questions in the negative. Public institutions need not choose between uncritically respecting adaptive preferences on one hand and flatly overriding them on the other. Nor must public institutions choose between valuing choice and cultural diversity and promoting deprived people's flourishing.

My project in this book is to offer what I call a "deliberative perfectionist approach" to public intervention in the lives of people with adaptive preferences, an approach that both prioritizes their flourishing *and* respects their right to lead the types of lives they want to lead. I attempt to show that people with adaptive preferences are simultaneously active choosers whose deeply held conceptions of the good deserve respect *and* participants in their own deprivation whose deprivation-perpetuating behaviors should be questioned. I also argue that there is a type of intervention in the lives of people with adaptive preferences that takes seriously both of these facts about people with adaptive preferences—that they are worthy sources of decisions about how to lead their lives and that they are vulnerable human beings whose flourishing needs support and attention. The women of El Pital accepted certain aspects of their own deprivation, but this does not mean that they were not reflective agents who could make meaningful decisions and care deeply about certain things. Still, the fact that the women of El Pital were reflective agents should not be taken to mean that their deprivation-perpetuating desires and behaviors were good for them. I argue in this book that public institutions should promote people's basic flourishing and that doing this requires public intervention in the lives of people with adaptive preferences. Yet this intervention need not be thought of as imposing an alien form of life on people who do not value their basic flourishing. Rather, the appropriate type of intervention can increase people's capacities to live in accordance with their deeply held desires for flourishing and their personal or cultural values.

My deliberative perfectionist approach is intended as a moral framework for this "appropriate type" of adaptive preference intervention. My approach permits representatives of public institutions, such as activists or development practitioners, to ask whether deprived people's preferences are consistent with human flourishing. Representatives of public institutions may treat desires and behaviors that seem inconsistent with a person's basic flourishing as suspect—that is, as worthy of scrutiny aimed at determining whether those desires and behaviors are likely to be adaptive. Development practitioners should interrogate such suspect preferences in order to understand the actual effects of those preferences on the flourishing of their bearers, and, in cases where preference transformation is appropriate, they should work *with* deprived people to come up with strategies for change.

Indeed, this is the type of intervention that PAEM engaged in with the women of El Pital. An activist from a nearby village, Maria Esther Ruiz, believed that the women of this community lacked both resources and power. She saw the women's acceptance of an unjust social order, not as an injunction to respect their desires for subordination, but rather as an invitation to engage these women as thinkers and deliberators who could be persuaded to choose more flourishing lives for themselves. She believed that they could imagine better lives for themselves on their own terms. The interventions she initiated were based on the belief that empowering the women to analyze and devise strategies for fighting their own subordination was the best way to change their lives (Rowlands 1997, 92–93). PAEM used reading materials based in local cultural values and a strong normative commitment to women's self-development to train women from El Pital to animate their own study circles—study circles that sometimes grew into educational circles on issues like reproductive health (Rowlands 1997, 96), sources of confidence to renegotiate relationships and resist their husbands' restrictions on their mobility (Rowlands 1997, 79–81), and the cores of income and food-generating activities (Rowlands 1997, 84). These interventions were not panaceas; the income-generating activities have not all been successful (Rowlands 1997, 74) and some of the women still face some (less severe) limitations on their mobility (Rowlands 1997, 80). And yet there is an important sense in which the women of El Pital have changed their lives by developing confidence to participate in public life. Deborah Eade, the Oxfam researcher who evaluated PAEM, noticed a change over the years where women went from covering their mouths and claiming they were too shy to speak to addressing whole crowds of other women (Rowlands 1997, 94).

The PAEM intervention in El Pital shows us that it is possible to treat people with adaptive preferences as involved in the undermining of their own flourishing and to engage them as agents who deserve to play a decisive role in determining the outcome of their lives. The deliberative perfectionist approach to adaptive preference intervention I offer in this book is an attempt to theorize the moral implications of interventions like PAEM's.

I have two more limited aims in this introduction. First, I sketch the book's argument in a fairly nontechnical way in hopes of illuminating its main points for readers who are not academic philosophers and providing a map of the book's argument for readers who are. Second, I show how my deliberative perfectionist approach responds to some of the key dilemmas facing attempts at a transnational feminist politics. Feminist theorists who want to write about the lives of third-world women and who endorse cross-cultural feminist interventions must be attentive to the various ways in which feminist theorizing about deprivation can function to obscure the agency of deprived people and misrepresent the causes of their deprivation. My second project in this introduction is thus to situate my deliberative perfectionist approach to adaptive preference intervention within a broader set of feminist concerns about women's agency and global justice.

Before I proceed to outline the book's argument and situate that argument within feminist conversations about global justice, I pause to make a few qualifying remarks about the terms and examples I use in the rest of this book. Specifically, I explain my usage of the terms "public institutions" and "third world" as well as my focus on examples of adaptive preferences held by third-world women. The deliberative perfectionist approach I offer in this book is intended to justify and guide adaptive preference-transforming interventions by representatives of public institutions. Readers may want to know what I mean by the term "public institution" here. Though I intend the term to include state actors, I use the term "public institution" in recognition of the fact that, in poor countries, many duties typically associated with the state in political philosophy are discharged by non-state actors. I intend the term "public institution" to include states in addition to non-state actors engaged in discharging state-like duties. These state-like non-state actors are often nongovernmental organizations (NGOs) charged with providing education for citizenship, basic social services, etc. in poor countries. I describe NGOs as public institutions both because they are entrusted with discharging state-like duties and because aid to governments is often disbursed through them.[2]

Though the term "third-world women" may strike many readers as outdated, I use it deliberately. One of my central reasons for using this term is my sense that neither of the key alternatives, "women from developing countries" or "women from the global South," accurately captures the geopolitical position of the women most frequently described in philosophical literature as possessors of adaptive preferences. I am uncomfortable with the term "women in developing countries," as it seems to suggest that traditional indicators reliably track a country's development—an assumption I am keen to reject, given that I reject the view that human flourishing can be reduced to access to income.[3] I am more comfortable with the term "women from the global South" and do occasionally use it.

However, I wonder whether the term "South" accurately captures the extent to which a defining feature of the South for many Westerners is the perception of the South as culturally backward. I believe this is a reason many feminists from the global South continue to use the term "third world"; they wish to emphasize that the perceived difference that marks them in the Western imaginary is not only a difference in income but a perceived hierarchical cultural difference. Since the approach I offer in this book is intended to be consistent with the claim that many non-Western cultural practices can promote objective human flourishing, I choose to retain a word that emphasizes that cultural difference and economic difference mark the countries we now typically refer to as the South. Finally, I choose to retain the term "third world" because I believe the numerical ranking explicit in it rhetorically frames global justice as a problem of severe *inequality* rather than poverty alone.[4]

I also wish to make a brief remark about my frequent use of preferences held by third-world women as examples of adaptive preferences. I have chosen to focus on adaptive preferences held by women in poor countries mostly because development interventions aimed at changing the adaptive preferences of third-world women are a common occurrence in our political world, and I am interested in asking about the conditions under which these real-world interventions might be morally justifiable. I do not believe that all third-world women have adaptive preferences and my position does not logically entail this belief. Nor do I believe that adaptive preferences are held exclusively by third-world women. It seems uncontroversial that women's adaptive preferences are part of the reason that patriarchal practices persist in the West. The justification of public intervention to transform adaptive preferences that I develop in this book logically justifies public intervention to transform the basic well-being affecting preferences of women in rich countries as well as poor countries.

What Public Institutions Owe to People with Adaptive Preferences: An Overview of the Argument

This book attempts to answer the question of what public institutions owe to people with adaptive preferences. It has two main aims: to explain why we should want an explicit definition of adaptive preference and to offer an approach to identifying and responding to adaptive preferences in practice based on a perfectionist definition of adaptive preference.

Why We Need an Explicit Definition of Adaptive Preference

One reason we need an explicit definition of adaptive preference is simply that we lack conceptual clarity about what adaptive preferences are. Earlier in this introduction, I asked what public institutions should do for women "like the women of El Pital." But to say that people with adaptive preferences are people "like the women of El Pital" is to gloss over the fact that ethicists and development practitioners constantly discuss adaptive preferences without being clear about what they are. Adaptive preference seems to have become a topic of discussion in development ethics in the 1980s, where the problem of adaptive preference was frequently discussed as a challenge to utilitarian theories of social distribution. The basic claim of these utilitarian theories is that we can measure how well people are doing by measuring how well their desires are satisfied. Theorists of adaptive preference, most notably Jon Elster (1987) and Sen (1988, 45; 2002, 634), problematized the metric of desire satisfaction by claiming that some people would *not* be doing well if their desires were satisfied. Desire satisfaction would "attach too small a value" to the "losses" of well-being "suffered by the dominated housewife, the hardened unemployed or the over-exhausted coolie" (Sen 1988, 45–46). The underlying idea seemed to be that it was counterintuitive to take the satisfaction of certain of desires as indicative of well-being.

But what was this class of desires? Sen was more interested in criticizing utilitarianism than answering this question, so he let our intuitive reactions to some examples make his case. Certainly, satisfying the desire for exhaustion of the over-exhausted coolie does not cause the coolie to achieve well-being, or so Sen expected our intuitions to lead us to conclude. Elster, on the other hand, explicitly defined adaptive preferences as preferences whereby a person unconsciously downgraded her desires for things she could not access, like the fox in the fable who believes the grapes he cannot reach are sour (Elster 1987, 117–119).

The concept Elster named is now widely discussed in development ethics and feminist philosophy, but the notion of adaptive preference animating contemporary ethical debates is not identical to Elster's. Martha Nussbaum offers a host of examples of supposedly adaptive preferences, many of which do not fit Elster's definition—for instance, the story of Vasanti, a poor Indian woman who remains in an abusive relationship because she believes she is condemned to suffer, not because she thinks a non-suffering life is not worth having (Nussbaum 2001, 112). Sen continues to discuss examples of adaptive preference that also fail to meet Elster's criteria—like people who *consciously* adjust their preferences. For example, he groups *deciding* that "it is silly to bemoan" one's lack of political freedom and using "heroic efforts" to be happy despite caste or race oppression with "coming to terms with adversities" (Sen 2002, 634).[5]

Beyond these theoretical discussions, we find attempts to describe what adaptive preferences would look like in real people. Sabina Alkire worries that people's adaptive preferences will introduce bias into participatory evaluations of well-being. She notes that poor women in Kerala highly value their roles as wives and mothers and that some scholars have asked whether this valuing is not simply an adaptation to a lack of opportunity outside the household and customs that place a high value on women's honor (Alkire 2007a, 20). Marilyn Friedman describes as adaptive the preferences of women who endorse "traditional norms of femininity only because they live under circumstances that penalize contrary choices" (Friedman 2003, 24–25). Deepa Narayan writes that a real-life case of adaptive preference would look like this: "a woman's perception of herself and her world may be so skewed by her circumstances and cultural upbringing that she may say and believe that she genuinely prefers things that she would not prefer if she were aware of other possibilities" (D. Narayan 2005, 34).

A truly diverse set of preferences has been grouped together under the adaptive preference rubric. We have preferences that are formed by conscious (Sen) and unconscious processes (Elster), as well as preferences described as adaptive without any discussion of whether they were consciously formed (Alkire, Friedman, and D. Narayan). We have preferences that seem to exist because of a lack of options (Friedman and Alkire) and preferences that seem to be formed because of a lack of awareness (D. Narayan). We have preferences that undermine or "skew" people's entire senses of self (D. Narayan and Nussbaum) and preferences that may not (Elster and parts of Sen).

It is puzzling to try to figure out what all of the foregoing preferences have in common. They seem to be shaped by social conditions and they seem to be bad indicators of what the well-being of their bearers would require. It seems right to say that if we want to know what the "dominated housewife" needs, we should not assume that her desire to be dominated straightforwardly answers the question. But is this intuitive definition sufficient to guide development practice? If development practitioners and activists are going to attempt to improve the lives of people with adaptive preferences, they need to know what adaptive preferences are.

A second reason that we need an explicit definition of adaptive preference is that without one, development practitioners are likely to identify adaptive preferences by consulting their personal intuitions. We should not expect individuals' intuitions to reliably identify adaptive preferences in practice.. Readers interested in what is wrong with authorizing development practitioners to identify adaptive preferences according to their personal intuitions should consult Chapter 1. I argue there that practitioners who rely on their intuitions alone to identify adaptive preferences are likely to misunderstand the causes of people's adaptive preferences or see adaptive preferences where none exist. Attempts to identify adaptive preferences in practice are susceptible to some basic types of confusion. To identify another person's adaptive preferences and attempt to respond to them is to make judgments about the effects of—and reasons behind—her behavior. In many cases, it is also to make such judgments across differences in class, culture, or gender. Activists and development practitioners who attempt to identify adaptive preferences engage in a complex, high-stakes practice of making judgments about those who are different from them. We do not always know why other people do what they do or how their behaviors affect them, and this difficulty is magnified when their life-contexts differ significantly from our own. In Chapter 1, I identify three "occupational hazards" of attempts to identify and respond to adaptive preferences—three ways real-life attempts at understanding adaptive preferences are likely to go wrong. Two of these occupational hazards involve misunderstanding the reasons behind people's adaptive preferences. I call these "psychologizing the structural" and "misidentifying trade-offs." Psychologizing the structural is treating people's beliefs and attitudes—that is, their psychologies—as the proximate causes of their deprivation. There are cases where people's beliefs and attitudes are the main cause of their oppression or deprivation, cases where people's beliefs and attitudes are only one cause of it, and cases where people's beliefs and attitudes play only an attenuated role in sustaining their deprivation.

Imagine that the husbands of the women of El Pital did not restrict their mobility—say, the women did not leave their houses because they were trained in norms urging female seclusion by mothers who came from a different generation in which female mobility was strictly punished by men. If this were the situation of the women of El Pital, their adaptive preferences would fall into the first group I described above; their beliefs and attitudes would be the primary cause of their deprivation, and changing their beliefs and attitudes would be the best way to promote their flourishing. The actual case of the women of El Pital seems to fall into the second group I described; the women's beliefs and attitudes were *part* of the cause of their lack of mobility. By changing their attitudes, the women were able to begin negotiating with their husbands, but their changed attitudes did not eliminate barriers to their mobility. Their husbands retained significant control over them despite the women's increased resistant consciousness. Now imagine a third case—where the women of El Pital are chafing at restrictions on their mobility but remain in the house because all the roads are washed out by rain; the women in this case are unlikely to experience improvements in their flourishing because of a consciousness-raising activity, because—quite simply—they need better roads, not better self-esteem. The attitudes of the women who lack mobility because of the absences of roads play only a much attenuated role—if any role at all—in maintaining their lack of mobility. Psychologizing the structural means mistakenly treating the women in this third group as though it is their beliefs, rather than social structures, that need to be changed. In practice, we should want to sort out preferences in this third group from preferences in the first and second groups; we will endorse ineffective and condescending interventions if we do not.

Another type of mistake development practitioners may make if they rely on their intuitions is that of "misidentifying trade-offs." The error here is similar to that of psychologizing the structural in that it involves misunderstanding the particular character of people's adaptive preferences. But where psychologizing the structural is about inappropriately treating the beliefs and attitudes of deprived people as the central cause of their deprivation, misidentifying trade-offs is about failing to see that adaptive preferences sometimes involve accepting less of one good to attain more of another. Those who cannot access flourishing in all domains of life, may be forced to sacrifice basic flourishing in one domain to achieve it in another. Imagine now that the women of El Pital do not leave the house very much only because their husbands will beat them if they do not. Here, the women may consciously trade flourishing in one arena of life (mobility) for flourishing in another (bodily health or freedom from violence). A development practitioner who approached these women under the assumption that their problem was a lack of value for mobility would ignore the extent to which values other than the value of mobility are implicated in the women's behavior. Such a practitioner would propose an intervention in the wrong domain of life; what these women likely need instead is a health, relationship negotiation, or income-producing intervention.

A third hazard of allowing development practitioners to identify adaptive preferences intuitively does not involve misunderstanding the reasons for people's adaptive preferences. Rather, it involves of seeing adaptive preferences where none exist. I call this occupational hazard "confusing difference with deprivation." Confusing difference with deprivation is treating unfamiliar preferences that are fully compatible with flourishing as though they were adaptive preferences. It is likely to occur when a development practitioner fails to understand the contextual meaning of a preference, or when a practitioner assumes that the way of flourishing to which she is accustomed is the only way. Imagine, for a moment, that the women of El Pital repeatedly talk about their desire to submit to the will of God. We can see a practitioner interpreting these comments as evidence of a fatalistic attitude that prevents women from resisting their oppression. The practitioner might think that these women only want to submit to the will of God because they have never been able to direct the courses of their own lives. We can imagine the practitioner being right about this, but we can also imagine her being dead wrong. For instance, the women of El Pital may believe that God wants them to flourish and that submitting to God's will means struggling for their own survival. Educational texts put together by PAEM send the message that God wants women to be empowered (Rowlands 1997, 107–109), so it is not too difficult to imagine women whose desire to submit to God promotes, rather than impedes, their flourishing. But a secular practitioner who simply consulted her personal intuitions in order to determine which preferences needed transforming might miss the positive effects of the women's religious beliefs on their flourishing.

Without an explicit definition of adaptive preference, representatives of public institutions are free to simply consult their personal intuitions to distinguish preferences that are reliable indicators of what deprived people need from ones that are not. In other words, deciding which preferences should be questioned because they are adaptive becomes a matter of development practitioner opinion. This can lead to morally objectionable outcomes; it can lead to treating people's preferences as adaptive just because they are different; and it can lead to ineffective interventions with inappropriate foci. There is a third reason that we need an explicit definition of adaptive preference, and it this: without a clear definition, development practitioners are likely to fall back on implausible commonsense ideas about adaptive preference that come with pernicious conceptual baggage; they suggest it is appropriate to treat people with adaptive preferences as incapable of making respect-worthy choices about their lives.

Two related commonsense conceptions of adaptive preference that we should reject are conceptions of adaptive preferences as autonomy deficits and conceptions of adaptive preferences as totally undermining an agent's self-worth. I argue against these conceptions in the second and third chapters, respectively. As I argue in the second chapter, adaptive preferences are often conceived as deficits of autonomy. In other words, we tend to think of adaptive preferences as preferences people did not choose to have. There are a number of reasons we might be inclined toward thinking of adaptive preferences as unchosen. We usually think that people's chosen conceptions of the good do a good job of telling us what their well-being would require. It would seem logical, then, if the underlying reason we think adaptive preferences are unreliable guides to people's needs were that people did not choose their adaptive preferences. Adaptive preferences are often described offhand as preferences that are "imposed" by social conditions on the people who have them, and imposition is the opposite of choice. Further, helping people move past their adaptive preferences is frequently described as giving people with adaptive preferences "real choices." If a person transforms her adaptive preferences by getting "real choices," it seems plausible to think of adaptive preferences as formed through some sort of false-choice process.

To see what it might look like to conceive adaptive preferences as choice deficits, we can return to our El Pital example. On an autonomy deficit view of adaptive preference, we might think that the women did not choose to think of themselves as unworthy of leaving the house, and we may think that this is why we do not see their initial preference not to leave their homes as a reliable guide to what their well-being would require. We might thus see their preference not to leave the house as somehow "imposed" or reflective of a lack of "real choice." However, there are real problems with treating adaptive preferences as unchosen. One of these problems is simply that it is incoherent to think of adaptive preferences as defined by their unchosen character. If we think that we can explain our intuition that adaptive preferences are not good guides to the needs of people who have them on the grounds that adaptive preferences are unchosen, then we should think that all unchosen preferences are unreliable guides to the needs of the people who have them. But we do not think this. There are plenty of unchosen preferences that we do not see as questionable indicators of people's well-being. If the women of El Pital uncritically decided to participate in public life because they lived in a society where women's participation in public life was the norm, we would not therefore think of their desire for mobility as adaptive.

Another problem with accepting the commonsense definition of adaptive preferences as unchosen is that it discourages us from treating people with adaptive preferences as the types of people who can make authoritative decisions about their own lives. To describe adaptive preferences as more "imposed" than other types of preferences is to ignore the fact that all of us have preferences that are shaped by our social conditions. To act as though having one's preferences shaped by social conditions is particular to deprived people is to put forward a conception of deprived people as less likely to make choices and reflect on their lives than people in positions of privilege. I see no good reason to credit this assumption. If development practitioners see people with adaptive preferences as passive bystanders in their own preference formation, they have little incentive to try to understand what deprived people's preferences mean to them and why they have the preferences they do. Further, we often think that people's capacity to make reflective choices is what protects them from being legitimate objects of coercion; public institutions should not flatly override the preferences of people who understand and identify with their preferences. Characterizing people with adaptive preferences as incapable of choice leads us toward seeing people with adaptive preferences as appropriate objects of coercion. If we see the women of El Pital as preferring to stay at home because they are incapable of choosing, we will be left with few arguments against coercing them.

Of course, having certain unchosen preferences does not turn a person into the type of being who is incapable of making choices. Even if we see adaptive preferences as unchosen preferences, it remains possible that people who are overall capable of choice can have certain preferences they did not choose to have. However, we cannot distinguish people's status as choosers from the chosenness of their preferences if we see adaptive preferences as affecting people's senses of self in a global way. The idea that adaptive preferences affect and undermine the *entire* selves of deprived people is the commonsense definition of adaptive preference I urge us to reject in the third chapter; this definition, too, is implausible and promotes morally objectionable attitudes toward people with adaptive preferences.

People with adaptive preferences are often described, and often describe themselves, as victims of a generalized belief that they are undeserving. We need look no farther for an instance of this than the narrative of the El Pital woman who says that she believed she was not worth much before her participation in PAEM (Rowlands 1997, 77) or the comment from Maria Esther Ruiz, PAEM's founder that women "devalue themselves" before they participate in empowerment programs (Rowlands 1997, 97). Like thinking of adaptive preferences as unchosen, it makes intuitive sense to think of people with adaptive preferences as lacking a sense that they are valuable. Why would a person not resist severe restrictions on her mobility? We might answer that it is because she does not have an adequate sense of self; if she had a sense of herself as a being with rights, she would not let other people push her around.

Despite the commonsense appeal of the notion that people with adaptive preferences lack general conceptions of themselves as worthy, I argue in the third chapter that we should think of adaptive preferences as *selectively* rather than *globally* affecting people's senses of self-entitlement. It is implausible that most deprived people have generally underdeveloped senses of self, so I suggest alternative ways of understanding adaptive preferences that do not require us to see the people who have them as lacking senses of self. Adaptive preferences sometimes affect only people's conceptions of self-worth relative to certain others or certain goods; indeed, women who begin to attend PAEM groups begin by being very critical of themselves *and each other* (Rowlands 1997, 95). This willingness to criticize other women suggests a sense of self-entitlement vis-à-vis other women, notwithstanding the lack of a sense of self-entitlement vis-à-vis men. It seems that what the PAEM women tend to describe as a general lack of self-worth is not a *complete* lack of it, since some of the women clearly think of themselves as superior to other women. Further, people with adaptive preferences may internalize negative self-concepts without this internalization being total or uniform; they may experience struggles within themselves to feel positively about themselves, and they may gain positive evaluations of aspects of their own identities through relationships with other people who are similarly oppressed or deprived. For instance, we can imagine women like those of El Pital having learned to view themselves positively as women through relationships with their mothers, and as continuing to look to the self-concepts generated by these relationships for self-worth—even while they are dominated by their husbands.

Moreover, a person may express a positive or ambivalent attitude toward her self-entitlement *through* her adaptive preferences. This will seem less puzzling if we acknowledge that there are often very real incentives for oppressed and deprived people to deprive themselves. Oppressed and deprived people are sometimes able to gain social recognition or achieve higher-order goals by impeding their own flourishing in certain domains of life. There are women all over the world who remain mostly in their homes like the women of El Pital but do so because adherence to norms of female seclusion increases their social status. It would be odd to describe a person who actively pursues social status as a person who does not experience herself as deserving—which is what a view of adaptive preferences as general deficits in self-worth would ask us to do.

It is not only that the commonsense view of adaptive preferences as general self-entitlement deficits is implausible; it also encourages us to take certain morally objectionable views of people with adaptive preferences. Development practitioners often describe transforming the lives of people with adaptive preferences as a matter of replacing deprived people's old senses of self or helping them to develop senses of self they previously lacked. I see this notion of development projects as creating senses of self for deprived people as mystical at best and morally problematic at worst. If people with adaptive preferences lack general senses of themselves as deserving, there are good reasons not to take their desires seriously. If people with adaptive preferences lack senses of self, it seems that they have no concept of what matters to them and thus no autonomous conceptions of the good that public institutions should attempt to respect. It is also disempowering to deprived people to have to work with development practitioners who are predisposed to treat all of their desires as suspect. Further, if we see adaptive preferences as making people's entire self-conceptions suspect, there is little reason to involve people with adaptive preferences in imagining better futures for themselves at all. If all of the desires of deprived people are self-undermining, any meaningful input by deprived people into the design of development projects is likely only to undercut those projects' success.

Thinking of adaptive preferences as global self-entitlement deficits occludes the possibility that people with adaptive preferences can come to adopt preferences that are consistent with their basic flourishing *and* consistent with their existing conceptions of what is important in life. If having adaptive preferences means not having a sense of self, or not having a respect-worthy sense of what matters and what one cares about, building strategies for preference transformation around the desires of deprived people is just a way of entrenching their deprivation. We should also be wary of strategies for adaptive preference intervention that discourage development practitioners from engaging people in designing responses to their own deprivation, because such strategies are likely to produce change that people with adaptive preferences do not *endorse*. Such strategies ask people to simply give up their existing senses of what matters to them in order to flourish, and they do so unnecessarily. Instead of asking deprived people to abandon their existing values, development practitioners should favor strategies that cultivate existing resistance and positive self-images on the part of people with adaptive preferences. They should do so for moral and pragmatic reasons; endorsement increases people's flourishing and increases the effectiveness of development interventions. People are more likely to adopt preferences consistent with flourishing if those preferences can be fit into their networks of existing values; the story of the women of El Pital embracing their own public self-representation for Catholic reasons is a case in point.

A Perfectionist Definition of Adaptive Preference and a Deliberative Perfectionist Approach to Adaptive Preference Intervention

In addition to explaining why we need a clear, non-autonomy-centered definition of adaptive preference, I offer a conception of adaptive preference that can guide more responsible adaptive preference interventions. This definition appears in the first chapter. I propose that we think of adaptive preferences as preferences inconsistent with basic flourishing that a person developed under conditions nonconducive to basic flourishing and that we expect her to change under conditions conducive to basic flourishing.

There are a few noteworthy contrasts between my definition of adaptive preference and the commonsense definitions of adaptive preference I discussed in the previous section. First, my definition of adaptive preference does not ask us to think of adaptive preferences as globally—or even very generally—affecting people's senses of themselves as deserving. Nothing in my definition excludes the possibility of a person having adapted some preferences but not others. We can imagine a woman who lives in a situation like that of El Pital who does not see herself as worthy of mobility but highly values her own nutrition and thus spends a large amount of her time engaged in subsistence agriculture behind her home. Indeed, my definition of adaptive preference does not say that adaptive preferences need to be experienced as self-esteem deficits at all. I have no doubt that some adaptive preferences are sustained by oppressed or deprived people's belief that they are unworthy; the El Pital women who describe themselves as afraid of speaking before people they see as more important than themselves are a case in point. But there are other forms of adaptive preference that do not involve the conscious perception that one is unworthy. For instance, some adaptive preferences may be based on simple lacks of information; we can imagine poor women in a situation like that of El Pital eating a nutritionally inadequate diet based on straightforward ignorance of the nutritional contents of their food.

A second noteworthy distinction between my definition of adaptive preference and the commonsense ones I listed in the last section is that I do not understand adaptive preferences as undermining people's capacities for autonomy. I believe that people can form adaptive preferences and remain autonomous agents with reflective capacities and senses of what matters to them. The definition of adaptive preference I offer is consistent with this belief. I define adaptive preferences as characterized by both substantive and procedural features; recall that adaptive preferences are preferences inconsistent with a person's basic flourishing that she developed under conditions hostile to her flourishing. Some adaptive preferences may be formed by nonautonomous processes, but many are not. Further, it is not the nonautonomy of the adaptive preferences formed by nonautonomous processes that makes those preferences worthy of public scrutiny. If nonautonomy is not the distinguishing feature of adaptive preference, we can avoid thinking of adaptive preferences as legitimately subject to coercive overriding and avoid thinking of people with adaptive preferences as lacking respect-worthy conceptions of what matters to them. If it is not autonomy deficiency that identifies adaptive preferences, we can coherently explain why some autonomy-deficient preferences strike us as adaptive while others do not; for instance, we can explain why the El Pital woman who accepts very limited mobility without questioning the norms of her society seems to have adaptive preferences whereas the woman who moves about freely without questioning the norms of her society does not.

This brings us to the third noteworthy difference between my definition of adaptive preference and other prevailing definitions: my conception of adaptive preference asks us to think of inconsistency with human flourishing as a defining feature of adaptive preferences. We can explain why unquestioning acceptance of norms of female seclusion strikes us as an adaptive preference while unquestioning acceptance of norms of female mobility does not by pointing out that the former preference is inconsistent with basic flourishing. I argue in this book that an adaptive preference has to sustain a form of life that is bad for a person. This is part of why the definition of adaptive preference put forth in this book qualifies as perfectionist. Moral perfectionists believe that there is an objective good for human beings and that this good lies in flourishing—developing and living in accordance with human nature. My approach says that one reason we think of adaptive preferences as bad guides to the needs of the people who have them is that there is an objective quality to people's needs for flourishing. If we think of adaptive preferences as *distorting* people's understandings of their needs, it is because we believe there is an objective truth about their needs that is capable of being distorted. A concept of human flourishing can provide us with an objective sense of what human beings need.

There is another important role that perfectionism plays in my definition of adaptive preference. I say that a preference is adaptive only if it is likely that a person will change it and endorse her change of it under better conditions. How can we claim that a person is likely to change and endorse her adaptive preferences under better conditions? On what grounds can we say that, given the fair value of the opportunity to express themselves in public, the women of El Pital are likely to want to do just that? Perfectionism asserts that it is in the nature of human beings to flourish, and this idea supports the claim that people are likely to choose preferences more consistent with flourishing under conditions conducive to it. If we can expect people's autonomously formed preferences to remain the same under any social conditions, there is no reason to assume that people with adaptive preferences will change their preferences under better conditions. But if we believe that people have an underlying tendency toward basic flourishing, we have reason to anticipate that they will adjust their preferences in favor of flourishing when they have opportunities to do so.

I call the idea that people tend to choose in accordance with their basic flourishing "the Flourishing Claim." The Flourishing Claim explains why we can reasonably expect noncoercive adaptive preference interventions to improve people's flourishing. This is not to say that adaptive preference intervention is always successful; people internalize flourishing-inconsistent preferences with varying degrees of depth, and some people probably have internalized such preferences so deeply that there is no hope of changing them. But it is to say that we can expect a high degree of coincidence between what people want and what is good for them. Looked at in a different light, the Flourishing Claim also helps us to make sense of certain commonsense ideas about adaptive preference. The Flourishing Claim helps us to understand why activists and development practitioners often refer to adaptive preferences as imposed by social conditions; perhaps what they mean is that people's adaptive preferences would not persist under conditions that supported flourishing human life. The Flourishing Claim also helps us to make sense of why development practitioners speak of adaptive preference interventions as giving people opportunities to make *meaningful* choices for the first time; perhaps what it means to have meaningful choices is not to have the subjective capacities necessary for choice but rather to have access to options that would allow one to flourish.

Once we recognize that a central problem with adaptive preferences is that they are adapted to conditions inappropriate for human flourishing, we can develop a more honest and responsible way of conceptualizing adaptive preference intervention. Absent the clarifications of the previous paragraph, speaking of adaptive preferences as somehow choice-deficient risks treating people with adaptive preferences as though something is deeply wrong with *them*—that is, as though their capacities for reflection and choice were impaired. This problem is not only a function of speaking of adaptive preferences as choice-deficient, I would argue. I would also suggest that it is a function of the very term "adaptive preference." The term suggests that adaptive preferences cannot reliably tell us what the people who have them need, because their preferences are adapted to social conditions. The term suggests that the only preferences adapted to social conditions are ones held by people who are oppressed and deprived. This is clearly false. To move us away from this type of confusion, I suggest a terminological shift. In the book, I speak of "inappropriately adaptive preferences" (IAPs) rather than simply "adaptive preferences." Motivating this terminological shift is my belief that adaptive preferences are complicit in perpetuating less than flourishing forms of life. The problem with adaptive preferences is not just that social conditions influence them; it is that *bad* social conditions influence people to form preferences that are *bad for them*.

But how do we know what "bad" social conditions are and what types of preferences participate in sustaining lives that are bad for people? We need a conception of human flourishing to answer this question. Presumably, lives that are bad for people are lives that are inconsistent with their basic flourishing, but what is basic flourishing? We need a conception of human flourishing for my perfectionist definition of adaptive preference to be of any practical use, and not just any definition of flourishing will do. If we want to be able to make judgments about adaptive preference across difference, we need a definition of human flourishing that is acceptable to a diverse group of people. Moreover, if we believe that people can have reasonably different conceptions of an excellent life without having adaptive preferences—which I think we do believe—we need a conception of human flourishing that focuses on its basic levels. That is, we may believe that some forms of life are not flourishing at a high level (i.e., excellent) without thereby committing to the belief that the persons who are not flourishing at this high level have adaptive preferences. Say we believe that excellence involves superior performance at competitive sports. Even if we believe this, we probably do not think that a person who does not enjoy competition and has not had many opportunities for competition has adaptive preferences. We may believe her life is not excellent, but we do not believe that her preference against competition distorts her needs.[6] The idea that adaptive preferences misrepresent the needs of people who have them suggests that we need a conception of flourishing that is basic in order to identify them.

I argue that my perfectionist definition of adaptive preference should be supplemented by a particular *type* of conception of human flourishing. I do not say what human flourishing is, but I do lay out some stipulations for what a conception that can acceptably guide development practice should look like. A conception of human flourishing that guides development practice should be a *deliberative* conception of human flourishing. By this, I mean that the conception of human flourishing should be the result of a cross-cultural deliberative process—both because we want the conception not to substitute *one society's* conception of flourishing for *human* flourishing and because we want people to be judged by a conception of flourishing that is widely perceived as legitimate.

It is because I believe that we need a cross-culturally acceptable conception of flourishing that I do not propose my own conception of human flourishing. My own reflection is not a cross-cultural deliberative process, and I do not expect it to stand in for one. But I do believe we can anticipate certain features of a cross-culturally acceptable definition of human flourishing. I believe that such a definition will be substantively minimal, justificatorily minimal, and vague. By substantively minimal, I mean confined to the basic levels of human flourishing; I believe it is safe to say that we have stronger agreement about what basic human needs are than what human excellence is. By justificatorily minimal, I mean not based on a culturally specific set of justifications and compatible with a variety of different justifications; for instance, we can support basic mobility on the grounds that it is God's will for us to be able to interact with one another or on the grounds that people have rights to mobility that should not be abridged. And by vague, I mean described at a very high level of generality; we should expect a deliberative conception of human flourishing to include items like "adequate nutrition" and "mobility" rather than "access to meat" or "the capacity to go to shopping malls."

A conception of flourishing with these features will restrict the range of adaptive preference interventions that are morally acceptable. If development practitioners work with a vague and minimal conception of flourishing, it will not always be obvious whether people's preferences are consistent with their flourishing, and there will not be a single, obvious strategy for transforming adaptive preferences into preferences more compatible with flourishing. The conception of flourishing itself cannot tell development practitioners whether people's preferences are inappropriately adaptive and what should be done about it if they are. This, I believe, gives us a strong reason to support adaptive preference interventions that involve deliberation with deprived people. If it is not obvious from looking at real-world preferences how those preferences affect the flourishing of the people who hold them, dialogue about those preferences can contribute valuable information about how those preferences' well-being effects should be interpreted.

More importantly, a vague conception of human flourishing *underdetermines* what strategies for adaptive preference change should be chosen in any case. PAEM activists may have known that the women of El Pital did not have sufficient income and that they had a fatalistic attitude toward this fact, but this does not mean they knew what any particular group should do to increase their income, and different groups of women in El Pital came up with different income-generation projects like growing vegetables, running a community mill, and cooking and selling food (Rowlands 1997, 74). Since the conception of flourishing does not dictate what should be done to improve people's flourishing in any particular case, the desires of people with adaptive preferences should shape strategies for change. There are a variety of ways a person or group of people can improve their flourishing; people with adaptive preferences should play an important role in deciding which flourishing-compatible course of action should be adopted. To say this with reference to an example, if there are a variety of ways to achieve a basic income, deprived people themselves should participate in determining what strategy for achieving a basic income they pursue.

The deliberative conception of flourishing and my perfectionist definition of adaptive preference are the moral conceptions that guide my deliberative perfectionist approach to adaptive preference intervention. Deliberative perfectionist interventions proceed from the idea that preferences inconsistent with basic flourishing developed under bad conditions are preferences people would likely change under conditions more conducive to flourishing. In the typical deliberative perfectionist intervention, a practitioner will begin by suspecting that a person's (or group of people's) preferences are inconsistent with their flourishing. The practitioner will then attempt to understand—through deliberation with the person or people—how those preferences affect their flourishing. If the practitioner's suspicion that the preference is inconsistent with flourishing is warranted, she will involve the people with adaptive preferences in normative discussion of the preferences and designing a strategy for change. It is this type of process that PAEM activists used to transform the adaptive preferences of women in El Pital. Maria Ester Ruiz began by suspecting that the women of El Pital lacked the confidence to negotiate relationships with men and participate in public life (Rowlands 1997, 92–93). She worked with them to create discussion groups in which they were encouraged to ask moral questions about their own subservience. Through these discussions, women envisioned their own strategies for change—strategies Ruiz sometimes did not anticipate. For instance, Ruiz was surprised to learn that some of the women prioritized learning how to negotiate sexual decisions with men (Rowlands 1997, 96). The women came to recognize their own subservience as a problem and design their own strategies for decreasing that subservience.

Readers may wonder why this deliberative perfectionist approach requires an objective conception of flourishing at all. Would interventions like PAEM's not do just as well without a conception of flourishing, as the conception is so vague? I ask readers concerned with this question to turn to Chapter 5 , where I discuss some of the difficulties of conducting adaptive preference interventions without an explicitly normative conception of empowerment. There, I show how a definition of adaptive preference that refers to a concept of human flourishing (i.e., a normative conception) can improve development interventions aimed empowering women. I demonstrate this by showing how my flourishing-based conception of adaptive preference responds to problems with contemporary empowerment interventions. Feminist development theorists and practitioners increasingly describe the lack of clarity about what empowerment is as a practical problem; the lack of clarity has allowed neoliberal development actors to present development projects that do little to change gender roles as "empowering" to women. Development theorists and practitioners also describe a number of practical difficulties that arise in attempts to identify states of empowerment and disempowerment in real people. I argue in Chapter 5 that these problems suggest a need for development practitioners to refine choice-based (e.g., very thinly normative) theories of empowerment. These theorists see defining empowerment as choice as requiring counterintuitive and morally problematic judgments about what the preferences of an empowered woman look like in the real world. Further, development theorists and practitioners note that the lack of an explicit conception of empowerment has justified foisting a culturally specific vision of the empowered woman on deprived people. I argue that concepts I have developed as a part of my deliberative perfectionist conception can motivate a more coherent and respectful development practice—one that can explain why not all chosen preferences intuitively seem empowering while simultaneously refusing to mold the lives of women with adaptive preferences according to a culturally specific vision of women's empowerment.

I believe that development practitioners cannot consistently and honestly respond to adaptive preferences without a conception of human flourishing, and this is why I advocate the deliberative perfectionist approach. But I also believe that development interventions can be normatively laden and express a high degree of respect for differences in people's conceptions of the good. We can accept the deliberative perfectionist approach and believe that individuals deserve the right to decide what types of lives they want to lead. We can also accept deliberative perfectionist adaptive preference interventions while believing that it is appropriate for different societies to promote different values. I urge readers who are interested in seeing how perfectionist adaptive preference intervention is compatible with moral diversity to turn to Chapter 4 (in this volume). In the Chapter 4, I show that *deliberative* adaptive preference interventions are fully compatible with a high degree of respect for individual autonomy; deliberatively encouraging people to make their preferences more compatible with flourishing does not involve coercing them and actually entails opportunities for them to build their capacities for autonomous agency. I also show that deliberative perfectionist adaptive preference interventions do not always require people to sacrifice values that are culturally important to them; instead, deliberative perfectionist interventions encourage people to imagine strategies for preference transformation that are compatible with their values *and* compatible with flourishing.

The Deliberative Perfectionist Approach and Transnational Feminist Politics

So far, I have described my deliberative perfectionist approach to adaptive preference intervention. The deliberative perfectionist approach understands adaptive preferences as preferences inconsistent with basic flourishing that are causally related to conditions nonconducive to basic flourishing. It understands basic flourishing according to a deliberative conception that is cross-culturally acceptable, minimal, and vague. The approach holds that practitioners should suspect preferences of adaptiveness based on a combination of their content and the processes by which they were formed, but it insists that deprived people must play a role in diagnosing their own adaptive preferences and envisioning strategies for change.

However, I have said very little about how an approach to adaptive preference intervention fits into the larger feminist project of achieving global justice. Though my goal is not to offer a complete feminist theory of global justice, I explicitly delimit the role of adaptive intervention in the struggle for global justice. Some other feminist philosophical projects focused on improving the lives of deprived people have unintentionally reproduced colonial attitudes toward third-world women. Taking a stance against deprivation without representing third-world women and third-world societies through a colonial lens is a more difficult task than it may originally seem. It is important for feminist interventions in global ethics to avoid the dangers of perpetuating colonial representations of third-world women, and it is for this reason that I explicitly discuss some of the dilemmas facing feminist theorists who wish to persuade public institutions to take seriously the grave deprivations that women the world over face without thereby encouraging those institutions to accept colonial representations of deprived people. In this section of my introduction, I spell out the implications of my project for three dilemmas of transnational feminist praxis: dilemmas I term "the global justice dilemma," "the agency dilemma," and "the culture dilemma."

The Global Justice Dilemma

It is a fact that our unjust global economic order is a major cause of the deprivation of many women in the South.[7] We live in a world in which poverty is not only widespread and debilitating but also gendered (Jaggar 2002). We also live in a world where Western feminists—and citizens of rich countries more generally—are complicit in perpetuating wide-scale deprivation, at least to the extent that their governments drive the unjust global economic order. Illuminating the injustice of the global economic order is an important task for feminist philosophers who are concerned with the deprivation of women in the global South. I do not take this to mean that we should never write about oppressions and deprivations that are not directly caused by the global economic order. But it does mean we should be wary of philosophizing about the oppression of women in the global South in ways that deflect attention from the injustice of the global economic order. We should be especially wary of deflecting attention from the global economic order given the potentially colonial tendency of Westerners to fail to understand the ways in which their governments promote the deprivation—economic and otherwise—of women in the South.

Given the reality of an unjust international economic system, a project like mine—focused as it is on justifying IAP intervention—may seem to get off on the wrong foot about global justice. It may seem to distract us from changing the global economic order. Indeed, it runs the risk of adding to two problematic trends in contemporary discussions of global justice: the feminist philosophical trend toward treating cultural practices as the main cause of Southern women's deprivation and the more widespread cultural trend of recommending individual solutions to structural problems. If adaptive preferences are primarily matters of women's complicity in perpetuating local patriarchal traditions, my project participates in creating the impression among Western academics that non-Western cultures—rather than the global economic order—are the primary source of women's oppression. And if I am claiming that adaptive preference intervention is the main solution to the deprivation of Southern women, I am guilty of proposing individual or community-level solutions to systemic problems—in precisely the way apologists for the neoliberal economic order often do. An important dilemma faces feminist philosophers who want to philosophize about the deprivation of women in the South without focusing on the global economic order. Is it possible to offer nonsystemic responses to women's deprivation without thereby occluding the systemic nature of global injustice?

My project in this book is to justify and provide a moral framework for IAP intervention, and it would be disingenuous of me to characterize it otherwise. However, I want to clarify how I see adaptive preference intervention as fitting into the larger struggle for global justice. I do not see adaptive preference as caused exclusively—or even mostly—by local cultural practices, and I do not hold that adaptive preference intervention is an adequate solution to our unjust economic order. Nothing in this book implies that it is primarily local cultural practices,

Southern men, or local income-generating inadequacies that cause the deprivation of women in the global South.

We can discern a somewhat problematic focus in recent feminist philosophical
writing on women in the global South. Susan Moller Okin's (1999) work on
global justice emphasizes cultural practices like polygamy, female genital cutting,
and child marriage, and the ways in which those practices undermine respect for
women as persons. Martha Nussbaum's work discusses the plight of poor women
in India but does not extensively analyze the causes of their poverty; rather,
Nussbaum (1999; 2001) emphasizes cultural impediments to their flourishing—
impediments like norms of female seclusion and submission and patriarchal religious practices and family law. Alison Jaggar argues that work like Nussbaum and
Okin's inaugurated a philosophical trend that describes cultural practices—rather
than poverty or global inequality—as a source of third-world women's deprivation (2005b). Jaggar describes Nussbaum and Okin's work as having the "nonlog-
ical implication" that third-world women are oppressed primarily by their cultural
practices.

This focus on cultural practices as the primary source of third-world women's
oppression is nothing new in Western feminist writing. Uma Narayan finds a similar focus in radical feminist discussions of first and third-world women's oppression from the 1960s and 1970s. Narayan identifies a disproportionate Western
fascination with oppression caused by the cultural practices of "other cultures."
She argues that discussions of *sati* (widow immolation) in India tend to represent
"Indian culture," rather than colonialism or economic motivations, as the cause of
sati (U. Narayan 1997, 84). Narayan argues that the portrayal of Indian culture as
the source of *sati* is both incoherent and inaccurate, given that there was no single
"Indian" culture prior to British colonization and given that *sati* seems to have
become more common in India after the British fascination with it marked it as an
"Indian cultural practice." Further, Narayan claims that the valorization of *sati* is
partly attributable to the economic motives of people who depend on maintaining
pilgrimage sites related to *sati* for their livelihood. Indeed, Narayan coins the term
"death by culture" to describe Western feminist understandings of the causes of
the more contemporary phenomenon of dowry murder. She does not see it as a
coincidence that a Western culture intent on proving its superiority represents
Indian *culture* as the source of Indian women's oppression.

My point in discussing this focus on culture in feminist global ethics scholarship is not to conflate Nussbaum and Okin's arguments with those of the radical
feminists of the 1970s whose beliefs clearly contained much more unquestioned
colonial residue. Nussbaum and Okin are clearly concerned about poverty as a
form of deprivation, and I am indebted to their pathbreaking work on feminist
global ethics. I also do not wish to suggest that Nussbaum and Okin are wrong

that oppressive cultural practices can function to impede women's flourishing; as the rest of this book makes clear, I hold that cultural practices that impede women's basic well-being are deeply wrong—and wrong in a way that merits public intervention.

Rather, the point I want to make is primarily epistemic. Many Western feminists tend to refer to different variables to explain third-world women's oppression than they do when explaining Western women's oppression. Specifically, Western feminists often treat cultural practices as the explanation of first resort of the deprivation of third-world women. Further, they tend to treat the cultural practices that cause women's oppression as practices specific to the third world and often fail to link the proliferation of oppressive practices to economic and political structures. For the purposes of our present discussion, I wish to point out—as Jaggar has done on multiple occasions—that the assumption that most deprivation of third-world women is caused by oppressive cultural practices may encourage feminist philosophers to draw false conclusions about what ending the deprivation of women around the world would require.

In order not to abet the belief that most oppression of third-world women is caused by their cultural practices, I wish to separate my focus on adaptive preference intervention from the idea that third-world women's *primary or only* source of oppression is their cultural practices. As I argued earlier, the view expressed in this book is compatible with the view that women all over the world—in both rich and poor countries—have adaptive preferences that are worthy of public scrutiny. For instance, many battered women in the United States rationalize their abuse, despite living under better economic conditions than many women struggling for basic nutrition and economic survival (Ferraro and Johnson 1983). Furthermore, cultural practices are not the only cause of adaptive preferences. A person may have adaptive preferences caused by poverty or social and economic marginalization. One of the examples of adaptive preference that Sen consistently repeats is that of the poor person who contents herself with what she has. Once we accept that the global economic order can encourage the poor to develop adaptive preferences, we recognize that discussing adaptive preferences does not require erasing the effects of the global economic order.

But seeing poverty as a cause of adaptive preference and understanding the structural causes of poverty are not the same thing. So even if my project does not treat cultural practices as the primary source of the deprivations of Southern women, it still may detract attention from the global economic system. A second problematic trend in Western perceptions of the deprivation of women—and men—in the global South is the trend of erasing or ignoring the systemic causes of poverty and the concomitant suggestion that individual charity is the best solution to the problem of global poverty. Andrew Kuper (2002) and Uma Narayan have both argued that this tendency is alive and well in the general field of global ethics. Narayan observes that philosophical discussions of global poverty tend to concentrate on persuading the rich to give charity to the poor—a focus which discourages Westerners from asking why the poor are poor in the first place.[8]

Outside academic philosophy there is a parallel trend toward providing small-scale solutions to systemic economic problems—a trend that may also encourage people to ignore the injustice of the global economic order. One place we encounter this trend toward small-scale solutions is in contemporary discussions of microcredit—both within development institutions and within the popular media. The public debate about microcredit is almost univocally celebratory, and microcredit has become "the primary *economic* component of the WID [Women in Development] agenda" (Poster and Salime 2002, 194, emphasis in original). Winifred Poster and Zakia Salime argue that the widespread celebration of microcredit as the *solution* to the deprivation of women in the South constructs a particular impression of what the *problem* is. Poster and Salime describe microcredit as an individualistic and neoliberal solution (Poster and Salime 2002, 194). If giving women small-scale credit is the best way to empower them, it may seem that the primary obstacle to their empowerment is a lack of credit (Poster and Salime 2002, 194). Further, if we see international banks and corporations as solving women's poverty by funding microcredit programs, we may lose sight of the ways in which those banks and corporations sustain an international economic order that is causing those women's poverty. Microcredit proposes a small-scale response to a structural problem, and Poster and Salime's analysis helps us to see how this type of feminist strategy can function to efface the causal role of the global economic order on women's deprivation.

Like a focus on microcredit, my focus on adaptive preference intervention may be taken to construct a false impression of what the causes of the deprivation of many Southern women are. If adaptive preference intervention is the solution, it may seem that the main problem of deprived women is their adaptive preferences. It may even seem as though I am suggesting that the beliefs and attitudes of deprived people are the main cause of their problems—that if deprived people just changed their beliefs, they would be able to flourish. I do not believe that either of these descriptions of the problem is accurate. I also believe that we can endorse adaptive preference intervention without accepting either of the above constructions of the causes of deprivation of women in the South. We can support intervention without believing that adaptive preferences are the main causes of women's deprivation in the South or believing that changing deprived women's beliefs and attitudes is always the best way to combat deprivation.

In order to see how this is possible, we need to clarify the role of a theory of adaptive preference intervention in a theory of global justice. I emphatically do not intend my justification of adaptive preference intervention as a complete theory of global justice. In fact, I believe that the basic premises of my argument for adaptive preference intervention weigh against treating adaptive preference intervention as the main method for combating global injustice. My justification of adaptive preference intervention is based on the broader assumption that public institutions should promote people's basic flourishing; a global economic order that impedes millions of people's basic flourishing is clearly objectionable on the grounds of this assumption. Adaptive preference intervention is also clearly an inefficient way of increasing the flourishing of all of the deprived people in the world. Further, even if small-scale adaptive preference interventions could successfully increase the flourishing of all of the world's deprived people, it would not follow that this set of arrangements was just. From the perspective of justice, there are clear reasons to prefer social arrangements that do not produce the types of inequalities and deprivations that make adaptive preference intervention necessary. In sum, I am not suggesting that adaptive preference intervention is *the* solution to the deprivation of women in the South; it is one small part of the solution.

Now let us turn to the idea that focusing on adaptive intervention creates the perception that it is the attitudes of deprived women in the South that are primarily responsible for their deprivation. If we think adaptive preferences are real, we think that people can participate in their own oppression and deprivation. When we acknowledge that people's desires can be complicit perpetuating in their deprivation, we always risk treating people's desires—rather than the conditions that shaped them—as the most proximate cause of their deprivation. This is a serious risk. However, my deliberative perfectionist approach to adaptive preference intervention takes this risk seriously and attempts to offset it. My approach insists that we cannot read people's reasons for their behavior off their preferences, and that development practitioners need to understand why people have the preferences they do in order to engage in effective interventions. My emphasis on deliberation encourages practitioners to ask whether changing people's beliefs and attitudes is a plausible response to their deprivation; adaptive preferences that are utility-maximizing adaptations to unjust conditions probably require interventions that are directly aimed at changing those unjust social conditions. Increasing the flourishing of people with adaptive preference will often require some combination of psychological transformation and social change, and the deliberative perfectionist approach encourages practitioners to see that this is possible. To say that adaptive preference intervention is part of the solution is not to say that changing individuals' attitudes will always bring about social change on its own.

My approach discourages development practitioners from treating deprived people's beliefs and attitudes as the first-resort explanation of their deprivation. Many cases of what seem to be inappropriately adaptive higher-order preferences will simply be inappropriately adaptive lower-order preferences that will only change under more just social conditions. My approach to adaptive preference intervention cautions explicitly against "psychologizing the structural"—that is, against assuming that people's attitudes are always the primary cause of their deprivation. However, I maintain that there are cases in which people's beliefs and attitudes are among the primary obstacles to their flourishing. People's adaptive preferences may be obstacles to social change, or they may hold onto adaptive preferences even after social conditions have already changed. So even if changing people's beliefs and attitudes will not always be the best way to improve their flourishing, there are cases where it will contribute positively to their flourishing. Adaptive preference intervention can play a limited but important role in a global ethics—that of guiding public institutions when they encounter people for whom some form of preference change is required for their basic flourishing.

There is another, more attenuated, role adaptive preference intervention can play in the struggle for global justice; adaptive preference intervention can motivate oppressed and deprived people to demand systemic change. Certain types of adaptive preferences—especially adaptive preferences that cause people not to see injustice against them as injustice—can prevent people from struggling for greater justice for themselves and communities. Many of the women of El Pital had these types of adaptive preferences. Recall the epigraph of this introduction, where a woman recalls not having understood "the situation she is living in" and having repressed her dissatisfaction with the conditions of her life until she began discussing her situation with other women. For these women, realizing that they had accepted injustice was the first step in a journey toward "becoming organized" and seeking social change on behalf of themselves and other women. Nussbaum writes, "to recognize the adaptive nature of one's preferences is the beginning of a search for independence" (Nussbaum 2001, 150). Adaptive preference intervention, then, may contribute toward changing structural injustices by helping people to *recognize* injustices so that they can begin to *organize* against them.

The Agency Dilemma

Feminists who theorize about oppression and deprivation are faced with a balancing act—that of trying to represent deprived people as agents without thereby obscuring the reality of their victimization. This dilemma is front and center when we attempt to theorize about adaptive preferences. When we say that a person has an adaptive preference, we are essentially saying that that person has become an agent of her own deprivation. But we can understand the meaning of the term "agency" here in different ways. We sometimes describe a person as an "agent" to mean that she is carrying out the will of another. Feminists often portray people with adaptive preference as agents in this sense—as engaged in doing the bidding of others who would seek to exploit them; in his famous claim that men seek not only women's obedience but also their sentiments, Mill describes women as the agents of men's desires rather than their own (Mill 2002, 135). Treating people with adaptive preferences as the agents of others has the advantage of foregrounding the fact that people's desires can be socially shaped. But it has the disadvantage, to use Uma Narayan's words, of making deprived people look like "prisoners"—people who are have "various forms of patriarchal oppression imposed on [them] entirely against [their] will and consent" (U. Narayan 2002, 418).

A way to get beyond this problematic portrayal of deprived people may be to use "agency" in a different sense. We may think of agency as the capacity to make decisions and shape one's world in accordance with what one cares about. If we think of agency in this way, we can see people with adaptive preferences as doing something other than univocally perpetuating their deprivation. We can see them as struggling to advance their own interests and desires, even if the struggle to do this must occur within the confines of limited opportunities. The recent trend in feminist scholarship about deprivation emphasizes this sense of the agency of deprived people (Mahmood 2005, 6). An advantage of valorizing agency is that it helps us see the desires of deprived people as rational and respect-worthy. But a disadvantage is that it does not help us see the conditions that shape people's desires and constrain their actions as a moral problem. Some feminist discussions of agency simply celebrate the fact that women who seem deprived do care about certain things and try to shape their worlds in accordance with the things they care about. If we accept the view advanced by this family of feminist discussions, however, we will have difficulty taking seriously the fact that oppressive conditions may encourage women to care about the wrong things or make it impossible for them to effectively advance their interests.

This is how we usually pose the agency dilemma in feminist theory: we ask, should we see oppressed people as agents whose choices are worthy of unquestioning respect or victims who cannot make genuine choices? But I think posing the question about adaptive preferences in these terms does not get us very far, because there are significant disadvantages to seeing deprived people in either way. If we see people with adaptive preferences simply as victims, we see them as needing to be completely reshaped into agents. Alternatively, if we see them only as agents whose choices we should celebrate, we cannot see anything particularly problematic about adaptive preferences. My approach to adaptive preference intervention describes people with adaptive preferences as both agents and victims. People with adaptive preferences make reflective choices and care deeply about certain things, but social conditions have encouraged them to sometimes choose and care about things that are not consistent with their flourishing. My contentions that adaptive preference affects people selectively rather than globally and that adaptive preferences do not destroy autonomy support a view of people with adaptive preferences as agents. But I insist that chosenness is not the only morally relevant feature of people's preferences. Adaptive preferences can be chosen and still worthy of public scrutiny because they inhibit people's flourishing.

But strong proponents of valorizing deprived people's agency will not be satisfied by the brief remarks above. In order to see how my approach to adaptive preference intervention does not deny the agency of people with adaptive preferences, I think we need to get clearer about what is at stake in the agency dilemma and why it might produce discomfort about adaptive preference intervention. We can understand two separate families of concerns as underlying the desire to treat oppressed and deprived people as agents. The first family of concerns, which I term "paternalism concerns," motivates a belief that respecting people with adaptive preferences as persons requires uncritically valorizing their agency. The second family of concerns, which I term "third-world positionality" concerns, motivates a belief that uncritically valorizing the agency of deprived people is the best way to counter a colonial tendency toward offering simplistic explanations of the lives and decisions of third-world women.

Let us begin with the paternalism concerns. Many feminist theorists who write in favor of valorizing deprived people's agency do so in the name of opposing coercion. Uma Narayan, for instance, sees policies designed to coerce deprived women into changing their behaviors as based on an "eclipsing of their agency" (U. Narayan 2002, 427). A better understanding of deprived women as agents— one that understood them as "bargaining with patriarchy"[9] rather than simply manipulated by it—would provide reasons to oppose coercive intervention in their lives.

This move toward valorizing agency responds to a very real problem in feminist theorizing about deprived people. There is a specific argument form that recurs in feminist philosophical debates about public intervention in the lives of women who seem to have adaptive preferences. The argument, which tends to happen in brief exchanges, goes something like this: one feminist philosopher argues for intervention in the lives of people with adaptive preferences. Another replies that women with adaptive preferences should not be subject to paternalistic coercion. I will not rehearse the many examples of this here, but I mention two of them, so that we might have a sense of what instances of this argument form actually look like. Okin, in her influential essay, "Is Multiculturalism Bad for Women?" argues that minority cultures in liberal states can function to undermine women's autonomy and seems to favor intervention in cultural practices that undermine it (Okin 1999). In a response to Okin, Azizah Al-Hibri brings up the example of Muslim veiling practices and asks rhetorically whether she should "organize to *force* those sisters to unveil their heads" (Al-Hibri 1999, 46, emphasis added).[10] Similarly to Okin, Susan Babbitt claims that people who lack senses of self would benefit from interventions that gave them greater opportunities (Babbitt 1993, 256–257). And similarly to Al-Hibri, Diana Meyers replies by wondering whether "*foisting* a new set of opportunities" on women who support female genital cutting "is an ethical and efficacious way to increase their autonomy" (Meyers 2000, 488, emphasis added).

Both sides in this debate trade on an ambiguity about the word "intervention" here. Interventionists like Okin and Babbitt do not seem particularly worried about what *type* of intervention they should endorse; they just want to answer the question of whether intervention should happen. Meanwhile, antipaternalists like Al-Hibri and Meyers rightly care about the type of intervention that should happen, and they thus focus their responses on opposing coercive intervention. I see many feminists who valorize agency as wanting to find a principled reason to side with the antipaternalists who oppose coercive intervention.

But I reply that it is possible to oppose the coercion of deprived people, valorize their agency, and support intervention that enhances their flourishing. We need not see intervention and support for agency as at odds. My deliberative perfectionist approach focuses on noncoercive intervention and on deliberative interventions that actively expand people's capacities for agency. Readers particularly interested in these paternalism problems can turn to my discussions of the implications of noncoercive intervention in the Chapter 4 and my view's implications for agency in Chapter 3. But for now, I want to simply state that my deliberative perfectionist approach says that preferences can be *suspect* of inappropriate adaptiveness without necessarily being so. Because my approach recommends intervention in part to determine whether people's preferences are inappropriately adaptive, it also insists that supporting intervention to improve the flourishing of people with adaptive preferences does not mean supporting coercion. When we separate suspicion and intervention from coercion, adaptive preference intervention seems less incompatible with a desire to respect the agency of deprived people.

Still, the compatibility of deliberative perfectionist adaptive preference intervention with valorizing agency depends on what we mean by "valorizing agency." If valorizing agency means uncritically accepting people's behavior as a guide to what their well-being would require, we cannot support adaptive preference intervention and valorize agency. My approach will not satisfy critics who insist on such uncompromising respect for agency. However, I ask whether uncritically respecting people's existing choices is the best way of respecting those people *as persons*. I argue this point in more depth in Chapter Four.

The second set of concerns motivating the desire to valorize agency are what I call "third-world positionality concerns." These concerns oppose a specific portrayal of deprived people as lacking agency: that of third-world women as, to use Chandra Mohanty's (1995) term, "unconscious reactors." Many third-world feminist scholars have pointed out a tendency in Western feminist theory and activism toward portraying third-world women as passive recipients of the norms of their patriarchal cultures. This view has at least two negative consequences for practice: it can function to relax the epistemic standards to which explanations of third-world women's oppression are held and it can create the impression that deprived third-world women are in need of "saving" by Westerners.

Each of these consequences has the potential to perniciously influence adaptive preference intervention. If practitioners see third-world women as passive recipients of their deprivation, they will offer simplistic explanations of adaptive preferences in third-world women. Third-world feminist scholars have repeatedly documented a type of *disproportion* in the epistemic standards used to understand the deprivation of third-world women. Where there is a tendency to see the oppression and deprivation of women in the West as stemming from complex and diffuse causes, there is a need to expand "debates about gender in non-Western societies beyond the simplistic registers of submission and patriarchy" (Mahmood 2005, 6). The oppression and deprivation of third-world women is also frequently chalked up to abstract and imprecise causes such as "culture," without a deeper examination of the economic and institutional structures that may cause deprivation or motivate third-world women's strategies for resisting and manipulating it. The idea of third-world women as victims can motivate development practitioners to apply similarly lax standards in order to understand the causes of deprived women's adaptive preferences.

The idea of third-world women as victims in need of saving by Westerners can also detrimentally impact adaptive preference intervention. At its most pernicious, it can disqualify third-world women from being seen as bearers of visions of the good life who can help people to overcome their adaptive preferences; conversely, it can make it seem as though Westerners are the only appropriate interveners. If third-world women are passive victims, the only people who are capable of opposing and seeing the oppression and deprivation of third-world women as such are outsiders. The notion of third-world women as victims whom only Westerners can "save" also promotes a type of adaptive preference intervention that treats all third-world women as though they have adaptive preferences, that ignores the objectiveself-interest that is expressed in certain adaptive preferences, and that assumes that adaptive preference explains all differences between third-world women's preferences and Western women's preferences. If Western interveners see third-world women as victims in need of Western saving, they are likely to view differences between third-world women's values and their own only as examples of adaptive preference—even in cases where third-world women's preferences do not negatively impact basic well-being.

To counter these tendencies, some third-world feminists suggest that scholars and activists should focus on portraying third-world women as agents. I agree with this suggestion. I offer the deliberative perfectionist approach contained in this book precisely in hopes of offering an approach to adaptive preference intervention that refuses to see third-world women simply as victims. Before I explain how my approach to adaptive preference intervention discourages development practitioners from seeing third-world women as in need of Western saving and from offering simplistic understandings of third-world women's deprivation, I clarify a couple of points about what my deliberative perfectionist approach does and does not imply about third-world women's agency. First, as I have already stated, nothing in my deliberative perfectionist approach implies that third-world women are the only people who have adaptive preferences and whom adaptive preference intervention would help to flourish. I have situated my project within conversations about development ethics that focus mostly on how to improve the lives of women in poor countries, but it is a logical implication of my approach that the basic flourishing of many Western women could be improved with deliberative perfectionist interventions. Similarly, my deliberative perfectionist approach does not imply that Westerners should be the primary interveners in the lives of third-world people who have adaptive preferences. I discuss this issue a bit more in depth in the final section of this introduction—the section on the culture dilemma. But for now, it is worth noting that many of the examples of adaptive preference intervention I cite as exemplary in this book are interventions initiated *by third-world women* in the lives of other third-world women. For instance, the PAEM movement in El Pital discussed in this introduction, was initiated by a Honduran activist, Maria Ester Ruiz.[11]

Let us return to the question of how my deliberative perfectionist approach encourages development practitioners to valorize the agency of deprived third-world women. Recall that one problem of seeing third-world women as victims is that it licenses development practitioners to apply lax epistemic standards in understanding their deprivation. My deliberative perfectionist approach insists that practitioners cannot assume out of hand that they know why deprived people make the choices they do. It encourages development practitioners to deliberate with deprived people to gain a clearer understanding of those choices. My approach thus asks practitioners to complicate the simplistic, victimizing judgments about people's behavior that they may initially be inclined to draw because of their (implicit or explicit) beliefs about the victim status of third-world women. A second insidious way in which the belief that third-world women are passive victims might influence adaptive preference intervention is by causing development practitioners to overlook resistance and assume that all differences constitute deprivation. My deliberative perfectionist approach also discourages interventions that overlook resistance. I argue that adaptive preferences have selective rather than global effects. This means that people with adaptive preferences may have preferences that harm their flourishing but may also retain partly positive self-images that IAP intervention should focus on helping them cultivate. If we see adaptive preferences as selective, we need not see oppression and deprivation as extinguishing people's desires to flourish. Thus, recognizing the fact of adaptive preference need not entail seeing people with adaptive preferences only as victims who have no idea what is good for them. My approach encourages development practitioners to look for resistance to oppression in the lives of people with adaptive preferences and to work with people with adaptive preferences to design strategies for change that build on this resistance. This is a significant departure from the view of third-world women as victims who need the conceptions of the good of outsiders to simply replace their existing ones.

The Culture Dilemma

Feminist philosophers interested in global justice face important dilemmas about how to characterize deprivation. We have already discussed two of these dilemmas: the global justice dilemma, which asks feminist philosophers to choose between addressing systemic injustice and promoting small-scale interventions to improve women's lives, and the agency dilemma, which seems to oppose recognizing deprived people's agency to recognizing that they may sometimes be complicit in their own deprivation. A third dilemma about how feminist global ethics should characterize deprivation is what I call the "culture dilemma." Simply put, the culture dilemma asks us to choose between opposing deprivation and respecting the cultures of oppressed or deprived people. The interest in respect for cultures responds to a serious tendency, on the part of Westerners in particular, to assume the superiority of their cultures and to force or encourage people in "other cultures" to adopt the values of Western culture. Meanwhile, feminist critics of "respect for cultures" point out that many cultural practices have the deprivation of women as their goal and claim that respecting cultures that harm women is morally irresponsible.

This conflict produces two separate sub-dilemmas for adaptive preference intervention: one ontological and one epistemological. The ontological culture dilemma poses the question, is it possible to oppose oppressive cultural practices and support the right of people to live according to culturally specific values? The epistemological culture dilemma poses the question, who is qualified to oppose cultural practices that promote deprivation? Given the tendency of outsiders to misunderstand the practices and values of cultural others, they are likely to see adaptive preferences where none exist. But given the likelihood that cultural insiders will not have developed critical perspectives on the sources of deprivation within their own cultures, they may be inclined not to condemn deprivations that are morally very serious.

Let us begin with the ontological dilemma. As I mentioned in my discussion of the global justice dilemma, Western scholars tend to represent the deprivations of third-world women as caused by their cultural practices. I have already agreed with the third-world feminist scholars who argue that this representation is harmfully reductive. But there is another important problem with representing "cultures" as the sources of people's deprivation. If we see cultures as the primary cause of people's deprivation, it may seem that the best way to improve their lives is to abolish their cultures. In "Is Multiculturalism Bad for Women?" Okin comes very close to suggesting that getting rid of deprived people's cultures would make their lives better. She writes that women who live in cultures that undermine their autonomy "*might* be better off if the culture into which they were born were to become extinct..." (Okin 1999, 22, emphasis in original). Okin does not suggest that this is the only solution; she also suggests that the culture altering itself is a potential solution (Okin 1999, 23). Still, she has been widely interpreted as suggesting that cultures whose practices deprive women of autonomy should cease to exist (Al-Hibri 1999, 41; An-Na'Im 1999, 64).

Deliberative perfectionist intervention will, in many cases, require opposing oppressive cultural practices and seeking to change them. But, I want to suggest, this is not tantamount to eradicating the cultures that sustain these practices. To suggest that changing a culture's harmful practices is the same thing as destroying that culture is to support some highly dubious idealizations about cultures. It requires assuming that change must cause cultural extinction. But this is clearly false; if change destroyed cultures, there would be no cultures. Cultures are perpetually changing and redrawing their boundaries (U. Narayan 1997; Tamir 1999, 51). Further, the view that change means destruction suggests that all forces that favor changing a culture are exogenous. Cultures are not monoliths, and it is doubtful that there are cultural practices that undermine basic flourishing that have univocal endorsement "within" cultures.

My deliberative perfectionist approach is based on a rejection of the idea that we have a choice between respect for cultures and flourishing. I claim that a vague and minimal conception of flourishing should motivate adaptive preference intervention. This has two significant consequences for the preservation of cultural values. First, because the conception of flourishing is minimal, my deliberative perfectionist approach only recommends changing preferences that are inconsistent with *basic* flourishing. My approach provides no imperative to change cultural differences in perceptions about excellence or the ultimate ends of human life.

Second, the conception of flourishing I advocate is vague and thus *underdetermines* the concrete strategy for changing adaptive preferences in any case. The deliberative perfectionist approach holds that it is a good thing for people with adaptive preferences to change their preferences into flourishing-compatible preferences they can endorse. But the vague conception of flourishing does not give an exhaustive list of what flourishing-compatible preferences will look like. Instead, it says that deprived people should participate in envisioning flourishing-compatible ways of life that allow them to retain the cultural values that matter to them. Maria Ester Ruiz of PAEM worked with women in rural Honduras to create a manual about women's empowerment that was rooted in Catholic values. This is a strategy that the deliberative perfectionist approach would embrace, and it is one that did not require the women to abandon Catholicism wholesale in order to embrace increased mobility and negotiating power within relationships. The deliberative perfectionist approach provides a framework for interventions that find flourishing-compatible strains of cultural values and build on them. This moves us beyond the false choice between preserving and destroying culture.

My answer to the epistemological culture dilemma is more complicated. Adaptive preference intervention usually requires third parties to make preliminary judgments about the adaptive preferences of others. Most people who seem to have adaptive preferences will be people who seem not to be resisting their deprivation, so third parties may have to be the ones who initiate questions about why they are not resisting and how they might lead more flourishing lives. Who is qualified to make decisions about the moral acceptability of culturally embedded preferences, if outsiders are likely to misunderstand them and insiders are likely to accept them? This is not a question that admits of a categorical answer, and I think we should avoid giving it one. I believe there are good prudential reasons to prefer insiders over outsiders in most cases, especially in deliberative perfectionist interventions. Good deliberative perfectionist interventions will be based on intimate contextual knowledge of the type that insiders are more likely to have. My deliberative perfectionist approach says that third parties are often right to intervene, but third parties need not be culturally foreign third parties.

On the other hand, I resist incorporating a categorical preference for cultural insiders into the deliberative perfectionist approach. There may be cases in which people with adaptive preferences do not want interventions from other members of their communities and would be uncomfortable being honest with them. This is particularly likely to be the case where communities contain significant hierarchies (Purkayastha 2002) or where cultural taboos initially prohibit discussion of certain preferences. Moreover, categorically preferring insiders means accepting a rigid dichotomy between insiders and outsiders. In reality, even cultural insiders who conduct interventions are often separated from people with suspect preferences by differences in class or education, and preferring cultural insiders does not eliminate the difficulties of understanding across difference. Accepting the insider/outsider dichotomy can also lead to the delegitimization of critics of flourishing-inhibiting cultural practices who are members of a culture. Conservative forces within cultural contexts often call insider critics "outsiders" in order to decrease the credibility of their criticisms (U. Narayan 1997, 22). The question of who should intervene is, in my view, largely a situational one that I do not seek to answer with my deliberative perfectionist approach. I do, however, hope to make clear that nothing in the deliberative perfectionist approach suggests that cultural outsiders—or Westerners in Southern contexts more specifically—are the best interveners. I believe that activists and development practitioners can be cultural insiders *and* critics, and that people like this are usually best situated to deliberate with deprived people about how to improve their flourishing.[12]

My overarching aim in this book is to offer a moral framework for identifying and responding to adaptive preferences. I began this introduction by summarizing the deliberative perfectionist approach. My approach is based on the belief that adaptive preferences are one type of preference incompatible with basic human flourishing. Practical attempts to identify and respond to them require a conception of flourishing, but not just any conception of flourishing will do. We need a conception that has been deliberated on and promotes deliberation with deprived people.

In addition to summarizing the deliberative perfectionist approach, I also hope to have given some sense of its role in transnational feminist praxis. I see adaptive preference intervention as only one part of the struggle for global justice—one that cannot take the place of action to reform the international economic order. I also see deliberative perfectionist intervention as compatible with the goal of seeing deprived people in general, and third-world women in particular, as agents. Finally, deliberative perfectionist intervention is based on the hope that it is possible for deprived people to transform their adaptive preferences without simply giving up their culturally particular sources of meaning.

I now turn to arguing for the deliberative perfectionist approach. My argument proceeds in the body of the book as follows. In Chapter 1, I describe the deliberative perfectionist approach and explain how it avoids many practical difficulties that face attempts at adaptive preference intervention. In Chapter 2, I attempt to show that my perfectionist definition of adaptive preference is superior to autonomy-based ones. There I conduct an extended demonstration of the incoherence of seeing adaptive preferences as autonomy or choice deficits. In Chapter 3, I focus on showing how people can retain agency despite having adaptive preferences and claim that the deliberative perfectionist approach promotes—and should promote—strategies for adaptive preference transformation that cultivate the existing agency of people with adaptive preferences. In Chapter 4, I defend the deliberative perfectionist approach against charges that it is incompatible with respect for people's capacities to decide what types of lives they want to lead. In the final chapter, Chapter 5, I examine some actual examples of adaptive preference intervention in more depth. I show that concepts I have developed as part of the deliberative perfectionist approach can help development practitioners move beyond some of the paradoxes of defining empowerment that make it difficult to identify real-world adaptive preferences.

1 A DELIBERATIVE PERFECTIONIST APPROACH TO ADAPTIVE PREFERENCE INTERVENTION

Adaptive preferences are a moral mystery. We encounter increasingly frequent mentions of them in contemporary development ethics. We read stories about battered women who do not see violence committed against them as wrong (Nussbaum 2001, 113), poor castes in India whose members resign themselves to lives of poverty (Appadurai 2004), and members of oppressed groups who internalize the belief in their own inferiority (Kabeer 1999, 441). We find social scientists worrying that the empirical data they collect about people's perceptions of well-being may be distorted because of the influences of deprivation on other people's desires (Alkire 2007a, 20; Clark 2003, 179). We also hear philosophers arguing that the phenomenon of adaptive preference makes utilitarian measures of well-being unreliable. They ask, how can injustice to the deprived register as bad, if well-being is simply a matter of desire-fulfillment and we know that people adjust their desires to bad conditions (Nussbaum 2001, 111–161; Sen 1984, 309; 1988, 45)?

Yet despite frequent mentions of adaptive preferences, we encounter few explicit discussions of what adaptive preferences *are* and what sorts of ethical problems they pose. We know that adaptive preferences are supposed to be distorting, unreliable accounts of what their bearers need. But we do not know what distinguishes adaptive preferences from other types of preferences we accept as reliable indicators of well-being—beyond some sense that adaptive preferences seem imposed by bad social conditions. Further, we do not know what development practitioners and activists should do when they run into real people with adaptive preferences.

I begin to fill in these gaps in our knowledge about what adaptive preferences are and what should be done about them. To answer the question of *what adaptive preferences are* and why they pose ethical problems, I offer a perfectionist definition of adaptive preference. On my perfectionist definition, adaptive preferences are (1) preferences inconsistent with basic flourishing (2) that are formed under conditions nonconducive to basic flourishing and (3) that we believe people might be persuaded to transform upon normative scrutiny of their preferences and exposure to conditions more conducive to flourishing. Underlying this perfectionist definition is the belief that people tend to seek their basic flourishing. To answer the question of *what should be done* about adaptive preferences in practice, I justify noncoercive public intervention aimed at promoting the flourishing of people with adaptive preferences. I offer a deliberative perfectionist approach to adaptive preference intervention. My deliberative perfectionist approach states that basic flourishing should be defined by some sort of cross-cultural deliberative process and that deliberating with people with adaptive preferences should be a key ingredient of adaptive preference intervention.

So, my central aims in this chapter are to offer a perfectionist definition of adaptive preference and to propose a deliberative perfectionist approach to responding to adaptive preferences in practice. The chapter is structured as follows: first, I argue that we need a conception of human flourishing to meaningfully distinguish adaptive preferences from nonadaptive ones. Second, I argue that the task of identifying adaptive preferences in practice is fraught with unavoidable epistemological difficulties. These difficulties include the likelihood of misunderstanding self-interested well-being trade-offs, treating deprivation caused by structural barriers as primarily caused by psychological problems, and mistaking unfamiliar ways of flourishing for instances of adaptive preference. We need a concept of human flourishing and an approach to adaptive preference intervention that acknowledges these difficulties rather than imagining them away. The deliberative perfectionist approach to adaptive preference intervention offers a framework for responding to adaptive preferences that is sensitive to the epistemological difficulties of real-life attempts to identify adaptive preferences. Third, I defend the deliberative perfectionist approach by claiming that involving deprived people in diagnosing and responding to their own deprivation is a good thing. I discuss both pragmatic and moral reasons for deliberating with people with adaptive preferences.

What Adaptive Preferences Are: A Perfectionist Account

As I have already mentioned, existing discussions of adaptive preferences in development tell us very little about what adaptive preferences are. Development theorists typically list preferences they would designate as adaptive without fully explaining the underlying similarity among them. They tend to list *examples* of adaptive preferences rather than define the term "adaptive preference." This lack of explicit definition makes sense once we notice the contexts in which theoretical discussions of adaptive preferences usually appear. Development theorists often discuss adaptive preferences within larger arguments criticizing utilitarian approaches to development.

Critics of utilitarianism in development typically cite the problem of adaptive preference in order to reveal problems with taking preference satisfaction as the end of social distribution.[1] Simply put, preference satisfaction theories of development hold that development should focus on giving people access to what they want. One problem with treating preference satisfaction as the end of development is that people can have preferences it seems morally questionable to fulfill. People's wants can become deformed by bad circumstances. Taking preference satisfaction as the end of development implies that we have an obligation to fulfill people's deformed preferences. This implication of preference satisfaction theories of social distribution is deeply objectionable, the critic of utilitarianism claims, and so we should be wary of utilitarian approaches. Adaptive preference features in this type of argument as a type of preference that utilitarianism commits us to fulfilling, but whose fulfillment we should find objectionable. For an example of such an argument, consider the following passage from Amartya Sen:

> The most blatant forms of inequalities and exploitations survive in the world through making allies out of the deprived and the exploited. The underdog learns to bear the burden so well that he or she overlooks the burden itself. Discontent is replaced by acceptance, hopeless rebellion by conformist quiet, and—most relevantly in the present context—suffering and anger by cheerful endurance. As people learn to survive to adjust to the existing horrors by sheer necessity of uneventful survival, the horrors look less terrible in the metric of utilities. (1984, 309)

In the passage, Sen brings up adaptive preferences to make a larger criticism of utilitarianism. The diminished desires of dominated or deprived people who learn to accept little serve as examples of preferences whose fulfillment should not be taken to constitute well-being achievement. Sen does not explicitly tell us *why* fulfilling these preferences would not constitute well-being achievement. Aiming social policy at fulfilling them just seems, well, *wrong*. Thus, I submit that the definition of adaptive preference in arguments like these is *intuitive*. We know that deprived people sometimes have desires that we would not expect them to have absent the deprivation—and that it seems morally questionable to commit political institutions to fulfilling. But we do not know what distinguishes these desires from other types of desires or *why* fulfilling them is morally problematic. Sen relies on our intuitions to supply the moral problem.

So Sen does not tell us what makes adaptive preferences different from other types of preferences, and he does not tell us why fulfilling adaptive preferences is objectionable. Why is this lack in Sen a problem? One reason intuitive definitions of adaptive preference pose problems is that they give us unreliable criteria for discerning cases of adaptive preference in the real world. We know from discussions like Sen's that some people problematically adjust their preferences because of deprivation, but by what criteria do we determine what is problematic, and how do we know who is engaged in problematic preference adjustment? Are the preferences in Sen's discussion problematic because they are deprivation-perpetuating? Are they problematic because deprived people seem to have very little choice in forming these preferences—that is, "sheer necessity" imposes the preferences on them? Are they problematic because they are not self-interested? Are they problematic because they are preferences that fail to express a desire for "more" than what a person already has?

Any of these explanations is plausible, and assenting to any of them will give us distinct criteria for identifying real-life adaptive preferences. For example, if we hold that adaptive preferences are unreliable indicators of well-being because they are deprivation-perpetuating, we will think that all people who go on health-threatening religious fasts have adaptive preferences regardless of why they are doing so. But if we hold that adaptive preferences are unreliable indicators of well-being because they are imposed, we will not see the fasting person as having adaptive preferences if she chose to fast, or if she had options other than fasting. Similarly, if we think that adaptive preferences are problematic because people's capacities to want "more" have been thwarted, we will think that the contented millionaire is a victim of adaptive preferences. If we think that adaptive preferences are problematic because the person who has them did not choose to have them, we will not see the contented millionaire's preferences as adaptive.

Without an explanation of why adaptive preferences are unreliable well-being indicators, we do not have a principled way of sorting adaptive preferences from nonadaptive ones. Further, if we lack an explicit conception of why adaptive preferences are problematic, we will not know what other ethical commitments our commitment to treating adaptive preferences as problematic entails. This is a second problem with relying on intuition to explain the problems with fulfilling preferences that seem to resemble the ones Sen described. So, for example, if we believe that adaptive preferences are inauthentic because they are not self-interested, we are committed to believing that well-being requires self-interest. If we believe that adaptive preferences are problematic because they are not chosen, we are committed to believing that people's judgments about their well-being are reliable only when they are chosen. We want to know what sorts of ethical consequences our judgments about adaptive preferences entail, especially because our intuitive judgments about adaptive preferences may entail ethical commitments that we eschew. Since we want consistency among our ethical commitments and our intuitions, we need greater ethical clarity about what adaptive preferences are.[2]

So we need a clearer definition of adaptive preferences than the one hinted at in arguments against utilitarianism like Sen's. Yet despite this need, the intuitive definition of adaptive preferences currently influences development ethics and policy. Many development practitioners already attempt to interrogate the adaptive preferences they encounter in practice. For instance, Solava Ibrahim and Sabina Alkire observe that adaptive preference poses problems for participatory evaluations of women's household decision-making power. They note that deprived people's accounts of their own well-being offer views that are "coming 'from' a delineated place such as a set of beliefs about what an empowered woman, man, or ethnic person does" (Ibrahim and Alkire 2007, 393). Although the first-person accounts of deprived people provide valuable information about well-being, in cases of adaptive preference, these accounts "should in some sense be 'cleansed' of this effect" (Ibrahim and Alkire 2007, 393). Similarly, Christopher Gibson and Michael Woolcock use the fact of adaptive preference to justify the use of deliberative processes in development (Gibson and Woolcock 2008, 153).

My aim here is not to criticize Sen or the practitioners who are acting according to an unclear sense of what adaptive preferences are. Sen, and other critics of utilitarianism like him, clearly does not intend to provide philosophically robust definitions of adaptive preference, and development practitioners need not wait for philosophers to tell them what concepts should inform their practice. But I do want to suggest that many of us are discussing, writing about, and creating policies to address adaptive preferences without a sufficient definition of what adaptive preferences are. The question of what adaptive preferences are is an urgent one for development ethicists, and philosophers more generally. We may currently be relying on some offhand remarks criticizing utilitarianism to define adaptive preferences, and, if we are, this may prevent us both from engaging in responsible policy prescriptions about adaptive preference and from engaging in rigorous moral reasoning about them.

Before I sketch a more explicit definition of adaptive preference, I respond to a potential criticism of my claim that the operative definition of adaptive preferences in development is intuitive and nonexplicit. It may seem that I have ignored existent attempts to explicitly define adaptive preference. Specifically, it may seem that I have failed to seriously engage the literature suggesting that adaptive preferences are unchosen and Jon Elster's explicit definition of adaptive preference. I acknowledge that I have yet not sufficiently discussed the existing idea of adaptive preferences as unchosen and simply ask readers who are interested in this line of thought to consult Chapter 2, which I devote entirely to exposing the problems with thinking of adaptive preferences as autonomy deficits.

Elster does provide an explicit definition of adaptive preferences, but his definition is not the one motivating contemporary development ethics. Elster understands adaptive preferences as preferences persons form unconsciously that downgrade options that are inaccessible to them (Elster 1987, 119). His definition is based on La Fontaine's fable of the fox and the grapes; the fox stops wanting the grapes because he cannot have them. I do not think it is accurate to think of development ethicists as simply having adopted Elster's definition. For one thing, some important development ethicists, like Martha Nussbaum, explicitly state that many preferences they consider adaptive would not fit Elster's definition (Nussbaum 2001, 158). For another, influential development theorists, like Nussbaum and Sen, cite as instances of adaptive preference preferences that are not adaptive on Elster's definition. For example, Sen calls up cases in which persons, unlike the fox in the fable, *consciously* adjust their preferences. For example, he groups *deciding* that "it is silly to bemoan" one's lack of political freedom and using "heroic efforts" to be happy despite caste or race oppression with "coming to terms with adversities" (Sen 2002, 634). Nussbaum also describes preferences not to protest poor sanitation that poor women have, "because they knew no other way" as adaptive (Nussbaum 2001, 113), but Elster's definition could not count them as such. Elster's fox has to have thought of the grapes as delicious before in order to "downgrade" them by calling them sour; conversely, the poor women in Nussbaum's example may never have known about the advantages of different sanitation practices.

Why We Need a Conception of Human Flourishing to Identify Adaptive Preferences

I have established that development needs a more explicit definition of adaptive preference. I now offer such a definition. One way of identifying the essential features of a phenomenon is to look at a variety of examples of the phenomenon and to ask what all of the examples have in common. I propose that the examples of adaptive preference described by a variety of development theorists and practitioners share a structure. The preferences we are most likely to discuss as adaptive are preferences that seem complicit in perpetuating people's oppression and deprivation that are held by oppressed and deprived people and were formed under conditions unconducive to their flourishing. Some examples are living without a clean water supply and not being upset about it (Nussbaum 2001, 113), thinking that one is not ill when objective indicators suggest otherwise (Sen 1984, 309), not complaining about the discriminatory wage structure one is subject to (Nussbaum 2001, 113), staying in an abusive marriage because one believes it is one's destiny (Nussbaum 2001, 112), not rebelling against one's tyrannical government—regardless of whether one can change it—(Sen 2002, 634), and achieving happiness in one's "limited life" despite caste or race oppression (Sen 2002, 634).

The preferences in this list all belong to oppressed and deprived people,[3] and they are all preferences that seem deprivation-perpetuating. But most descriptions of adaptive preference do not simply cite instances of deprivation-perpetuating behavior by deprived people; they also make claims about the subjective states of the people who have adaptive preferences. Theorists of adaptive preference do not simply note the coexistence of oppression and oppression-perpetuating preferences. They also suggest that people with adaptive preferences have developed them for reasons that have more to do with circumstance than with authentic endorsement. Adaptive preferences appear imposed on their bearers, or as somehow not belonging to them. In the long excerpt from Sen I cited earlier, Sen refers to people with adaptive preferences as "adjust[ing] to the existing horrors by sheer necessity of uneventful survival" (Sen 1984, 309). Similarly, Naila Kabeer describes women with adaptive preferences as having lacked the capacity to imagine themselves otherwise (Kabeer 1999, 442). When Nussbaum discusses the lives of the Indian women who accept poor sanitation and domestic abuse, she emphasizes that the women "knew no other way" (Nussbaum 2001, 113).[4] It is as though Nussbaum wants to highlight a difference between doing something because one has chosen it after considering the options and doing something because one is ignorant of other options.

In discussions like these, I want to suggest, we are asked to activate two different moral intuitions: intuitions about the badness of impeding one's own flourishing and intuitions about the badness of not being the author of one's own values. If adaptive preferences seem morally distinct—if they seem like a category of preferences that are particularly worthy of questioning by public institutions— it is both because they are flourishing inconsistent and because they seem "imposed" on their bearers. Remove either feature from a case, and we no longer seem to be left with adaptive preference. Imagine a preference that a person has not reflected on or consciously chosen but that is consistent with her flourishing. For instance, imagine a woman who learns how to read so that she can better understand her interactions with public agencies but does so simply because this is "what everyone is doing." We would hardly describe this woman as possessed of adaptive preferences. We may think of her as somehow nonautonomous, since she has not subjected her first-order desires to reflective scrutiny or sought harmony between her first- and second-order desires. But we do not think of her as falling into the same category of the "dominated housewife" or the poor person who has a diminished "capacity to aspire." If we imagine an "imposed" preference that is consistent with flourishing, we do not find a case of adaptive preference. We thus cannot isolate *processes* of preference formation that make adaptive preferences what they are.

Now let us imagine a preference that does not seem "imposed" but is inconsistent with flourishing. We might imagine a woman who has access to conditions for flourishing across a variety of domains, who reflects upon her decisions, and who decides in spite of it all to spend the rest of her life engaging repeatedly in a sport that is likely to kill her—say bullfighting. Like the woman who learns to read just because everyone is doing it, this woman seems not to have adaptive preferences. We may have paternalistic desires to prevent her from bullfighting, but we would not think of her preference as adaptive if social conditions did not seem to have unduly influenced this choice.

In judgments about real-life cases of adaptive preference, intuitions about the problematic nature of flourishing-inconsistent preferences and intuitions about the problematic nature of not being in control of one's own life do not only *accompany* one another; we also find one intuition *eliciting* the other. When dealing with actual cases, we typically notice that somebody has a well-being-inconsistent preference under bad conditions, and then we wonder whether that preference can be authentically said to belong to her. We recognize a flourishing-inconsistent preference and wonder about why someone would choose that preference; the choice of a flourishing-inconsistent preference in the face of bad social conditions makes us further wonder in what sense the person was in control of her decisions. Nussbaum's discussion of the Indian women who accepted poor sanitation and malnourishment "because they knew no other way" (Nussbaum 2001, 113) is one example. Nussbaum recognizes the seemingly flourishing-inconsistent behavior (accepting malnutrition and poor sanitation) and then wonders why someone would choose it (because he or she knew no other way).

Another telling example comes in Marilyn Friedman's discussion of women's participation in cultural practices that are harmful to them. Friedman writes, "If a group of women consistently choose to live in ways that violate their own rights, we should first try to assess the conditions under which the women are making their choices" (Friedman 2003, 192). Like Nussbaum, Friedman observes women's well-being-inconsistent behavior and wonders whether these women's choice to perform them was somehow impeded. It is helpful to think of judgments like Nussbaum and Friedman's as motivated by a type of counterfactual reasoning.[5] Perhaps harmful preferences formed under bad conditions seem unchosen, because we have difficulty imagining that a person *would have formed* those preferences under conditions conducive to flourishing.

We suspect that people's preferences somehow do not belong to them when those people have preferences inconsistent with flourishing formed under conditions nonconducive to flourishing. I believe that this is the basic structure of judgments about adaptive preference. If I am right about this, seeing adaptive preferences as a problem requires moral commitments best described as *perfectionist*. Before I explain why, I pause briefly to explain my understanding of perfectionism. Following Thomas Hurka, I take perfectionism to be the idea that "what is good, ultimately, is the development of human nature" (Hurka 1993, 3). Perfectionism holds that a person leads a good life if she is flourishing—that is, if she is exercising certain valuable capacities that it is in the nature of human beings to exercise. Leading a flourishing life is not identical with living a life one is satisfied with, because one can become satisfied with a life that does not exercise valuable human capacities, or that exercises them in a less than human way. I do not mean anything much stronger than this when I speak of perfectionism, and I especially do not mean to endorse Aristotle's (1998) ideas about what constitutes a flourishing human life—as many perfectionists do. Also, in saying we need certain perfectionist commitments to see adaptive preferences as problematic, I do not mean to say that we must commit to a complete perfectionist theory of politics in order to want public institutions to promote the flourishing of people with adaptive preferences; I believe that the perfectionist commitments we need are compatible with a liberal commitment to personal autonomy, as I argue in the Chapter 4.

Why does seeing adaptive preferences as a problem require perfectionist moral commitments? I believe there are two reasons. First, the idea that a person can experience satisfaction with her form of life and yet not be doing well requires a criterion of well-being other than pleasure or desire-satisfaction. Second, seeing well-being-inconsistent preferences as evidence of inauthentic choice requires a view of human beings as having a natural tendency toward flourishing. Let us begin with the first reason. If we think adaptive preferences pose an ethical problem, we think it is possible for a person to have desires that are inconsistent with her well-being. This implies that we think of desire-satisfaction and well-being as distinguishable from one another. The destitute person who no longer has the "capacity to aspire" may want only the insufficiently nourishing diet she receives. If we judge that she is not doing well in spite of her apparent desire for undernourishment, it is because we do not treat well-being and desire-satisfaction as coextensive. Perfectionism holds that human beings need to perform certain valuable capacities in order to flourish, where feeling satisfied is not the only valuable capacity. A perfectionist who believes that people need adequate nutrition to flourish can consistently say that a person who is content with malnutrition has her desires satisfied but is not flourishing.

Admittedly, perfectionism is not the only moral theory that refuses to treat desire-satisfaction and well-being as identical. There are a number of ways utilitarians might attempt to distinguish desire-satisfaction from well-being. A hedonic utilitarian might claim that satisfying desires for pain rather than pleasure does not produce pleasure—so that the malnourished person who wants to be malnourished is not doing well if she is subjectively suffering from her malnutrition. Similarly, a utilitarian who took a long-term view of the content malnourished person's life may want to say that malnutrition will frustrate other desires the person has, and thus that the frustration of her future desires prevents her from having well-being—in purely utilitarian terms.[6] I think that these permutations can account for the apparent inauthenticity of some adaptive preferences, but many preferences we intuitively classify as adaptive may not produce psychological suffering or frustrate future desires. Nussbaum's Jayamma, who works in a brick kiln with a discriminatory wage structure and does not protest (Nussbaum 2001, 113), may not find that her adaptive preference frustrates future desires. If she desires only what her current income can give her, she can make very little money and persist in having a very high level of desire-satisfaction. Moreover, her desire for only what she can get need not be construed as a desire for subjective suffering; she may gain immense subjective pleasure from the small mercies in her life. Perfectionism, unlike these variants of utilitarianism, distinguishes desire-satisfaction from well-being in a way that makes sense of the apparent inauthenticity of a wide range of adaptive preferences. Through a perfectionist lens, the poor person who is content with malnutrition, Jayamma who does not protest wage discrimination, the poor women who see nothing wrong with the poor sanitary conditions under which they live, and the battered woman who believes she deserves abuse[7] can all unambiguously be said to have achieved a certain level of desire-satisfaction without thereby flourishing.

Let us turn to the second reason I think seeing adaptive preferences as a problem requires perfectionist commitments. As I argued above, when identifying real-life cases of adaptive preference, we usually move from noticing a flourishing-inhibiting preference formed under bad conditions to wondering whether a person "really chose" to have that preference. In these judgments, we treat flourishing-inconsistent preferences as *markers* of some sort of lack of choice. For example, we encounter a person who does not boil her water before drinking it and think her choice not to boil her water might reflect a lack of information. Underlying judgments like this, I think, is the belief that when people have options for flourishing, they tend to choose in accordance with their flourishing. If we thought all types of choices were equally likely under conditions of procedural autonomy, we would not think flourishing-inconsistent choices were more likely "imposed" than flourishing-consistent choices. We would not think of oppressed and deprived people's self-harming preferences as more likely to have been imposed than their flourishing-promoting preferences. Call the underlying idea here the "Flourishing Claim." According to the Flourishing Claim, people tend to pursue their basic flourishing, and preferences that impede people's basic flourishing are unlikely to be their deep preferences. By "deep preferences," I mean preferences they would retain under conditions conducive to flourishing that a person recognizes as such. I will explain this notion of deep preference a bit more in the coming section. For now, let us note that the Flourishing Claim is perfectionist, because it points out a natural tendency toward the good in human beings, and perfectionism holds the good to lie in the development of human nature.

Toward a Perfectionist Definition of Adaptive Preference

I began this chapter by pointing out that many of us who think about oppression and deprivation are writing about adaptive preferences without great clarity about what they are. I have just argued that seeing adaptive preferences as unreliable guides to what constitutes the well-being of their bearers requires certain perfectionist commitments. I believe that acknowledging these perfectionist commitments can give us a clearer definition of adaptive preference. I propose the following definition of adaptive preference.

> An adaptive preference is a preference that (1) is inconsistent with a person's basic flourishing, (2) was formed under conditions nonconducive to her basic flourishing, and (3) that we do not think a person would have formed under conditions conducive to basic flourishing.

In order to identify adaptive preferences in practice, however, we need a *prospective* understanding of this definition. I propose this one:

> Representatives of public institutions can reasonably suspect a preference of adaptiveness if (1) that preference is inconsistent with basic flourishing, and (2) it was formed under conditions unconducive to a person's flourishing, and (3) we believe it is possible for the person to change the preference into a preference more consistent with flourishing and endorse the change.

Three concepts I have used in this definition require further explanation: the concepts of "preference," "preference incompatible with flourishing," and "endorsement." Let us begin with the concept of preference. On my definition, both expressed lower-order preferences (like the action of drinking unboiled water for instance) and higher-order preferences about preferences (like the belief that drinking unboiled water is healthy or good) count as preferences. This means that either type of preference can count as adaptive. A woman's preference to drink unboiled water because she knows no other way may be accompanied by a higher-order preference for health or it may be accompanied by a higher-order preference for submission to the suffering fate to which she believes she is condemned. My definition says that the expressed preference to drink unboiled water arrived at under conditions nonconducive to flourishing is likely adaptive, independent of what higher-order preferences accompany it. But it also says that higher-order preferences, like the preference to submit to suffering, can be adaptive as well. Clearly, higher-order adaptive preferences will require different types of interventions from lower-order adaptive preferences, and this is an issue I will discuss in more detail shortly. For now, the important point is that both higher and lower-order preferences can count as adaptive on my definition.

Now let us turn to the terms "preference inconsistent with basic flourishing" and "endorsement." A preference inconsistent with basic flourishing is a preference that a person who was flourishing at a basic level would not express. A preference may be *inconsistent with* basic flourishing without being the *primary cause of* a person's lack of basic flourishing. A woman who does not boil her water before she drinks it may not boil her water because she has insufficient access to fuel; in a case like this, her preference is inconsistent with flourishing but her beliefs and attitudes are clearly not the main cause of her precarious health. Finally, when I say that an adaptive preference is amenable to being reversed and endorsed, I mean that an adaptive preference is amenable to being changed in way that a person who previously had adaptive preferences feels positively about and recognizes as a part of her own projects. So, if the woman who does not boil her water and has access to fuel learns about how this will prevent disease and feels positively about her increased capacity for health, she has endorsed her preference change.

My definition characterizes adaptive preferences according to both the conditions under which they were formed and the content of the preferences themselves; in other words, they are defined by both procedural and substantive criteria. In order to make explicit the fact that adaptive preferences are defined by both procedural and substantive features, I accompany my new definition with a terminological shift. Rather than speaking of "adaptive preferences," I think we should speak of "inappropriately adaptive preferences."[8] The term "adaptive preference" suggests that the very adaptation of a person's preferences to her social conditions is a problem. "Inappropriately adaptive preference" (IAP) helps us to see that it matters that the preferences are *harmful* to their bearers, and adapted to *bad* social conditions.

Taken together, this definition of IAP and the Flourishing Claim stated earlier furnish a reason for public institutions to intervene in the lives of people with adaptive preferences in order to promote their flourishing. On the basis of the Flourishing Claim, we may say that if a person holds a preference contrary to her basic flourishing, and she lacks opportunities for basic flourishing, it is possible that she is committed to a conception of the good that does not value flourishing and that will not change even under better social conditions. But it is more likely that the person in question is managing a bad option set or acting according to a set of values to which she is not deeply attached—that is, that would change with new knowledge and/or better conditions. Faced with a woman who accepts malnutrition and poor sanitation, for example, public policy can reasonably proceed from the assumption that her preference to eat less than is healthy does not likely express an unchangeable deep desire. This type of judgment can be appropriately based on the presumption that people have a tendency to value their basic flourishing. Indeed, this tendency is strong enough that we expect most people to express preferences consistent with their basic flourishing when opportunities for flourishing they recognize as such are available to them.

More generally, we may say that if people have a tendency toward their basic flourishing, preferences that are inconsistent with their flourishing and formed under conditions nonconducive to basic flourishing are likely not "deep" preferences. That is, non-flourishing preferences formed under bad conditions are not only amenable to being changed; it is likely that people with adaptive preferences can come to endorse changes that will increase their capacities to flourish. This provides a warrant for public institutions to intervene to improve the lives of people with IAPs.

However, the Flourishing Claim does not justify *indiscriminate* intervention in the lives of people with adaptive preferences. It justifies noncoercive intervention, both because we can accept it without abandoning the principle of respect for persons (as I argue in Chapter 4) and because it is difficult to identify adaptive preferences in real-life situations. It is to describing the epistemological difficulties endemic to real-world attempts at adaptive preference identification that I now turn.

The Deliberative Perfectionist Approach to IAP Identification

I have put forth a perfectionist definition of IAP as well as a perfectionist justification of public intervention in the lives of people with IAPs. But even if we understand something about the basic structure of IAPs, we may not be able to easily identify IAPs in practice. Understanding whether a person's behaviors and/or desires are consistent with basic flourishing is trickier than it may initially seem. Part of this difficulty arises from general facts about human psychology; it is difficult to read a person's desires from her behavior. Without a detailed understanding of a person's option set and her perception of it, third parties will not be able to determine from the content of a person's preferences how those preferences impact her flourishing. A person who does not protest her malnutrition may do so because she erroneously believes that she could not ask for more or because she correctly believes that she should conserve her energies for work when protesting her malnutrition is unlikely to change anything. I would argue that both preferences are adaptive and yet they require radically different interventions. Yet it would be difficult to distinguish them in practice, since the preferences may seem identical to a third-party; both preferences are preferences to eat an inadequately nourishing diet by people who have lived under conditions of deprivation. Another part of the difficulty of identifying adaptive preferences in practice stems from the problems associated with making cross-cultural judgments about flourishing. Third-parties who are insufficiently familiar with the life-contexts of deprived people will always risk confusing *unfamiliar forms* of flourishing with the *absence* of flourishing.

We cannot simply read people's reasons for having the preferences they do or the effects of their preferences on flourishing from their behaviors. These facts about the world make IAP identification in development practice susceptible to specific types of error. In the remainder of this section, I name three epistemological difficulties that development practitioners face in identifying adaptive preferences. I also claim that these difficulties suggest something about the *type* of conception of human flourishing we should endorse if my perfectionist justification of IAP intervention is to guide public policy. I argue that what I call a "deliberative perfectionist approach" to IAP intervention allows public institutions to take the flourishing of people with IAPs seriously without denying the epistemological difficulties of IAP identification.

The Epistemological Difficulties of Adaptive Preference Identification

We might think of error in IAP identification as something like an occupational hazard of development practice. An occupational hazard is a risk encountered as a normal part of a practice because of the nature of that practice. The nature of cross-cultural interpersonal interaction makes it the case that development practitioners risk misunderstanding the effects of people's preferences on flourishing.[9] The limitations that cause this risk of misunderstanding do not admit of easy elimination: we cannot read people's reasons for their behavior from their behavior, and we cannot always understand how the behaviors of people who are different from us affect their overall lives. We can distinguish three different ways development practitioners and activists are likely to misunderstand the effects of people's preferences on basic flourishing—three occupational hazards of IAP identification. Call these occupational hazards "psychologizing the structural," "misunderstanding trade-offs," and "confusing difference with deprivation."

Occupational Hazard 1: Psychologizing the Structural

A person living under unjust conditions may express lower-order IAPs while having higher-order preferences that are perfectly consistent with flourishing. Her expressed preferences may be a way of making the best of a situation under which basic flourishing is not available and may persist unaccompanied by a set of inappropriate higher-order beliefs and desires. Since we cannot discern the reasons for people's behavior on the basis of their expressed preferences, it is possible to wrongly assume that lower-order IAPs reflect higher-order ones—that actual choices inconsistent with basic flourishing reflect a lack of value for flourishing. Brooke Ackerly accuses Nussbaum of precisely this error. Nussbaum suggests that an impediment to women's participation in Bangladesh Rural Advancement Committee (BRAC) literacy programs is their lack of appreciation for the value of education (Nussbaum 1995, 91). Ackerly counters that her personal interactions with over 800 Bangladeshi women involved in BRAC and programs like it have made clear to her that a lack of value for education is not the main reason these women do not choose to pursue their own literacy (Ackerly 2000, 107). Rather, these women value education, but education requires a financial investment on their part—a financial investment it is more rational for them to make on their children's behalf than on their own (Ackerly 2000, 107). If the Bangladeshi women have only limited resources to spend on education, they will spend them on their children and do so out of rational self-interest. The returns from education, such as income, will be higher for their children than for them, as they can gain from their children's education over the long term. In short, Ackerly thinks that Nussbaum has mistakenly treated women's illiteracy as evidence of a lack of value for education, where it is actually an attempt to manage a limited option set in a world where sufficient opportunities for schooling for all family members are not available.[10]

How might lower-order preferences inconsistent with flourishing (like the preference not to educate oneself) fail to manifest adaptive higher-order preferences—that is, adaptive values and attitudes? The answer is that people may do their best to manage limited options and simultaneously judge that their options are unacceptable.[11] If this seems puzzling, perhaps it is because we have overlooked a basic fact about what revealed preferences can tell us about people's desires. A revealed lower-order preference can only tell us how a person ranks *available* options, not how she ranks unavailable ones. So, for a woman to choose to educate her child rather than herself under conditions where she cannot educate both tells us little about what that woman would choose if she could. Put more formally, that a person prefers y over x tells us little about how she feels about z. A woman who prefers to educate her son may also have a separate, or higher-order, preference to live in a world in which both she and her child could pursue educations.

We can see the conflict between Ackerly and Nussbaum as a dispute about how we should interpret the behavior of people who seem to be living in non-flourishing ways. It seems likely that some people have flourishing-inconsistent behaviors because of low-level adaptations to bad conditions and others have them because of higher-order adaptive beliefs and attitudes. Undoubtedly, higher-order IAPs where a person nearly completely devalues her flourishing and the types of preferences Ackerly describes are points on a continuum; not all structural constraints are equally limiting, and people may be complicit in perpetuating their deprivation to varying degrees. But Ackerly's comments alert us to a particular type of danger—a danger we might call "psychologizing the structural."[12] We psychologize the structural when we incorrectly assume that a person is failing to flourish primarily because of problems with her psychology (her values, desires, etc.) rather than because of her structural environment. If we accept Ackerly's criticism of Nussbaum, we can say that Nussbaum is right that poor South Asian women who do not become literate have IAPs[13] but also wrong about what motivates those IAPs. Nussbaum psychologizes the structural by seeing South Asian women's values, instead of their limited opportunities, as their primary reasons for not becoming literate.

Development practitioners and activists need to be particularly wary of psychologizing the structural, because it can cause them to overlook well-being-directed agency on the part of deprived people, and because it promotes ineffective development interventions. Interventions aimed exclusively at changing people's values and attitudes—like helping people build self-esteem, for instance—will likely do little on their own to improve the lives of people whose flourishing requires expanded options or structural change. IAP interventions in the lives of people who are simply constrained by bad options will likely have to focus more on changing social conditions than changing people's higher-order values.

Occupational Hazard 2: Misidentifying Imposed Trade-offs

One reason development practitioners may make mistakes in responding to IAPs is that they may incorrectly attribute people's oppression to psychological—rather than structural—factors. Another reason is that they can wrongly treat flourishing as a single vector—something that is either present or absent. Rather than being simply present or absent, flourishing is likely plural—that is, comprised of a number of disparate goods or capacities. If flourishing has plural constituents, it is possible for a person to be flourishing in some domains and not others. The danger of treating flourishing as though it were a single vector is that a person who is failing to flourish in some domains may seem not to be trying to flourish *at all*.

Take as an example the case of a woman who risks HIV exposure in order not to anger her husband. Studies of women's sexual health behaviors all over the world indicate that women tend not to ask their male partners to wear condoms for fear of angering them—particularly under circumstances where their partners' favor guarantees women access to goods like food, income, and freedom from shame and abuse. A common explanation of the high prevalence of HIV among married women in sub-Saharan Africa is that women do not negotiate condom use with their husbands because of economic and social dependency.

A woman who risks HIV exposure under conditions where doing so guarantees her access to other goods may or may not have inappropriately adaptive attitudes toward her health. She may wish she could protect her bodily health by engaging in safer sex. We may speak of the woman in this case as facing an *imposed* well-being trade-off. She wants to be able to flourish in all domains, but given the current circumstances, she does what she can to flourish in some. She, like the woman who educates her children rather than herself out of necessity, has higher-order preferences that are consistent with basic flourishing. But it would be easy for a development practitioner to miss this fact. Imagine a development practitioner who believes she can read people's attitudes about flourishing *in general* from people's behavior. This practitioner might look at a woman's choice not to prevent HIV exposure and conclude that that person does not value her own well-being. But a lack of value for one's own flourishing is not the only reason one may have lower-order preferences consistent with flourishing in some single domain. One reason it does not follow is that flourishing across all relevant domains may be impossible. The development practitioner who assumes that failing to flourish in one domain reveals a global lack of desire for flourishing has succumbed to an occupational hazard we might call "misidentifying imposed trade-offs."

Like the development practitioner who psychologizes the structural, the practitioner who misidentifies imposed trade-offs is likely to recommend ineffective interventions. In some cases misidentifying trade-offs will be one way of psychologizing the structural; an intervention aimed at changing the beliefs surrounding sexuality of a woman who values her sexual autonomy but does not express it because she will lose income if she angers her husband is one motivated both by a psychologization of the structural and a misidentification of trade-offs. Sometimes, however, misidentifying trade-offs will not be a version of psychologizing the structural. For instance, a woman may not negotiate condom use with her husband only because she believes she must rely on him for income since women are hopeless entrepreneurs. In this case, the woman's deprivation is largely perpetuated by deformations in her higher-order beliefs and desires. Both types of cases of misidentified trade-offs are likely to lead to ineffective development interventions. The practitioner who misidentifies trade-offs is likely to recommend interventions that are ineffective because they are targeted at the wrong domain of life. In the foregoing case of the woman who does not avoid HIV exposure, is the best intervention one that teaches her how to use condoms? Or, might it be better to work on ensuring her access to income and social recognition that would help her bargain with her husband? The latter would arguably be more effective, but a practitioner who misidentified imposed trade-offs would likely pursue the former.

Occupational Hazard 3: Confusing Difference with Deprivation

A third occupational hazard of real-life attempts at IAP identification is not caused by misjudgments about *why* people who are not achieving basic flourishing are not achieving it. Rather, it is caused by misjudgments about *whether* certain—higher- or lower-order—preferences are consistent with flourishing. It is difficult to tell whether another person is flourishing—especially if that person's life-context is unfamiliar because she is from a different cultural background, gender, or social class. It is one thing to know in the abstract what basic flourishing is; it is quite another to know when it is and is not happening in practice. To put this differently, a development practitioner may know what general capacities are constitutive of human flourishing without knowing how a person's actual behaviors impact her exercise of those capacities. Imagine that our conception of human flourishing includes items like the capacity to be adequately nourished, to develop one's cognitive and affective capacities, and to make decisions about one's sexual life. In the real world, we do not typically encounter people as "adequately nourished," "developing cognitive and affective capacities," or "making decisions about their sexual lives." We encounter people who are eating mangoes, hamburgers, noodles; people who are attending schools, watching soap operas, counting money, telling stories; people who are having arranged marriages, going out with "sugar daddies," going to visit the "circumciser," having few or many children. When a development practitioner observes that a person has never attended school, does it follow that she has underdeveloped cognitive capacities? Having an abstract sense of what flourishing is can furnish only part of the answer to this question. To answer it responsibly we also need to understand the context of the person's life: is she doing other things might reasonably be interpreted as developing her cognitive capacities?

It is not always obvious how a person's behaviors impact her flourishing. Moreover, real people are probably used to recognizing flourishing in very culturally and class-specific behaviors. So a person from a cultural world in which marriages are not arranged may perceive a fundamental incompatibility between having one's parents play a role in choosing one's partner and being able to make decisions about one's sexual life, and a formally educated person from the city may not notice all of the ways a poor female merchant exercises cognitive capacities in her daily life-regardless of whether she knows how to read or write.

The development practitioner who thinks a person has IAPs may be wrong because she has misapplied the abstract concept of human flourishing to a real-world case—or, specifically, because she has failed to distinguish the essential features of flourishing from the contingent ones given by her own life-context. Call the occupational hazard here "confusing difference with deprivation"—inaccurately capturing the effects of a preference on flourishing because of differences between the life-context of the practitioner and the seemingly deprived person. Confusing difference with deprivation may involve misunderstanding the sense in which a deprivation is a deprivation, or, in more clear-cut cases, it may involve seeing deprivation where there is none at all. Vandana Shiva's work on Indian women and subsistence agriculture charges Western development discourses with seeing deprivation where none exists. According to Shiva, many pernicious agricultural policies in development are traceable to a view that confuses a Western conception of flourishing with flourishing as such. Specifically, Westerners understood lives not centered on technology, conspicuous consumption, and participation in cash economies to be essentially deprived. They could thus not recognize well-being in lives focused on subsistence farming (Shiva 1988, 4). If we imagine a Western urban development practitioner intervening in a rural community focused on subsistence farming, we can think through what mistaking difference with deprivation might look like in an actual case. This urban practitioner might see the focus on subsistence agriculture primarily as evidence of severe poverty—rather than as a way of accessing food security in a context where cash income is unreliable, or as a way of life that allowed people to achieve other objectively valuable goods like interpersonal relationships and connectedness to the natural environment.

The practitioner who confuses difference with deprivation is likely not just to propose ineffective interventions but to propose interventions where none are necessary. In the worst case, the practitioner who mistakes difference for deprivation will propose interventions that do not improve—or even decrease—people's well-being. Rather than improving people's lives, interventions motivated by an implicit desire to diminish difference will focus on making the development participants more like the people in the community of the development practitioner's origin. Many critics read the history of development practice as full of interventions focused on making people more similar to the "developers" rather than actually improving the well-being of deprived people.[14] We might think of interventions that homogenize without a moral warrant—to the extent that those interventions are conducted in some semblance of good faith—as motivated by a failure to adequately distinguish flourishing from familiarity.

The Deliberative Perfectionist Approach to Identifying IAPs

I have identified three ways development practitioners are likely to misunderstand the effects of people's preferences on their flourishing. I have called these "occupational hazards," suggesting that these dangers are inextricable from practical attempts to identify IAPs. Do the epistemological difficulties of IAP identification make the task of attempting to identify IAPs in practice hopeless? I believe we can answer this question in the negative. Rather than giving up on attempts to improve the lives of people with IAPs, we need an approach to identifying them that takes the epistemological difficulties inherent in IAP identification seriously and attempts to offset them. I sketch a "deliberative perfectionist approach" to identifying IAPs that may reduce the risk of error and of ineffective/morally objectionable interventions in the lives of people with IAPs.

Defining the Deliberative Perfectionist Approach

I argued in the first section that we needed a conception of human flourishing to identify IAPs. I also argued that public institutions should intervene in the lives of people with IAPs to promote their flourishing. But I said little about what *type* of perfectionist conception should motivate these interventions. I propose that development practitioners should employ a "deliberative perfectionist conception" of human flourishing to diagnose and respond to IAPs. I call this type of conception "deliberative," first, because it is arrived at through a cross-cultural deliberative process. I will not specify the type of deliberative process by which the conception should be generated beyond saying that it should be an *actual* rather than *hypothetical* deliberative process. Subjecting a proposed conception of human flourishing to actual deliberation allows proposed content to be critically evaluated by several parties who come from different moral frameworks. It is unlikely that one person can adequately consider alternative conceptions of flourishing through a deliberative exercise in her imagination. More important, employing actual, rather than hypothetical, deliberation to arrive at the conception lends legitimacy to that conception (Benhabib 2002; Fraser 2008). We want to know that the conception *is* actually or *could actually come to be* acceptable to a wide variety of people—not just that some person thinks the conception *should* be acceptable to a wide variety of people.

We can anticipate that, in a moral world as diverse as ours, a conception of flourishing on which we can agree will possess the following three features: a concern with basic levels of functioning, justificatory minimalism, and vagueness. We expect that a cross-culturally acceptable conception of flourishing will confine itself to *basic* flourishing, because, as is often argued in the literature on global ethics, there seems to be greater consistency across cultures about what basic flourishing requires than about what excellence requires.[15] Indeed, as philosophers like Nussbaum (1992; 2001)[16] and Michael Walzer (1996) have suggested, different cultural perspectives appear to converge more neatly on conceptions of the bad than the good. A conception that grows out of a shared sense of what impedes human flourishing rather than a shared vision of human excellence will confine itself to the more fundamental levels of human flourishing.[17]

The diversity of existing cultures and belief systems also gives us reason to suppose that a cross-culturally acceptable conception of the good will be justificatorily minimal. That is, the conception will stipulate constituent components of basic flourishing without saying much about why those components are valuable. I borrow the term "justificatory minimalism" from Joshua Cohen (2004), who uses its adjectival form to describe conceptions that come unaccompanied by comprehensive moral justifications and are therefore compatible with a variety of comprehensive moral justifications. I use the term "comprehensive" in Rawls's (1996) sense to refer to metaphysical views of the good that cover most domains of human life. A conception of flourishing that emerges from cross-cultural deliberation is likely to be justificatorily minimal, because our agreement about *which* functionings constitute basic human flourishing is stronger than our agreement or *why* these functionings are important. As I noted earlier, it seems quite plausible that there is broad agreement about what *basic* flourishing is. On the other hand, it seems quite *im*plausible that there is broad agreement about what the ultimate ends of human life are. Controversy about the ultimate ends of human life need not preclude agreement about what the basic needs and desires of human beings are, however. As Cass Sunstein (1995) has argued, our chances of reaching moral agreement may be enhanced if we are willing to leave the deepest theoretical questions unresolved. A conception of flourishing that is cross-culturally acceptable will most likely rest on what he might call "an incompletely theorized agreement."

It may seem that the conception of flourishing required for the flourishing argument cannot be justificatory minimal because of its ties to a conception of human nature.[18] However, there is compelling reason to believe both that a cross-culturally acceptable conception of flourishing would be articulated in a moral language that makes the human being central and that this fact alone would not compromise the justificatory minimalism of the conception. In the status quo, we have a level of cross-cultural agreement on the normative concept of the human being; it is the human rights regime. People from different cultures flesh out the deeper moral significance of the human rights in different ways while agreeing on the core moral commitment to a normative conception of the human being.[19] The Flourishing Claim required by my approach demands a commitment to a normative concept of the human being, but referring to the human nature as exerting a moral claim is not a justificatorily maximalist move in the moral world we actually inhabit.

We can anticipate that a conception of flourishing that receives cross-cultural endorsement will be vague as well as justificatorily and substantively minimal. By saying that we should expect such a conception to be vague, I mean that we should expect it to describe the functionings constitutive of basic human flourishing in a highly general fashion. This is because the process of reasoning about these functionings moves from identifying specific instances of them to generalizing about what these instances have in common. Describing the functionings in a way that makes them applicable to human beings as a group will require distilling away some particularities that make them realizable only by certain persons in certain contexts. As Sabina Alkire aptly writes, "Actualized functionings will always have a particular form. One cannot drink 'nutrition' through a straw. One must drink a mango milkshake, or eat a plate of biscuits" (Alkire 2002, 138). However, we believe that a person can be adequately nourished without drinking mango milkshakes. Given this, we should expect the items contained in a cross-culturally acceptable conception of flourishing to be very generally formulated ones, like "access to adequate nutrition" rather than specifically formulated ones, like "access to mango milkshakes." It would be absurd to think of access to mango milkshakes as a constituent of *human* flourishing, even though consuming mango milkshakes may help particular human beings in particular contexts to flourish.

A deliberative, cross-culturally acceptable conception of flourishing will likely be vague, justificatorily minimal, and concerned with basic levels of flourishing. Furthermore, if it is vague and justificatorily minimal, the conception of flourishing will be deliberative in another sense: it will usually require local-level deliberation to be used in practice. If the conception of basic flourishing is vague, it will often be difficult for third parties to ascertain whether a given preference is consistent with it or not. In order to make determinations about whether to treat—or continue to treat—a certain preference as suspect, public institutions must understand the role that preference plays in its particular context. Arriving at this type of understanding will frequently entail taking into account the first-person narratives of the persons in question.

The vagueness of the deliberative perfectionist conception does not only stipulate that deliberation will usually be necessary to determine how people's preferences affect their flourishing. The vagueness also makes it the case that the perfectionist conception tells us little about what IAPs should be changed *to*. To put this point differently, the deliberative perfectionist conception *underdetermines* any vision of how people with IAPs should live. The deliberative perfectionist conception might tell us that people with IAPs need adequate nutrition, but it will not tell us whether they need mango milkshakes, noodles, or hamburgers. It may tell us that people need opportunities to develop their cognitive capacities, but it probably will not tell us much about what the content of school curricula should be. Once we recognize this, we see another reason for local-level deliberation. Absent a moral imperative for the practitioner to decide what people's preferences should be changed *to*, deprived people should participate in imagining more just futures for themselves, and their imaginings should guide the choice of strategies for change.

Offsetting the Epistemological Difficulties of IAP Identification

To recapitulate, I am arguing that development interventions aimed at transforming IAPs should be guided by a deliberative perfectionist conception of flourishing—a conception arrived at by a cross-cultural deliberative process that is substantively minimal, justificatorily minimal, and vague. This conception and my perfectionist definition of IAPs together motivate a deliberative perfectionist approach to IAP identification. A development practitioner guided by the deliberative perfectionist approach may use the perfectionist conception to *suspect* that certain preferences that seem inconsistent with flourishing are IAPs. But initial suspicion is not a warrant for indiscriminate intervention, so she will attempt to understand the preferences in context in order to get clearer about whether they are actually IAPs. Conversation with people who seem to have IAPs about why they have the preferences that they have will often be an essential part of this process. After all, a suspect preference is not necessarily an inappropriately adaptive one. If discussion reveals that the person does not have IAPs, no further intervention may be in order. However, if people do have genuine IAPs, the practitioner should deliberate with them to imagine a more just future for themselves; she should attempt to find out what they deeply value and help them craft a flourishing-consistent set of preferences that also appeals to the people's extant sources of meaning.

What exactly constitutes deliberation? It is important to note that not all development interventions hailed as participatory would meet the requirements of my approach. There is increasing consensus in the development community on the idea that interventions can be enhanced by participation, but the meaning of the term is unclear. Sometimes participation simply means development practitioners reporting to communities about decisions made on behalf of those communities. In other cases participation is much more robust—involving local-level bodies that design and implement courses of action and democratic institutions that link these bodies in a network. Though I cannot offer a theory of morally appropriate deliberation here, the moral framework I have set out here commits me to something like David Crocker's "deliberative participation." In deliberative participation, "non-elites (sometimes among themselves and sometimes with elites) deliberate together, sifting proposals and reasons to agree on policies that at least a majority can accept" (Crocker 2008, 344). Crocker's conception makes clear that interventions appropriately called "deliberative" involve people reasoning together about courses of action rather than implementing a predetermined course of action. Deliberative perfectionist interventions should have roughly the character Crocker describes, since the deliberative perfectionist conception of flourishing underdetermines the appropriate course of action in any given situation, and since there are prudential and moral reasons to engage deprived people in choosing the appropriate strategy (which I discuss in the next section).

We saw how deliberation might help development practitioners understand the reasons for people's preferences and how it can help deprived people transform their preferences through our PAEM (Programa Educativo de La Mujer) example in this book's introduction. The following example can show us how deliberation with the deprived can determine what their preferences should be changed *to*. Sabina Alkire describes an Oxfam-funded rose cultivation project in the village of Arabsolangi, Pakistan. Oxfam began work in the village without much prior knowledge of it by assuming that persons in it needed basic income (Alkire 2002, 152), but participatory processes played a significant role in designating rose growing as the income-generating project of choice (Alkire 2002, 272). The strong investment the participants developed in the project reflected the extent to which this project fit into their existing sets of values and culturally specific views about the world. For example, it fit well into the high value participants placed on community religious life; some of them described feeling particularly connected to this work, because it reflected their conception of *sawab* or holy work (Alkire 2002, 278).[20]

I believe that my deliberative perfectionist approach embodies a strategy for IAP identification and intervention that can help offset the occupational hazards I described in the previous section. Recall that two epistemological difficulties of IAP identification are psychologizing the structural and misidentifying trade-offs. Both of these difficulties arise from a basic fact about human interaction—that it is difficult to read a person's higher-order preferences based on her lower-order expressed preferences. Just because a person is engaging in behaviors that we do not imagine a flourishing person would engage in does not mean that she does not want to flourish. To return to our old example, a woman's reason for not avoiding HIV exposure may be that she has to keep her husband happy to maintain access to food and shelter rather than that she believes that women should always submit to their husbands' sexual wishes. How can a development practitioner tell the difference between the woman who is not asking her partner to wear a condom because of lower-order IAPs and the woman who is not doing so because of inappropriately adaptive higher-order values? The deliberative perfectionist approach suggests that the development practitioner should actually ask her. The practitioner can use the deliberative perfectionist conception as grounds for preliminary suspicion that this deprived woman has IAPs, but the practitioner is not justified in taking her own preliminary judgment as authoritative. She should not treat understanding higher-order preferences as a matter of inference from lower-order ones; she should try to find out why the deprived person has the preferences she has. Information gathered from the first-person perspectives of people with IAPs can help development practitioners distinguish lower-order IAPs focused on managing limited option sets from higher-order IAPs.

The deliberative perfectionist approach can also help development practitioners avoid confusing difference with deprivation. There are two separate reasons for this. The first is relatively straightforward. A development practitioner whose conception of basic flourishing is simply the thick conception of flourishing her own culture prescribes will be prone to incorrectly assuming that people who are different from her are deprived and just do not happen to know it. For instance, a development practitioner who thinks that farming is drudgery because she is from the city may look at a subsistence farmer and assume she is not flourishing; when the farmer objects that this helps her lead a good life, the practitioner can simply chalk it up to IAP—contentment with less than adequate options. The deliberative perfectionist approach can begin to mitigate this danger by justifying only intervention that is done on behalf of a conception of the good that is *cross-culturally acceptable*. A practitioner motivated by the deliberative perfectionist conception is explicitly asked to distinguish her personal or cultural conception of the good from the "right" one.

There is another reason my deliberative perfectionist approach can help minimize the dangers of confusing difference with deprivation. The approach recommends that development practitioners ask people with suspect preferences about their preferences and what they mean. At its best, this encounter can encourage the practitioner to challenge her own conceptions of what flourishing looks like in the real world. It is possible, through discussion, for people who seem to have

IAPs to persuade practitioners that what initially seemed like deprivation is actually a different way of living out the human flourishing described by the deliberative perfectionist conception. For another example from development practice, we can turn to Priya Chopra's (2004) ethnographic research on women who use their cognitive capacities in creative ways but are technically counted as illiterate. Chopra excerpts a narrative from Naj Jamal Khatoum, a woman who is running for public office but has little formal education. This woman says, "I have studied Urdu in my village madarsa, and can sign my name in Urdu and write my address in Hindi... People should not think if a person cannot read and write, they have no brains. I am 'illiterate, but that does not stop me from doing my work. I use my brains to move forward' " (Chopra 2004, 47–48). We can imagine a development practitioner who equates literacy with cognitive capacity who sees Naj Jamal Khatoum as a victim of thoroughgoing cognitive deficiency. But this practitioner would miss the fact that this woman frequently participates in politics and deliberately accesses information through visits to political offices (Chopra 2004, 46). Chopra refuses to see Khatoum's illiteracy as a marker of complete cognitive deficiency; she uses Khatoum's narrative to challenge the idea that illiterate people cannot offer sophisticated analyses of their lives (Chopra 2004, 52–53). Without saying that illiteracy is not a deprivation, we can see in Khatoum a different way of utilizing cognitive capacity for practical reason—rather than its mere absence.[21]

Of course, it is not easy for most people—especially not people in positions of power—to learn to challenge their own ideas about what flourishing looks like. As many theorists of participatory development and I myself have argued, elsewhere (Khader 2011) development practitioners will need to acquire specific virtues to learn to hear and be open to voices that are different from their own. But the deliberative perfectionist conception of flourishing forces practitioners to at least recognize that there are manifold ways of flourishing.

Why Deliberate with the Deprived?

I have argued that IAPs are preferences inconsistent with basic flourishing that a person would reverse and endorse under conditions conducive to basic flourishing. I have also developed an approach to public intervention aimed at helping people who have IAPs flourish. My approach recommends that deprived people should be involved in diagnosing and developing strategies for responding to their own IAPs. I hope the preceding discussion has made clear why the first-person narratives of people with suspect preferences matter to IAP diagnosis. We cannot understand why people are doing what they are doing merely by observing them, and their descriptions of what they are doing can paint a more complete picture of the reasons behind their preferences. Further, development practitioners who know why people are not protesting their own deprivation will be able to tailor interventions more strategically. Ibrahim and Alkire explain this point as follows:

> Consider a local government that wished to enhance women's autonomy but did not know whether to invest in conscientization of women about their deplorable state, or in direct interventions to invest in change, such as providing training for advocacy for child care [sic] facilities and maternity leave on jobs. Which of these interventions will prove most helpful? If the women are truly chafing at their situation, further conscientization is not necessary and could seem a waste of time, so the second option would be chosen; if, on the other hand, the women were demurely satisfied with their role as housewives, then they would not participate in the advocacy work, so conscientization would be a necessary first step. However, to choose between these requires an undertstanding of women's own "positionally objective" views. (Ibrahim and Alkire 2007, 394)

It is fairly clear why deprived people should be involved in *diagnosing* their own IAPs. It may be less clear, however, why deprived people should be deliberatively involved in transforming their own futures. After all, if we know what basic flourishing is, and the struggle for flourishing is something human beings share, why prefer courses of action infused with the "thick" values of the deprived? Are not all flourishing-compatible courses of action equally good, regardless of whose thick values motivate them?

We should not only care whether interventions aimed at transforming people's preferences offer alternative preferences that are compatible with flourishing. We should also care whether those alternatives can be "owned" by deprived people. There are both moral and pragmatic reasons that development practitioners should deliberate with people with IAPs and strive to generate strategies for preference transformation that draw on those people's existing values. The clearest imperative, and the one most frequently cited by theorists of participatory development, is a pragmatic one. Development interventions whose intended beneficiaries feel alienated from them are just unlikely to work. Deprived people are unlikely to participate in projects they see as compromising values that are important to them. If people see no link between a development project and their needs, they also will probably not take advantage of it.

Ethnographer of literacy practices, Brian Street recounts the story of Winnie, an illiterate South African activist (Street 2005, 63–64), which can help us see how people can react negatively to interventions that are foisted upon them.[22]

According to Street, Winnie was a local leader of the anti-apartheid movement who began to take government-sponsored classes aimed at helping illiterate women gain reading skills. However, Winnie's participation in the literacy classes declined because she did not see literacy as her primary need; she had enrolled in the classes because she thought they would help her build on her skills as a community worker. Instead, the literacy project ignored the skills she already had and adversely affected her self-esteem; practitioners and other participants in the literacy project continually undermined her sense of her own competence. We may imagine that there are many stories like Winnie's—stories of people who do not participate in development interventions because those projects do not build on their existing systems of meaning. In Winnie's case, part of the problem was a literacy project that failed to connect literacy instruction to her existing competencies and life aspirations. Another part of the problem seems to be that participating in these classes entailed a loss to her sense of competence. More generally, we might say that development interventions can be ineffective because they fail to create opportunities for flourishing that deprived people recognize as such.

The fact that development projects that deprived people do not recognize as meeting their needs are unlikely to work furnishes pragmatic reasons to support deliberation. There are also at least two moral reasons for development practitioners and activists to deliberate with people with IAPs about what should be done to increase their flourishing. First, deliberation can help people develop agential capacities. Participating in public discussions can help people develop more robust senses of who they are and what they care about, and they can help them develop intrinsically valuable skills—like the skills of public self-representation, reasoning, and speech. When public discussions function well, the people who are participating in them are not simply recounting pre-established values. Rather, participants are clarifying their values by incorporating or rejecting the perspectives of others and sometimes even forming new values. A participant may learn things like the following: that she is not the only one who experiences a particular deprivation, that she strongly disagrees with others about what the community's priorities should be, or that she wants to question her established social role. An important advocate of this view of deliberation as good for people is Sen, who describes "political and social participation" as having "intrinsic value" (Sen 1999a, 10) and public debate as helping people form values (Sen 199b).

If deliberation helps people develop important agential capacities, development practitioners can help improve the lives of people with IAPs simply by deliberating with them. *Ceteris paribus*, an intervention that helps people develop agential capacities *and* develops their capacities for flourishing by transforming IAPs is generally morally preferable to one that only works on transforming IAPs by imposing new opportunities; the latter intervention develops agency, which adds moral value. I think Sen is correct that deliberation generally adds moral value to development interventions. By pointing this out, however, I do not mean to suggest that more deliberation always improves people's lives. There are certainly circumstances under which deliberation may actually do little to improve people's agential capacities. For instance, a person who already has ample opportunities to participate in public life probably stands to gain little marginal value from a public meeting about what type of plumbing should go into a public building. Situations where deliberation is actually harmful to people are not unimaginable, either. For example, a woman in an extremely patriarchal context may be seriously shamed for challenging her gender role in the presence of men; it is not clear that she will gain a more robust sense of herself as an agent if her exercise of deliberative capacity is responded to with shame. Similarly, a person who overburdened with work to the point of exhaustion may not benefit from opportunities to deliberate, *ceteris paribus*. The imperative to deliberate with deprived people because it helps them develop agential capacities that improve their well-being is not unqualified.

A second moral imperative for deliberating with deprived people is not based on a belief in the *intrinsic* value of deliberation. Rather, it is based on the belief that interventions that have been deliberated upon are more likely to be interventions people identify with and support. I claimed above that this fact generated a pragmatic imperative for deliberation; projects people do not identify with may simply flop. But I think the fact of greater support for projects that have been deliberated about also generates a moral reason for deliberation. In order to understand this moral reason, we need to understand a particular idea developed by liberal perfectionist philosophers—the concept of endorsement as a component of well-being. The view of endorsement as a component of well-being holds that a person is doing well if she has certain objectively valuable goods *and* has a positive attitude about their presence in her own life (Raz 1988; 1994; Scanlon 2003).

This idea of endorsement as adding value to a person's life is fully compatible with the perfectionism entailed in my definition of IAP. We can make it so just by saying that endorsement is one objectively valuable functioning among others. To be sure, this adds a subjective element to flourishing, but to say that the possession of certain subjective attitudes are *one component of* human flourishing is not to say that those attitudes are *constitute* human flourishing. We can say that a life in which a person is objectively flourishing across multiple domains and endorses the conditions of her life is better than a life in which a person is flourishing across multiple domains but does not endorse the conditions of her life. A woman who starts negotiating condom use with her husband because she believes her health is valuable is doing better than a woman who negotiates condom use with her husband because "this is how things are now," or because she will lose access to other services provided by a development project if she does not attempt to protect herself from HIV.

People are more likely to endorse courses of action that they have participated in designing, and this furnishes a moral reason for practitioners to deliberate with the deprived.[23] The endorsement reason for deliberating with people with IAPs is slightly stronger than the pragmatic imperative it resembles. Both the endorsement and pragmatic reasons say that it is undesirable for deprived people to feel alienated from interventions that could improve their lives and that development practitioners should focus on participatory interventions to prevent this from happening. But, where the pragmatic reason demands only non-alienation, the endorsement reason asks development practitioners to strive for stronger subjective endorsement. This means that the endorsement reason promotes deliberation in a larger set of cases. Practitioners driven by the pragmatic imperative only have reason to deliberate when nondeliberation would doom the intervention to failure. Practitioners driven by the endorsement reason have an incentive to deliberate even when a project might succeed at improving flourishing in some domains without deliberation.

For a more concrete explanation of this, let us return to the different reasons a woman might begin negotiating condom use in a case like the one I described above. For practitioners motivated by the pragmatic reason—that is, absent a notion of endorsement as morally valuable—there is little reason to deliberate with women about how to reduce their HIV risk in cases where the practitioners can reasonably expect that the women will start negotiating condom use if the practitioners give them the impression that this is just "the way things are these days." Practitioners motivated by the endorsement imperatives will have reason to deliberate, even if they can reasonably expect women to change their behavior without deliberation. Endorsement-driven practitioners prefer an outcome where women change their HIV-risking behaviors for reasons that matter to them over one in which they change their HIV-risky behaviors grudgingly. To be sure, encouraging people to change their behaviors grudgingly will often lead to changes that are unsustainable, and this gives pragmatic reason-motivated practitioners some reason to deliberate even in cases where they foresee only grudging change. Perhaps women will continue to negotiate condom use only for a short period if they do it because this is "just the way things are these days." But I do not think behavioral changes that were initially undertaken grudgingly are always unsustainable. The endorsement imperative asks practitioners to deliberate in the interests of producing endorsement even in cases where sustainable unendorsed behavior change seems likely.

How does the endorsement reason for deliberating weigh in favor of the deliberative perfectionist approach? My deliberative perfectionist approach holds that there are certain objectively good activities constitutive of human flourishing, but it also leaves open the possibility of a variety of different ways of flourishing in the concrete. This is what I mean when I say that the deliberative perfectionist conception of flourishing *underdetermines* what should happen in any particular intervention. People's lives will be better if their IAPs are transformed into preferences more compatible with flourishing, but there are many different types of flourishing-compatible preferences. The endorsement imperative gives us reason to favor flourishing-compatible outcomes grounded in people's existing desires. It asks development practitioners to favor flourishing-compatible outcomes grounded in local values and practices over flourishing-compatible outcomes perceived as foreign or alien. Deliberative perfectionism-motivated practitioners who care about endorsement will attempt think creatively with deprived people about ways in which flourishing-compatible preferences can be embedded within people's existing systems of meaning.

A qualifying remark about the endorsement imperative is in order. Endorsement-motivated practitioners face an imperative to pursue strategies for change that will win the endorsement of affected people, *not* strategies that challenge nothing about the local status quo. In cases where deprived people want to oppose tradition on a large scale, neither the endorsement reason nor my deliberative perfectionist approach authorizes practitioners to protect the local culture at the expense of the interests and desires of the participants in that culture. So the endorsement imperative promotes flourishing-compatible courses of action embedded in local values *only insofar as the people whose lives are affected care about those values.* For a practitioner to impose on people with IAPs her vision of what is worth preserving about a local culture is undoubtedly morally objectionable.

What types of strategies for improving flourishing while respecting deprived people's systems of meaning can development practitioners and deprived people imagine together? A project employed by Kenyan activists working against female genital mutilation (FGM)[24] illustrates something like the deliberative perfectionist approach in action. Before I explain how the approach manifests deliberative perfectionism in action, I should be clear that the preference to have one's daughters' genitals cut is not, strictly speaking, an IAP; my definition is restricted to self-regarding preferences. Further, even though girls who desire it may be said to have IAPs, the political implications of this fact are different from those of the IAPs of adults because they are children and thus reasonably conceivable as nonautonomous. Still, what follows is an example of a way of involving people in developing a strategy for changing widely held preferences against flourishing in a way that does not compromise their larger worldview. In the early 1990s the Kenyan nongovernmental organization (NGO), Mandaleo Ya Wanawake, saw the need for local-scale interventions to decrease the prevalence of female genital cutting (clitoridectemy sometimes accompanied by the removal of the labia, more specifically). Local community-level interventions are often effective in combating female genital cutting, because the prevalence of female genital cutting is often strongly tied to an intermarrying group's standards of what makes a girl marriageable. Parents are most likely to stop having their daughters cut once they have the impression that a critical mass of parents in their communities are doing the same; uncut daughters are less likely to face unmarriageability if a number of families commit to refusing to cut their daughters (Mackie 2003, 141).

Though they entered local communities with the intention of decreasing the prevalence of FGM, the Mandaleo Ya Wanawake activists did not enter with a specific vision of what should be done. Rather, they seem to have presumed, as Diana Meyers recommends practitioners should, that the people involved had "some understanding of what matters to them and how best to proceed in light of their values and commitments" (Meyers 2000, 489). The NGO engaged in extensive participatory research with community members to determine what the appropriate intervention might be (Chege, Askew, et al., 2001). Together with community members, they created a ritual called "Circumcision Through Words." Girls who participate spend a week in seclusion together learning "traditional teachings about their coming roles as women, parents, and adults in the community" as well as about "personal health, hygiene, reproductive issues, communication skill [sic], self-esteem, and how to deal with peer pressure" (James 1998, 1045). This creative new cultural practice demonstrates how the deprived people can invent new types of flourishing-compatible preferences. Unlike simply eliminating coming-of-age rituals—as an outsider practitioner is likely to have suggested on her own—"Circumcision Through Words" does not require the community to abandon the coming of age practices and cultural knowledge it values in order to ensure that women's capacities for sexual pleasure are preserved.

As the case of "Circumcision Through Words" demonstrates, we can imagine strategies for IAP transformation based on a universal conception of what human beings deserve that nonetheless take seriously the particular values and desires of deprived people. This intervention began from the assumption that FGM undermined young women's chances for flourishing, but Mandaleo Ya Wanawake activists did not begin with a preset plan of *how* to decrease FGM. The strategy for decreasing FGM grew out of the values of the people in the affected communities.[25] Effectively and responsibly responding to IAPs will often require this type of creative and collaborative thinking that creates new cultural practices partly out of existing thick, culturally particular values. But it will also require a normative conception that makes it possible to identify IAPs and that helps distinguish alternatives that are compatible with human flourishing from those that are not. I propose the deliberative perfectionist approach to IAP intervention as the type of flexible moral framework that allows for negotiation between an abstract commitment to human flourishing and the thick, culturally embedded desires of real people. I believe that responsible strategies for transforming IAPs—strategies that take seriously the struggle for flourishing of people with IAPs without denying the richness and complexity of our diverse moral world—require such a flexible framework.

ADAPTIVE PREFERENCES AND CHOICE: ARE ADAPTIVE PREFERENCES AUTONOMY DEFICITS?*

Adaptive preferences can seem to be imposed on their bearers. The woman who undernourishes herself to feed her husband, the poor laborer who does not speak out against her unjust working conditions, and the woman who risks HIV exposure because of patriarchally prescribed beliefs about women's sexuality may all seem to have had their preferences foisted upon them by adverse social conditions. The very term "adaptive preference" suggests that the problem with adaptive preferences is that they are "adapted to"—in other words, "formed in reaction to"—social conditions. Miriam Teschl and Flavio Comim cast the difference between nonadaptive and adaptive preferences as a difference between what people "really prefer and what they are made to prefer" (Teschl and Comim 2005, 236). If we follow Teschl and Comim's line of thought, we may think that our moral problem with adaptive preferences is that they are preferences that the agent did not choose to have. After all, the opposite of being "made to" do anything is to do it out of one's own volition.

Once we realize this, we may think we have an answer to why inappropriately adaptive preferences (IAPs) are unreliable indicators of people's well-being; perhaps the moral problem with IAPs is that they are unchosen, or, more technically, *procedurally nonautonomous.* Procedural theories of autonomy hold that a preference belongs to a person only if the process by which she developed the preference allowed her independence of mind—that is, if she arrived at the preference motivated only by desires that are her own. Thinking of IAPs as problematic primarily because they manifest procedural autonomy deficits has a certain intuitive appeal. It allows us to say that adaptive preferences merit public interrogation without sacrificing our commitment to choice. We want public institutions to help people achieve their chosen goals, we might say, but adaptive preferences are not chosen.

Why, then, have I offered a definition of adaptive preferences that is not autonomy-centered? Recall that in the previous chapter I claimed that IAPs were preferences formed under conditions inhospitable to a person's flourishing that are causally related to conditions inconsistent with basic flourishing. My perfectionist definition of adaptive preference does not suggest that a person's procedural independence must have been interfered with in order for her preferences to be inappropriately adaptive. My definition also suggests that a major reason we see IAPs as worthy of public interrogation is that they undermine their bearers' flourishing. My perfectionist definition of IAPs thus does not hold IAPs to be procedural autonomy deficits.

I have offered a perfectionist definition of adaptive preferences rather than a procedural autonomy-centered definition, because there are serious problems with thinking of adaptive preferences as autonomy deficits. In this chapter, I illuminate these problems. In the first section, I argue against defining adaptive preferences as procedural autonomy deficits. I show that attempts to define adaptive preferences as procedural autonomy deficits—despite the intuitive appeal of such attempts—yield conceptions of adaptive preference that are intuitively implausible, unsuited for use in development practice, and/or morally objectionable. If the problem with adaptive preferences is that they are unchosen, we should think that all unchosen preferences are worthy of public interrogation. I will demonstrate that we do not.

After rejecting the view of adaptive preferences as procedural autonomy deficits, I turn in the second section to whether we should characterize adaptive preferences as *substantive* autonomy deficits. Substantive theories of autonomy hold that a preference is autonomous if it reveals a person's commitments to certain objectively good values. Though there are important resonances between my perfectionist definition of adaptive preferences and the view of adaptive preferences as substantive autonomy deficits, I also briefly argue against conceiving adaptive preferences as substantive autonomy deficits. If we think of adaptive preferences as substantive autonomy deficits, we will recommend morally objectionable strategies for preference transformation, or so I will claim. In particular, we will find ourselves advocating coercion of deprived people and encouraging deprived people to simply abandon their existing systems of value.

Before I begin to argue against conceiving adaptive preferences as autonomy deficits, a terminological clarification is in order. In Chapter 1, I recommended that we shift from using the term "adaptive preferences" to the term "inappropriately adaptive preferences" in order to highlight the fact that IAPs are characterized by their harmful content. In the remaining chapters of this book, I continue to use the term "IAP." In this chapter, however, I shift back to the language of "adaptive preferences" so as not to prejudice our current discussion against the view that adaptive preferences are autonomy deficits.

Are Adaptive Preferences Procedural Autonomy Deficits?

There are good reasons to want to define adaptive preferences as procedural autonomy deficits. One such reason is the prospect of being able to support adaptive preference intervention at no cost to our commitment to liberalism. If adaptive preferences are unchosen preferences, there is no conflict between respecting people's choices about their lives and interrogating adaptive preferences. As Cass Sunstein (1991) argues, attempts by public institutions to make persons' preferences more autonomous are perfectly consistent with a public commitment to protecting *autonomously formed* conceptions of the good. If adaptive preferences are procedural autonomy deficits, we can easily preserve traditional liberal commitments—like the commitment to opposing intervention to change people's autonomously formed preferences and the commitment to public neutrality among conceptions of the good. If adaptive preferences are procedural autonomy deficits, public institutions need not separate adaptive preferences from nonadaptive ones on the basis of the conceptions of the good those preferences reveal. Preferences with *any* contents can be immune to public questioning—as long as they result from free choice. Adaptive preference intervention becomes a matter of changing how deprived people stand in relation to their preferences, not a matter of changing preference content.

So defining adaptive preferences as procedural autonomy deficits allows us to conceptualize real-life adaptive preference interventions in a particular, liberalism-compatible way. Questioning people's adaptive preferences becomes a way of making sure they have choices rather than steering them to choose in a particular way. We hear this type of normative justification in the strain of development theory focused on "empowerment." Development anthropologist Andrea Cornwall argues that the concept of empowerment that pervades contemporary development discourse equates empowerment with "the act of making independent choices" (Cornwall 2007a, 165). Similarly, development theorist Naila Kabeer argues that empowerment is a process of change" by which deprived people gain "the ability to make choices" (Kabeer 1999, 436–437).

The normative force behind the idea of empowerment in development seems to come from the idea that deprived people live in states of internalized oppression where they cannot make their own choices.[1] The process of "empowerment" enables them to make their own choices for the first time. The notion of development interventions as empowering people to make their own choices for the first time appears frequently in contemporary gender and development discourse—especially in discussions of microcredit, where we read claims that development interventions do things like "create the context for them to think, make their own choices and participate equally in the reproductive decision-making process with their spouses" (Hadi 2001, 28). If we can understand adaptive preference interventions as simply empowering people to choose, supporting adaptive preference intervention is not tantamount to asking public institutions to promote a vision of the good life.[2]

If we define adaptive preferences according to procedural criteria, we also have a feasible account of our intuition that not all self-sacrificing preferences are adaptive. This is a second reason we may find a procedural definition of adaptive preferences appealing. We certainly do not think that all preferences with contents that harm a person's well-being are adaptive. We are often asked, in discussions of development ethics, to distinguish forms of deprivation that seem externally imposed from forms of deprivation that seem self-imposed. For instance, Martha Nussbaum states, "there is a difference between fasting and starving" (Nussbaum 1999, 44). We may plausibly conclude that the difference between fasting and starving is the chosenness of the former. If adaptive preferences are procedural autonomy deficits, we may be able to say that the poor woman who undernourishes herself to feed her male relatives has an adaptive preference while the fasting Buddhist does not, and to do so on the grounds that the woman in the former case did not choose to have her preference.

Problems with Defining Adaptive Preferences as Procedural Autonomy Deficits

However appealing we may find defining adaptive preferences as procedurally nonautonomous, we cannot do so a way that is coherent and provides useful guidance for development policy. In order to make this case, I turn to revealing the shortcomings of definitions of adaptive preferences as procedurally nonautonomous. We want to know whether we can coherently understand adaptive preferences as procedural autonomy deficient. I will ask whether four different versions of procedural autonomy can identify adaptive preferences in a way that is practically useful and consistent with our intuitions. To ask whether a given definition can account for adaptive preferences in a way consistent with our intuitions, we can examine cases of preferences that seem intuitively to be adaptive and ask whether our definition can identify them as such. In what follows, I use this method to demonstrate that we cannot find a procedural autonomy-based definition of adaptive preferences that identifies them in a way consistent with our intuitions. I refer repeatedly to four examples of preferences described by development theorists and practitioners as "adaptive," "deformed," or instances of "internalized subordination." They are as follows:

Case 1: Women and Microcredit

ACTIONAID workers on Bhola Island, Bangladesh noticed that the majority of poor women in its microcredit program transferred their loans to their husbands (Archer and Cottingham 1996 4.1.1). This is not an uncommon outcome of microcredit programs targeted at poor women in South Asia (Goetz and Sen Gupta 1996, 49; Mahmud 2003). Such preferences are often attributed to women's limited beliefs about what they deserve and are capable of (Fermon 1998).[3]

Case 2: Female Genital Cutting in Saharan and Sub-Saharan Africa

Development practitioners in various areas of Africa describe women's own highly positive attitudes toward clitoridectemy as significant obstacles to eradicating the practice (COGWO, Nagaad, et al. 2004; Mandaleo Ya Wanawake 2000; Yount 2002).

Case 3: Intrahousehold Food Distribution

Development theorists and practitioners throughout Asia worry that women's behaviors and beliefs concerning intra-household food distribution contribute to their disproportionate undernourishment (Papanek 1990; Ramachandran 2006; Sen 1990).

Case 4: Lack of Perceived Injustice in Women's Subordination in West Africa

The Guinean women in a study by Paul Shaffer (1998) recognize "gender inequalities in terms of women's heavier workloads and men's dominance in decision-making" but do not consider these inequalities to be unjust (Kabeer 1999, 440).

Adaptive Preferences as Rationality Deficits

We can begin with the idea that autonomy is rationality—that, in order to be truly chosen, preferences must be rationally formed. Thinking of adaptive preferences (APs) as revealing rationality deficits finds much support in the rhetoric of empowerment, particularly in the strand of it influenced by Paulo Freire's thought. Freire describes disempowerment as a lack of consciousness. Below, I examine three different understandings of autonomous preferences as rational preferences to see whether they help us arrive at a coherent procedural autonomy-based definition of adaptive preference.

Rationality as Full Information

What type of rationality can APs be said to lack? One way to differentiate rational from adaptive preferences might be to call preferences that are not fully informed "adaptive." Perhaps people with adaptive preferences are simply unaware of the consequences of their lifestyles or the options available. So, for example, the Bangladeshi women in the microcredit example may give their loan money to their husbands because they are unaware that women can and do start small enterprises in their own names. Similarly, women who seem to manifest adaptive attitudes about severe genital cutting may simply be unaware of its health risks.

Thinking of adaptive preferences as information-deficient is appealing, because it facilitates thinking of public intervention to transform APs as interfering only with persons' *instrumental* preferences. The preferences being transformed are not preferences about what a good human life *is*; they are just preferences about *how* to bring about the individual's own conception of a good life. Interventions can appear as simply offering people non-normative instruments with which to achieve normative goals they already have. Clare Chambers offers this type of justification for public intervention in the lives of women who support clitoridectemy. According to her, women who support clitoridectemy have a higher-order goal of pursuing their own health; they are just unaware that clitoridectemy promotes ill health (C. Chambers 2008, 213).[4]

Yet there are significant problems with thinking of adaptive preferences as simple information lacks. First, it seems simply false to say that all adaptive preferences are sustained by information lacks; some of them are certainly sustained by *normative* beliefs. It may seem plausible to say that women who lack medical knowledge want to be healthy but do not know how. But it is disingenuous at best to claim that the seemingly adaptive preferences to give one's money to one's husband or to view one's submission to one's husband's decision-making authority as required are based on non-normative knowledge deficits. These types of preferences are quite likely sustained by elaborate networks of beliefs about how good women behave.

Second, if adaptive preferences were simply information deficits, we would expect adaptive preferences to disappear when deprived people are exposed to new information. Practice tells us that changing adaptive preferences often requires more than information. Transforming the preferences of a woman who gives her loan to her husband, for example, may not just be a matter of telling her that some women do otherwise. It may require support for the creation of social networks that celebrate her growing financial independence or educational programs that allow her to experiment with a new sense of competence.[5]

Third, if adaptive preferences are primarily information deficits, all cases of information deficit should strike us as adaptive. But they do not. Take cases where persons' uninformed preferences seem to be good for them and cases where persons' uninformed preferences are morally trivial, for instance. It probably does not arouse our intuitions about adaptive preference when a woman does *not* want to undergo genital cutting, even if she is ignorant of the statistics about its complications. If we believed information-deficiency defined APs, we would think all choices made about genital cutting without knowledge of its risks and its potential benefits (e.g., increased marriage prospects) were adaptive. Similarly, a woman microcredit participant who makes the uninformed choice to eat bananas rather than pineapples (within the context of a nutritionally acceptable diet) does not strike us as adaptive.

The difference between inadequately informed preferences that seem adaptive and those that do not is likely traceable to preference content. Uninformed preferences that are *deprivation-perpetuating* seem more adaptive than uninformed preferences that promote—or simply do not impact—flourishing. Once we say that nonharmful preferences arrived at without adequate information are autonomous, however, we are embroiled in judgments about the goodness and badness of preferences. If we are going to distinguish adaptive preferences in a way consistent with our intuitions, we must see them as characterized by something more than information deficiency. It looks like this *more* may have to come from a theory of the good—not procedural autonomy.

Rationality as Reflectiveness

We may be able to coherently to think of APs as rationality-deficient if we change our definition of rationality from information to reflectiveness. We may say that APs are unchosen preferences because they have not been subject to higher-order reflection. This is consistent with Gerald Dworkin's definition of autonomy as the capacity to "raise the question of whether I identify with or reject the reasons for which I act" (Dworkin, 1988, 15). It is also a way of understanding the strand of development practice devoted to the "conscientization" of development participants. According to it, once persons reflect on their lives, they will discover their acquiescence to power structures to which they should not want to acquiesce and decide to change their preferences (de Koning 1995, 34–37). The movement away from AP is a movement from unreflective preferences to reflective ones—from "unquestioning acceptance of the social order to a critical perspective on it" (Kabeer 1999, 441).

However, thinking that unreflectiveness characterizes APs reveals a dangerous and unwarranted empirical assumption—that people with APs reflect on their behavior less than everyone else. The main argument I see in its favor is that many individuals with APs have little formal education.[6] It is implausible, however, that one needs formal education to be able to reflect on situations, make decisions, and have preferences about one's lower-order preferences. It is difficult to imagine independent adults getting through life without having developed these minimal capacities. We know well that deprived people routinely exercise reflective capacities. We need only return to the example of Naj Jamal Khatoum from Chapter 1 (who has no formal education but is running for public office and offering reasoned criticisms of the government's requirement that political candidates be literate) to see how reflective uneducated people can be.

Even when they are not criticizing institutions, most deprived people make reflective decisions on a daily basis—even if they are sometimes decisions among rotten options. Deprivation means that a person has to decide among bad options, but it need not mean that her rational capacities are impaired. Bina Agarwal describes rural Indian women who covertly resist patriarchal intrahousehold food distribution norms by feigning spirit possession to obtain foods they would otherwise be denied (Agarwal 1997, 24). These women demonstrate enormous reflective ingenuity.

Another reason to reject the assumption that there is a strong connection between education and the absence of AP is that there exist preferences that intuitively seem adaptive but occur in persons with formal education. Battered women in the first world who prefer to stay with their abusers because they feel they deserve the abuse provide just one example.[7]

Even if we drop the idea that education is a requirement for reflectiveness, it remains the case many APs manifest higher levels of reflectiveness than their nonadaptive counterparts. The woman who systematically malnourishes herself to feed her husband exhibits an extremely reflective attitude toward her food consumption. It would be odd to view her preference as less adaptive than that of the woman who consumes adequate calories without thinking much about it. The woman who insufficiently nourishes herself may even have developed philosophical beliefs about why she should eat less. Hannah Papanek describes the networks of beliefs that sustain gender-biased intrahousehold food distribution in a particular community in Java. An elderly Javanese woman recalled being told as a child that women needed to discipline themselves, because they were superior to men who could not control themselves. Papanek adds that this idea could be easily supported by a web of religious beliefs encouraging self-deprivation as a spiritual discipline (Papanek 1990, 172). Complicated and reflective beliefs may sustain preferences that intuitively appear to be adaptive.

All of this suggests that defining APs as unreflective does not help us identify them in a way consistent with our intuitions; if APs are simply unreflective preferences, the unreflective preference to eat sufficiently should strike us as adaptive, and the reflective preference to undernourish oneself to feed one's husband should strike us as nonadaptive. But this is the opposite of what our intuitions suggest.

Further, the assumption that people with APs are unreflective has pernicious practical consequences. It absolves development practitioners of the obligation to treat people with APs as though there were reasons behind their preferences. As Seyla Benhabib writes, "all understanding…must begin with a methodological and moral imperative to reconstruct meaning as it appears to its makers and creators" (2002, 34). Development practitioners who think that intended development beneficiaries are unreflective may think that they can adequately reconstruct the psychologies of beneficiaries without any genuine encounter with them.

Treating persons with APs as unreflective also decreases the extent to which practitioners and activists will see persons with adaptive preferences as possessed of perceptions that might be valuable in constructing strategies for improving their lives. Indeed, the claim that the unreflective state is "animal" or less than human sometimes appears in the rhetoric of conscientization in development (Barroso 2002, 6–7). Viewing people with adaptive preferences as unworthy of consultation is a problem, because it encourages practitioners to adopt strategies for preference transformation that fail because they are based on misunderstandings of local specificities and because of a lack of participant ownership.

A proponent of the autonomy-as-reflectiveness view of APs might retort that I have misrepresented her conception of what adaptive preferences are. The real issue, she might say, is that persons with APs are not *critically* reflective. I would reply that this may be the right way to characterize APs, but it is not a procedural conception of autonomy. The difference between critical consciousness and reflective consciousness must be a difference in the contents of that consciousness. We might be tempted to believe otherwise if we assume that one cannot endorse existing power structures *and* be highly reflective. But in a world where eloquent defenses of institutions like patriarchy and colonialism—even from people who are harmed by these institutions—abound, there seems little reason to credit this assumption.

Thinking of APs as unreflective shares two other flaws with thinking of APs as uninformed. Both conceptions of adaptive preferences as rationality deficits stipulate that all irrational choices, even trivial ones—like the unreflective choice to eat mangoes rather than bananas—merit public concern. Both also suggest that people should want all their preferences to be based on true judgments about the world. In this sense also, neither definition is really indifferent to the content of people's conceptions of the good. Some types of preferences—particularly preferences not to reflect or to be denied information—would always count as adaptive on these definitions. Many religious preferences are preferences against information. Some preferences of this sort—like the preference not to know one's options for education because one believes it is God's will that women be cloistered—might seem adaptive. But many preferences to act unreflectively or without full information do not—like the preference not to think about the severity of one's illness because one because one's religion demands constant hope, for instance.

Rationality as Self-Interest

Perhaps we might salvage our attempt to think of APs as irrational by redefining rationality as self-interest. Maybe APs seem unchosen because they are contrary to persons' interests, and no rational person would choose against her interests. Let us assume that self-interested acts are those that a person can reasonably expect to increase her utility. If we think of APs as irrational and rationality as self-interest, we can think of preferences that do not advance a person's interests as adaptive.

If we define utility subjectively, however, APs can be self-interested. Preferences that intuitively seem adaptive can increase people's overall utility. The woman who undernourishes herself to feed her husband may experience an increase in utility even if she is starving. She may, for instance, feel proud of acting as a "good woman" should. As Papanek asserts, part of learning to live with less food on one's plate is internalizing the "compulsory emotions" that are meant to accompany it (Papanek 1990, 163). An adult woman who has lived her entire life this way may gain more utility from the boost to her self-image generated by her renunciation than she would gain from eating. Similarly, Elaine Gruenbaum's fieldwork indicates that some women in rural Sudanese communities where female genital infibulation is common perceive women with infibulated genitals as beautiful and sexually attractive and women without them as ugly (Gruenbaum 2006). A woman who feels that she is beautiful from undergoing infibulation certainly gains utility from this feeling. Nothing in subjective utility requires these women to value nonstarvation or access to sexual health over their feelings of satisfaction.

What if we give objective content to utility? This is notoriously hard to do, but let us suppose for the sake of argument that actions that jeopardize one's bodily health are not self-interested. Even with this supposition in hand, we cannot capture many preferences that our intuitions deem adaptive. It is easy to imagine cases of people whose choices harm their bodily health according to some objective metric and simultaneously advance their interests. A woman may malnourish herself for reasons other than that it contributes to a certain self-image. She may do so because if she does not nourish her husband above a certain level, he will not make it through the workday and neither of them will have food. Or she may do it because she knows that if her husband suspects her of taking more than her "fair share" he will beat her. In cases like these, intuition tells us that the woman's choice to malnourish herself is adaptive. Despite this, she expresses the most self-interest with regard to bodily health that she can express under her circumstances.

We may think that fleshing out objective utility can solve this problem. Perhaps, for a person to act out of self-interest, she must not only be doing the best she can to secure some given good or set of goods but must also desire the *quantity* of that good that would help her flourish. A person with APs is not just deprived of some good; she thinks that she does not need more of it than she has. This is the type of AP manifested by the Guinean women who do not see their husband's authority over them and the unequal division of labor as unjust; they do not think they need more household decision-making authority than they already have.

However, whether this preference appears adaptive with regard to rational self-interest depends on what is on our list of goods people are expected to want and how they are *ranked*. It remains possible that the preference not to be troubled by one's mistreatment secures access to other objective goods. Perhaps, if the Guinean women let themselves become angry, they will not feel able to stop themselves from protesting against their husbands. Perhaps they correctly think that if they do this, their husbands will expect more household labor from them rather than less. Or it may be that if they start seeing injustice, they will not be able to sleep at night and thus become less effective at fulfilling the daily tasks that contribute to their survival. Accepting that this is just the way things are may provide these women with an opportunity for—as Elster would put it—"reducing cognitive dissonance" (Elster 1987, 110), which will help them to perform the tasks required by daily life more efficiently.

More important, giving such robust content to objective utility—even if it may help us identify adaptive preferences—moves us away from offering a procedural autonomy-based account. Attempting to coherently think of APs as non-self-interested leads us down the same path as our other attempts to coherently think of APs as rationality-deficient; it leads us to refer to a conception of the good. As we have just seen, we need a normative conception of what persons should desire in order to begin to come up with a definition of APs as non-self-interested that identifies APs in a way consistent with our intuitions. This normative conception of what people want cannot be supplied by a theory of procedural autonomy alone.

A final problem with thinking of APs as self-interest-deficient is that it classes too many preferences as adaptive. For example, if eating is constitutive of self-interest, and rational acts are self-interested, we cannot avoid thinking of the preference to engage in religious fasting under conditions conducive to flourishing as adaptive. This is one more defect that the attempt to define APs as self-interest-deficient shares with other attempts to define APs as rationality-deficient.

Adaptive Preferences as Deficits in the Capacity to Live According to a Life-Plan

We have seen that defining APs as irrational does not identify APs in a way consistent with our intuitions and fails to provide useful guidance for development practice. APs may still be procedurally nonautonomous on other definitions of procedural autonomy, however. We may alternatively define procedural autonomy as the capacity to live according to a life-plan. Diana Meyers defines a type of autonomy called programmatic autonomy. For her, programmatically autonomous people ask the question "How do I want to live my life?" and answer with consistency (Meyers 1987, 624). They live in ways consonant with their answers to this question. Such a definition of procedural autonomy could yield the following definition of APs: APs are preferences inconsistent with people's life-plans.[8]

Life-Planning as the Understanding of Personal History

One way to define APs as preferences inconsistent with people's life-plans is to say that APs are preferences a person initially formed unconsciously—rather than as part of the deliberate life-planning process. Elster claims that APs are different from preferences that manifest "character-planning." Forming APs "is a purely causal process" of adaptation, taking place "behind the back" of the person concerned (Elster 1987, 117). In line with a view like his, we might think that APs are preferences that fail to be part of people's life-plans, because the only preferences that can be part of life-plans are preferences that people consciously form on the basis of their values.

However, this way of thinking of APs commits us to a dubious metaphysical position. This is the position that there is one authoritative narrative about why a person forms a preference at the moment that it happens. So, for example, we would have to assume that there is a "true" reason the fox in LaFontaine's fable now thinks the grapes he used to desire are sour. This may not be problematic for the fictional fox, but it is problematic for real people. Is the "true" reason a woman initially chooses to give her micro-loan to her husband that she does not enjoy public sphere activity or that she is unconsciously afraid that she will not succeed at it? Is the "true" reason a woman initially chooses to support genital cutting that she believes that it will increase her beauty or that she is afraid she will never get married if she does not? These questions about the origins of preferences do not seem readily answerable—at least not in practice.

There may be a more practically plausible way of determining whether people's preferences have been formed unconsciously rather than through conscious character-planning processes. According to Elster, "where APs typically take the form of downgrading the inaccessible options, deliberate character-planning would tend to upgrade the accessible ones" (Elster 1987, 119). But this way of thinking of APs distinguishes them in a way inconsistent with our intuitions. Many potential APs *upgrade* existing options; women who malnourish themselves, accept unequal work distributions, get their genitals cut, or transfer their loans to their husbands may do so because they think being a "good" woman is better than being a "modern" one, for example.

It may seem that the distinction between upgrading accessible options and downgrading inaccessible ones is linguistic. Perhaps no upgrading of available options can occur without the downgrading of unavailable ones. But I do not think this is true; for it to be true, all acts of valuing would have to be acts of ranking alternatives in relation to one another. But even if upgrading accessible options does imply downgrading inaccessible ones, there is a further problem with identifying APs as preferences that downgrade inaccessible options—where downgrading inaccessible options is the marker of a preference that a person did not plan in accordance with her character. It is this: we cannot meaningfully speak of *downgrading* options without again leaving the domain of procedural autonomy for a conception of the good. The notion of "devaluing" goods is incoherent without some idea of objectively valuable goods.

We might think that we can get around this problem by defining downgrading as a decrease in the individuals' positive evaluation of a good over time. However, positively unadapting one's preferences can happen by the same process. The woman who changes her attitudes toward genital cutting may, for example, begin by believing that genital cutting increases women's beauty and later come to believe that it actually decreases their beauty. This "devaluation" is the move from a seemingly adaptive preference to a nonadaptive one. Another way we might try to get around the need for a theory of the good to explain downgrading would be to say that downgrading is relative; that is, we could say that a person downgrades an inaccessible option if she values it less than the accessible one. But this last move casts an overly wide net for adaptive preferences; surely it is not the case that every time a person prefers the available option to the unavailable one it is because she has adapted her preferences. The notion of adaptive preferences as preferences that a person cannot have formed in accordance with her character because they downgrade inaccessible options either generates an impractical definition of adaptive preference or requires a theory of the good to make sense of the word "downgrading."

Life-Planning as Living According to a Life-Plan

We may instead think that APs are nonautonomous, because they manifest conflicts between how a person *wants* to live and how she actually lives. This would be consistent with Harry Frankfurt's (1988) notion of autonomy as endorsement. A view like Frankfurt's does not require us to think that life-plan-consistent preferences must be consciously formed at a single moment in time. Further, the view of APs as preferences inconsistent with a person's life-plan has the advantage of allowing us to hold that some preferences can be rationally self-interested and adaptive at the same time. A woman may prefer to give her micro-loan to her husband rather than be beaten by him for refusing, for example. However, at the level of life-planning, she may wish she had other options. Perhaps what she would really prefer is to be able to leave her husband without shame and keep the money for herself. Or perhaps she would prefer to be able to persuade her husband to accept her maintenance of the loan in her own name. The choice to give her loan to him is therefore worthy of public interrogation, because it does not reflect her real conception of the good life—or so an autonomy as life-planning definition of adaptive preference would suggest.

However, we should not assume that APs cannot be endorsed as parts of life-plans. Others with whom I discuss this project often insist that nobody could possibly endorse certain preferences. They typically describe the preferences in normatively laden language that does make it difficult to imagine anybody wanting those preferences. It is difficult to imagine a person who wants to "starve herself." But it is much less difficult to imagine someone who wants to make sure the people she cares about eat enough or who wants to learn to be less demanding like a good woman should. If we hold that only unendorsed preferences can be adaptive, many intuitively APs will not count as such.

It may still seem that preferences like the preference to undernourish oneself are not *real* preferences—even if they are higher-order preferences. Nussbaum demonstrates sympathy for the idea that adaptive higher-order preferences are not real when she claims that when persons seem to manifest APs for their conditions of deprivation we should "probe more deeply" (Nussbaum 2001, 42). Perhaps she believes that if we just ask questions at a high enough level of abstraction, we will find nonadaptive preferences.

However, the idea that higher-order preferences—that is, preferences about preferences and so on—are necessarily less adaptive than first-order preferences is questionable. Theories of ideology suggest that the case is sometimes the opposite—that persons' descriptions of their reasons for their behavior often uncritically reflect social norms, even when their behavior itself challenges them. For an example of this phenomenon, consider the following account of the attitudes of Kisii women in Kenya toward household decision-making authority. When asked about household authority, the women in Silberschmidt's (1992) study reply by claiming that men "own them" and describe men as the "heads of households" (Kabeer 1999, 447). Despite this spoken assent to male dominance, the women's behavior resists male dominance. For instance, when they disagree with their husbands' ideas about how seeds should be planted, they do not voice their disagreement. Rather, they simply plant the seeds as they see fit. If their husbands complain, they apologize and claim that they planted the seeds elsewhere because the seeds did not germinate in the husbands' desired spots (Kabeer 1999, 447; Silberschmidt 1992, 249).

Perhaps Silberschmidt got this answer because she had not yet probed deeply enough. We can imagine these women's beliefs changing through some sort of consciousness-raising intervention. But is this change just the exposition of higher-order preferences these women already had, preferences that constituted these women's genuine life-plans? We should be cautious about this way of justifying preference transformation. It may be that the only way practitioners can know when they have "probed deeply enough" is when beneficiaries express the "right" preferences. If the rightness of the preferences indicates the depth of probing, the content of preferences matters to preference adaptiveness. Once again, we are surreptitiously using a theory of the good rather than procedural autonomy to distinguish APs.

Furthermore, thinking of inconsistency with life-plans as the defining characteristic of APs again classes too many preferences as adaptive. If any preferences inconsistent with a person's life plan are adaptive, akratic preferences are adaptive. Surely the preference to eat chocolate when one is on a diet—though potentially nonautonomous—is not an AP.

Saying that APs are inconsistent with life-plans for reasons *external* to persons does not eliminate the problem. The fact that an individual adjusts her life-plan to the opportunities available to her in her society is not itself problematic.[9] John Rawls goes so far to suggest that public institutions can reasonably *expect* individuals to adjust their life-plans to available opportunities, because social cooperation sometimes requires us to demand less for ourselves than we would want in an ideal world (Rawls 1996, 186). He concludes this in the context of a discussion of expensive tastes. Justice may require a person whose life-plan involves drinking champagne on a daily basis to content herself with drinking grape juice if her society has limited resources. Rawls does not think this sacrifice subjects the champagne lover to an injustice, and we probably do not see her resultant preference for grape juice as worthy of public suspicion.

The difference between the preference adjustment of the woman who undernourishes herself to feed her male relatives and that of the champagne lover seems to be that the former decreases a person's basic well-being and the other does not. Sen writes that the well-being losses of people with adaptive preferences are *muted* by preference-satisfaction theories of welfare (Sen 1988, 46); conversely, the well-being losses of people with expensive tastes seem *exaggerated* by preference-satisfaction theories of welfare. Underlying the idea that well-being can be muted or exaggerated by desire-satisfaction theories seems to be an objective conception of well-being. If we try to distinguish adaptive preferences from nonadaptive ones on the basis of how objectively they represent what a person's well-being would require, we can explain why the champagne lover seems not to have adaptive preferences, while the woman who undernourishes herself does. But thinking of APs as preferences that diminish people's well-being in ways preference-satisfaction theories cannot account for once again requires us to leave the realm of procedural autonomy for a theory of the good. If only well-being-muting preferences inconsistent with people's life-plans can count as adaptive, we are sorting adaptive from nonadaptive preferences partly on the basis of their contents.

Adaptive Preferences as Agency Deficits

A third family of procedural autonomy-based approaches to defining APs with a conception of autonomy asks us to think of autonomy as agency. We might posit that APs are distortions in persons' conceptions of their own agency. According to agency-based approaches, people with APs view themselves as incapable of advancing their own interests. An agency-based definition of APs helps make sense of the autobiographical narratives of some people who have undergone preference transformation. These people often report an increase in feelings of self-worth and an expansion of the field of activities of which they think they are capable. We can find one instance of such improved self-worth in the testimony of a poor woman participant in an Oxfam-funded literacy project in Khoj, Pakistan. According to Sabina Alkire, this woman—identified as "Shabnam"—said, "Women think that they are like a bud—that they do not understand with their own eyes. But we are not buds, we are mountains. We can do anything with out lives. So I tried to open my eyes, and my eyes were opened" (Alkire 2002, 233). Narratives like Shabnam's are not uncommon.

Conceptualizing APs as distortions in people's conceptions of their own agency also plausibly explains of how people can seem not to want things that we imagine they would want under different conditions. That a person is not actively seeking some good may not mean that she does not want it. Rather, it may mean that the person erroneously believes that she is *incapable* of securing the good. The woman who transfers her microcredit loan to her husband may not believe that she is capable of managing the loan, for instance.

Agency as Self-Esteem

Much development discourse describes this constricted view of one's own agency as a lack of self-esteem. Persons whose preferences seem adaptive, according to self-esteem views, lack the sense that they are worthy or capable in general. Nussbaum speculates that women who acquiesce to injustice or domination sometimes do so because they lack "concept[s] of [themselves] as...person[s] with rights that could be violated" (Nussbaum 2001, 113). We might think that people with APs simply think they are unworthy of having their interests advanced. For example, one might venture that the woman who chooses genital cutting does not think she deserves sexual pleasure or that the woman who malnourishes herself does not think she deserves to eat.

This explanation is just too simple to be plausible. Self-esteem is an excessively global concept. It is implausible that most persons with APs think that they are unworthy human beings who cannot make claims on others. Many participatory development facilitators notice that groups of women who otherwise seem to lack self-esteem still attempt to dominate one another during sessions (Gujit and Shah 1998; Kothari 2001). It is likely that the same South Asian women who seem to acquiesce to not having enough food on their plates will demand humble service from their daughters-in-law in old age.

As I discuss further in Chapter 3 (in this volume), people's apparent levels of self-esteem change depending on whom they are interacting with or comparing themselves to. Sen's concept of "cooperative conflict" helps account for this. Sen argues that we must understand people's differential senses of entitlement not only with reference to their attitudes toward goods but also with reference to their relations to one another (1990). What appears as a general lack of self-esteem may be more aptly described as a lack of a sense of worthiness relative to some specific other person or persons.

Persons' levels of self-esteem vary with the field of life they are operating in as well as according to whom they are interacting with. A woman who is a confident business owner may manifest APs about her bodily health. A woman with high self-esteem about her sexuality may also think that a formal education would be wasted on her. Suggesting that self-esteem across *all* domains is a requirement of nonadaptive preferences will not help, because it is impossible for a person to possess self-esteem across all domains.

Even if it were possible to be confident across all domains, preferences that demonstrate lack of self-esteem in certain domains do not intuitively appear adaptive. That a person does not think she can be a successful soccer player or actress or mother does not seem in itself problematic. We are again left with a definition of adaptive preference that includes a large number of preferences that do not intuitively seem to be adaptive. Perhaps we can get around this problem by specifying important domains and levels of self-esteem. This may indeed allow us to use a conception of self-esteem to diagnose APs, but, once again, we will have gone beyond a procedural conception of autonomy.

Agency as the Capacity for Self-Representation

Another way of thinking of APs as agency-deficient may be to specify one domain in which self-esteem is particularly important—perhaps by saying that APs distort people's perceptions of their own political agency. A person who has APs does not see herself as capable of representing interests in public forums or making claims on public institutions. Admittedly, this definition of empowerment is not fully procedural. It is content-sensitive, because it indicates that persons should exhibit the preference to participate in public life. However, this type of sensitivity to preference content may be particularly consistent with liberalism, because people must represent their interests in public to sustain democratic social institutions.

However, describing APs as the absence of competence or desire to participate in public life suffers from the opposite problem of describing APs self-esteem deficits. Where self-esteem is an excessively broad concept, political participation is an excessively narrow one. Many intuitively APs are unrelated to a desire to participate in political life—and may happily coexist with a desire to participate in political life. If we take seriously Sen's idea that one's self-confidence in a particular arena is related to one's position relative to others in that arena, we must entertain the possibility that a woman may quite competently represent her interests in a women's self-help group and continue to malnourish herself at home.

Moreover, there is another class of preferences our intuitions deem adaptive that seem simply unrelated to the confidence to represent one's interests in public. APs about sexual life potentially fall into this class. It is perfectly imaginable that a woman could participate in public life and choose to have her genitals cut out of a belief that women's sexuality is shameful. Thus attempts to define APs as deficits in people's capacity for self-representation classify too few preferences as adaptive.

Adaptive Preferences as Deficits in Access to Flourishing

Instead of defining procedural autonomy as agency, we might define it as living under conditions that promote flourishing. This is admittedly a very idiosyncratic definition of autonomy, given that we usually understand autonomy as an aptitude of subjects rather than a feature of conditions. It is also clearly an insufficient definition of autonomy, given that people may have good opportunities and still make nonautonomous choices. A definition of autonomy as access to conditions that promote flourishing must be combined with some other stipulations about subjective states (such as rationality) in order to be complete.

Still, the language of theorists of AP often suggests that they take access to flourishing to be a constituent component of autonomy. Sen claims, for example, that poverty can be a form of coercion, just as tyranny can (Sen 1999b, 3). In responding to critics who claim that her list of capabilities justifies intervention in the lives of poor women who did not ask for it, Nussbaum writes:

> Choice is not pure spontaneity, flourishing independently of material and social conditions. If one cares about autonomy, one must care about the form of life that supports it, and the material conditions that enable one to live that form of life. Thus the approach [of using a capabilities list] claims that its own comprehensive concern with flourishing is a better way of promoting choice than the liberal's concern with spontaneity alone. (Nussbaum 1999, 50)

Nussbaum does not discuss what she means when she says that access to flourishing conditions promotes autonomy. We have good reason to suppose she does not mean that it is impossible to develop the rational capacities needed to reflect on one's preferences absent a very minimal level of nutrition and education. The conception of flourishing embodied by her capabilities list includes much more than the minimal conditions for practical reason (the capacity to enjoy the natural world, for example, does not seem to have an effect on persons' rational capacities). Nussbaum must think that non-flourishing conditions inhibit people's capacities for autonomy in some other way. I will not venture to fully explain what it is, but there is intuitive resonance to the idea that bad conditions force us to choose things we would not otherwise choose. The idea seems to be that a certain range of options must be available to individuals—who also have sufficient rational capacities—for their choices to count as autonomous.

One problem with thinking of APs as preferences formed under sub-flourishing conditions is familiar to us by now. Thinking of APs as preferences formed under sub-flourishing conditions does not do a good job sorting preferences that we intuitively think are adaptive from those we think are not—even the cases about which we are most sure. Deprivation can produce in persons the determination to resist, and this is the very opposite of AP. Feminist scholarship has provided a plethora of analyses of preferences that members of oppressed groups have developed under unjust conditions that actually work to empower them. For example, in an interview with John Foran, a Salvadorian anti-poverty activist called "Maria" describes the hunger and extreme poverty in which she grew up as motivating her to fight the injustice that produced them. "This life has allowed me to see many unjust things.... So this inequality and poverty is what made me decide to lead this [activist] life" (Bhavnani, Foran, et al., 2003, 23).

This first problem is a problem for the philosopher trying to account for our moral intuitions about APs, because it suggests that the conditions under which the preferences were formed are not the root of our worries about them. But it is not necessarily a problem for the practitioner trying to figure out which and whose preferences seem adaptive. This is because the preferences that escape definitions of APs as preferences formed under sub-flourishing conditions—preferences that have adapted in a good way—are not preferences a development practitioner is likely to have suspected in the first place. So, for example, the preferences of women whose own experiences of genital cutting have led them to become women's rights activists are unlikely to appear adaptive to practitioners. On the other hand, the preferences of women whose experiences of genital cutting have caused them to believe that they should always submit to their husbands' sexual desires are likely to seem adaptive. The fact that practitioners are unlikely to suspect good preferences formed under bad conditions of adaptiveness reveals this problem: making access to conditions for flourishing a requirement for nonadaptive preferences does not distinguish APs in a content-neutral way.

There is another problem with taking the conditions under which a preference was formed to define APs in the development context. In many contexts other than development, it makes perfect sense to use the conditions under which preferences are formed as a way of deciding if those preferences are autonomous. In the context of medical decisions, for example, it seems plausible enough to say that a person's decision to have a surgery because the doctor intimidated her is not autonomous. However, it seems more questionable to say that a woman who transfers her micro-loan into her husband's name because she is afraid of making him angry is not autonomous. One reason for this is that she may have made an autonomous decision to be in this particular relationship. It is difficult to identify a moment of decision when we speak of persons' preferences for certain modes of life without falling into an infinite regress problem.

Lessons: The Need for a Conception of the Good

I began this chapter by noting the appeal of defining APs as procedural autonomy deficits. Defining APs as unchosen preferences makes sense of the rhetoric of empowerment that describes AP transformation as giving people choices. It also gives us an obvious path for supporting development interventions aimed at transforming APs without compromising our commitments to liberalism and respect for moral diversity. Yet, however appealing it may be to define APs as procedural autonomy deficits, the foregoing discussion suggests that we cannot do so in a coherent fashion. We have asked whether any of four different conceptions of procedural autonomy—as rationality, life-planning, agency, and access to conditions for flourishing—can yield a definition of AP that is both consistent with our intuitions and practically applicable. We have seen all four conceptions fail. The following table (Table 2.1) summarizes the results of our investigation:

Table 2.1 Problems with Defining APs as Procedural Autonomy Deficits

Conception of Procedural Autonomy	Problems
Rationality A—Full Information	1. does not justify interventions that do more than provide information 2. identifies APs inconsistently with our intuitions by saying all uninformed preferences are adaptive
Rationality B—Reflectiveness	1. elitism 2. encourages seeing bearers of APs as unworthy of consultation 3. identifies APs inconsistently with our intuitions by saying all unreflective preferences are adaptive
Rationality C—Self-Interest	1. assumes APs cannot contribute to utility 2. identifies APs inconsistently with our intuitions by saying all non-self- interested preferences are adaptive
Life-Planning A—Understanding Personal History	1. assumes single authoritative narrative of individuals' personal histories 2. cannot coherently explain upgrading and downgrading of goods without attention to preference content 3. identifies APs inconsistently with our intuitions by saying all preferences based on incomplete understandings of personal history are adaptive

Life-Planning B—Living in Accordance with Life-Plan	1. identifies APs in a way inconsistent with our intuitions
	  a. higher-order preferences cannot be adaptive
	  b. preferences manifesting weakness of will must be adaptive
	  c. preferences to correct expensive tastes count as adaptive

Agency A—Self-Esteem	1. identifies APs in a way inconsistent with our intuitions by saying all persons with APs lack self-esteem
	2. empirically implausible that people either possess or do not possess self-esteem
Agency B—Public Self-Representation	1. identifies APs in a way inconsistent with our intuitions by ignoring APs that do not directly affect political representation
Access to Conditions Conducive to Flourishing	1. identifies APs in a way inconsistent with our intuitions by saying all preferences formed under sub-flourishing conditions are adaptive
	2. not neutral to preference content in practice

Each of the notions of procedural autonomy we have examined yields a definition of adaptive preference that is inconsistent with our intuitions, practically inapplicable, or both. But the lesson to be learned from this fact is not simply a negative one about how *not* to define APs. We can also glean a lesson about how *to* define them. In our foregoing discussion, an important pattern emerged. Almost every time we attempted to defend a notion of APs as procedurally nonautonomous against potential criticisms, we found ourselves supplementing procedural autonomy with a theory of the good. We found ourselves saying that the content of preferences matters to whether or not they are adaptive. Specifically, we found ourselves describing preferences with "bad" contents that seem imposed by deprivation as APs. To identify APs, we need to be able to distinguish good preference content from bad. The conception of human flourishing built into my perfectionist notion of IAP is such a theory of the good.

Are Adaptive Preferences Substantive Autonomy Deficits?

There remains a third way to define APs that is neither my perfectionist definition nor a procedural autonomy-based definition. This alternative would be to define APs as *substantive* autonomy deficits. Where theories of procedural autonomy state that only preferences formed or endorsed by certain processes are autonomous, theories of substantive autonomy state that only agent-endorsed preferences with certain motivational contents can be autonomous. The most famous substantive conception of autonomy can be found in Kant's idea that only actions performed out of respect for and in accordance with the moral law are autonomous. More contemporary theories of substantive autonomy suggest that autonomous preferences must have motivational contents that do things like demonstrate a value for independence (Friedman 2003, 19), aim at achieving a good life (Raz 1988), or criticize social norms according to appropriate normative standards (Benson 1987).

Substantive notions of autonomy have conceptions of the good built into them; though these notions differ about which preferences count as "good," they agree that only preferences consistent with some conception of the good can be autonomous. Given this, it may seem that substantive notions of autonomy can succeed at defining adaptive preferences where procedural ones fail. Defining APs coherently seems to embroil us in distinguishing good preferences from bad ones; and substantive theories of autonomy say that autonomous decisions manifest themselves in good preferences. Imagine we define APs as substantive autonomy deficits using a substantive definition of autonomy that says that autonomous preferences manifest a sense that one is capable of being wronged. If we define APs in this way, we have a plausible explanation of why women who do not critically analyze their subjugation seem to have APs while women who do not critically analyze baseball statistics do not seem to have them.

Further, if we can coherently define APs as substantive autonomy deficits, we need not give up the idea that APs are unchosen; we simply create more robust standards for what constitutes a chosen preference. In fact, treating APs as substantive autonomy deficits can help us to make sense of the tendency in development ethics to describe people with APs as lacking some special *type* of choice, rather than lacking the capacity to choose as such. Development theorists often qualify their use of the word "choice" when explaining the type of choice APs seem to fail to manifest. For example, Kabeer recognizes that some form of choice is available to people with APs but maintains that people with APs lack the capacity for "*meaningful* choices" (Kabeer 1999, 42). Perhaps having meaningful choices means being able to choose in a way consistent with one's own good, as substantive theories of autonomy suggest.

But defining APs as substantive autonomy deficits comes with its own problems, or so I want to suggest. Existing theories of substantive autonomy, like theories of procedural autonomy, yield definitions of AP that identify APs in a way inconsistent with our intuitions. I do not believe that this is a problem for all theories of substantive autonomy, however; we can imagine a theory of substantive autonomy that identifies APs in a way consistent with our intuitions. Yet regardless of how successful they are at identifying APs in a way consistent with our intuitions, substantive autonomy-based definitions of AP are problematic for a set of reasons procedural autonomy-based definitions are not. It is difficult to imagine a substantive autonomy-based definition of AP that identifies APs in a way consistent with our intuitions *and* allows us to retain our liberal commitments to respect for persons and moral diversity. To better see this, let us briefly examine three conceptions of substantive autonomy and the definitions of APs they yield.

Substantive Autonomy as Independence

One substantive conception of autonomy holds that agents act autonomously when they act in ways that value their own independence. On views like these, preferences to subordinate oneself cannot manifest autonomy, unless a person chooses to subordinate herself "for some higher nonsubordinate purpose which continued to be her own in the condition of servitude" (Friedman 2003, 19). People who do not see themselves as the source of their own values and who consistently prioritize achieving the ends of others over achieving their own ends fail to act autonomously. To define APs as nonautonomous on an independence view of substantive autonomy would be to say that APs are preferences motivated by a desire to subject oneself to the authority of another(s).

This view has the advantage of seeming to make sense of the intuition that APs do not really belong to the people who have them. On a substantive independence conception of autonomy, APs do not seem to belong to people, because a person can only have her *own* desires if she perceives herself as a source of her own values and if she perceives her ends as distinct from those of others and worthy of being pursued. A substantive independence-centered definition of AP can indeed explain why some preferences we intuitively declare adaptive seem to be so. For instance, a woman may undernourish herself to feed her husband because she perceives their interests as fused, because she believes she must always submit to her husband's desires, or because she feels like it is her fate to suffer. If she is motivated by any of these beliefs, she sees herself primarily as a vehicle for pursuing the ends of some other(s)—in the former cases the welfare of her family, in the latter, the ends of some higher power—and is therefore not autonomous.

However, a substantive independence-based definition of APs shares with procedural autonomy-based definitions of AP an inability to identify APs in a way consistent with our intuitions. It seems right to say that many APs are preferences to subject oneself to the will of another. Yet not all preferences that seem adaptive exhibit this structure. As I suggested earlier, a woman who undernourishes herself to feed her husband may do so because it helps her feel like a good and respectable woman. In a case like this, the woman's views about her own independence are ambiguous. She may engage in self-depriving behavior primarily in order to achieve her goal of feeling good about herself, and the higher-order goal of feeling self-worth is not obviously inconsistent with her valuing her own independence. Her preference seems adaptive, but it does not obviously manifest a lack of substantive independence autonomy.

Further, a substantive independence-based definition of APs defines as adaptive an entire class of preferences we do not intuitively consider to be so: voluntary self-sacrificing preferences made under conditions conducive to flourishing. Imagine a person who has opportunities to flourish but chooses to enter the military or a religious order. This person clearly cedes authority over many of her decisions to a party outside herself, and may do so because she believes that she is not a good judge of what should happen to her. On a substantive independence-centered definition of AP, this preference is adaptive—despite the fact that it intuitively does not seem to be so.

If we define APs as substantive independence autonomy deficits, we must also compromise some of our commitments to respect for persons and diversity among conceptions of the good. There are two particular points of tension between our liberal intuitions and a substantive independence-centered definition of AP. First, if people whose preferences do not manifest a value for their own independence are not autonomous, public institutions may reasonably coerce those people into changing their preferences. Since we have established that a substantive independence-based definition of APs will define all self-subordinating preferences as adaptive, public policies motivated by this definition will tend to justify coercion of people with APs (like the preference to undernourish oneself to feed one's husband) and people with other self-subordinating preferences (like the preference to join the military).

If we are committed to the principle of respect for persons, we will likely find this prescription morally problematic. Even if we think that APs are unreliable indicators of what people's well-being requires, we may oppose coercion of the people who have them. If we value people's capacities to live the types of lives they want, or if we oppose the use of force to encourage people to live according to a conception of the good, we will be uncomfortable with calling people with APs nonautonomous. If we are uncomfortable with the use of public coercion to promote a conception of the good, we will be less comfortable with calling people with APs substantively nonautonomous than calling them procedurally nonautonomous. There is some intuitive appeal to overriding the decisions of people who lack basic rationality, or who cannot evaluate information; however, it is much more intuitively objectionable for public institutions to override the decisions of people who do not happen to value their own independence. Since the coercion problem is a general problem with using a substantive conception of autonomy to define APs, I will revisit the question of whether defining APs as substantive autonomy deficits justifies objectionable coercion later. For the moment, I want only to note that saying that people with APs are nonautonomous seems to leave public institutions without a principled reason to refuse to coerce them.

A second reason a substantive independence-centered conception of AP falls foul of our commitment to respect moral diversity is that it encourages public institutions to question all preferences that do not conform to what may be a culturally specific conception of the good. If substantive independence autonomy requires consciously valuing one's own independence, substantive independence autonomy is a relatively controversial value. Philosophers and social scientists frequently suggest that consciously valorizing one's independence from fate and from others is a particularly white, middle-class, Western, and/or masculine type of self-conception (Apffel-Marglin and Sanchez 2004; Friedman 2003, 23; Iyengar and Leper 1999; Saharso 2000). For instance, some schools of Buddhism urge their practitioners to strive to decrease their investment in controlling their fates—a task that is clearly incompatible with a consistent conscious valorization of one's independence and self-direction. It is important to distinguish the conscious valuing of independence from having a conception of what matters to one or having a conception of oneself as separate from others. The latter two conceptions seem more culturally generalizable than the first, and I see little reason not to treat the latter two conceptions as sufficient for autonomy. A growing body of work in cross-cultural psychology suggests that people can be self-directed without consciously valuing independence (Chirkov 2007).

Defining APs as lacks of substantive independence may mean asking public institutions to suspect preferences simply because they belong to members of certain cultures, rather than because they are objectively "bad" preferences. Of course, to assert that a conception of the good is controversial does not demonstrate that the conception of the good is false. However, absent conclusive evidence or arguments that the failure to consciously value one's independence is somehow harmful to people or choice-inhibiting, it is not clear why we should encourage public institutions to question preferences that do not manifest substantive independence. Absent a clear reason to promote substantive independence as a necessary condition of autonomy or well-being, those of us who believe people should be allowed to pursue their own visions of the good life lack a good reason to endorse public suspicion of preferences that do not manifest a conscious value for independence.

Substantive Autonomy as Being Motivated by Good Norms

A different substantive theory of autonomy we might use to define APs understands autonomous preferences to be those motivated by an agent's endorsement of true or "good" norms. Paul Benson (1987) and Natalie Stoljar (2000) argue that oppressed people can have difficulty forming autonomous preferences because they internalize false norms. On conceptions of substantive autonomy like theirs, autonomous agents need to apply the correct norms when they are making decisions. Oppressed people who have internalized unjust norms come to lack the capacity to appropriately scrutinize those unjust norms, and this causes them to act badly. If we use a definition of substantive autonomy as the capacity to be motivated by true norms to define APs, we can think of APs as preferences motivated by false norms.

To be sure, we need an account of the distinction between true and false norms to use a good norms conception of autonomy to identify APs. Yet even without such an account, we can still identify some problems with a good norms definition of APs. As in the case of a substantive independence definition of AP, treating people motivated by false norms as nonautonomous leaves public institutions with little reason not to coerce them. We can also surmise—even without an account of the difference between true and false norms—that a good norms definition of AP would fail to identify many preferences that intuitively seem adaptive. Certainly, some APs—like a woman's choice to undergo clitoridectemy because she believes that her sexuality will take over her life if it is not curtailed—are motivated by false norms. But it seems that many APs are not *motivated by* false norms, even if they are complicit in reinforcing them. A woman may undergo clitoridectemy in a society that values it because she wants social recognition or because she wants to do what her peers are doing. In either case, it is not clear that she is motivated by false norms, even if a society that promotes false norms places her in a situation where genital cutting is a means to friendship and social recognition.

It may be retorted that she must be motivated by false norms even if she does not know it. But this idea is problematic in its own right, for a woman like the one in our example is probably motivated by both false norms (about women's sexuality) and true ones (about the value of belonging to a community). Further, she seems more proximately motivated by true ones. To say that all preferences complicit in perpetuating false norms are motivated by them fails to distinguish proximate causes of people's behavior from more attenuated ones. Even if a woman who gets her genitals cut to receive social recognition is partly motivated by false beliefs about women's sexuality, she is more directly motivated by a desire for community belonging. Practically speaking, a view that reduces her decision to motivation by false norms will likely produce development interventions with an ineffective focus—that focus on teaching her that she needs to feel positively about her sexuality rather than creating new modes of social recognition.

Furthermore—and this point is more controversial—treating false social norms as the most proximate cause of all APs does not allow for the maximal amount of respect for moral diversity compatible with the autonomy and flourishing of individuals. If we are serious about respecting cultural variety in conceptions of the good when these do not conflict with the basic autonomy and well-being of individuals, we should focus on changing "cultural practices" only when they *cause* some sort of harm or wrong to individuals. But false social norms may circulate in society without causing serious harms to the people to whom those norms apply. For instance, anthropologist Astrid Christoffersen-Deb discusses the persistence of a form of genital cutting that does not inhibit sexual functioning among young Abagusii girls in some regions of Kenya (Christoffersen-Deb 2005, 402). Some of the norms that cause the persistence of this practice are clearly misogynistic; one of them, for instance, is the belief that women's sexuality is voracious and needs to be controlled (Christoffersen-Deb 2005, 412). And yet the harm done to the young girls who undergo minor genital cutting are certainly less severe than the harms of clitoridectemy or infibulation, and arguably no more severe than the harms Western women inflict on their young daughters by encouraging them to be thin or to participate in child beauty pageants. A very large percentage of things women in patriarchal societies do can be viewed as influenced by bad social norms.

My point here is emphatically not that there is no harm in oppressive social norms that encourage women to shape their lives around the goal of being desired by men; I strongly oppose such norms wherever they are found and believe that they have negative consequences for women, even if these consequences do not directly translate into serious harm. Nor am I trying to say that misogynistic norms that are prevalent in the West do not affect women's basic flourishing; plenty of battered women in the West have their basic flourishing compromised daily, and Western cultural practices help us to explain why this happens. Rather, my point is to show that some choices motivated by oppressive norms do not cause serious harm to oppressed people. The warrant for liberal institutions to intervene in choices motivated by oppressive norms that do not cause serious harm is not apparent.

When justifying AP intervention—particularly cross-culturally—we should focus on serious harm. We likely do not have cross-cultural agreement about what constitutes flourishing above the basic levels. Further, when we judge that a person has an AP, I do not think we are merely saying that that person lives according to a conception of the good with which we disagree. Rather, we are saying that a person's preferences are preferences that we cannot imagine many people really wanting to have. It seems disingenuous to claim that we cannot imagine people wanting to believe in *any* oppressive social norms—even if it seems plausible to believe that we cannot imagine people wanting to give up their basic well-being or their capacities to choose the kinds of lives they want to lead.

Identifying APs as any preferences complicit in perpetuating bad social norms makes an implausibly large number of preferences adaptive. It also encourages interventions aimed at changing highly general social norms rather than changing the proximate causes of people's nonautonomous or nonflourishing preferences. I have already mentioned that these types of interventions are often ineffective. But if we want to respect cross-cultural moral diversity, we may also find such interventions morally objectionable. For when they focus on changing social norms that do not directly cause the APs they are trying to transform, they will diminish cultural diversity without a pressing moral warrant for doing so.

Substantive Autonomy as the Capacity to Choose the Good

Joseph Raz suggests a conception of substantive autonomy that is based neither on rejection of false norms nor on valuing independence. Rather, Raz distinguishes between the "autonomy we value" and procedural autonomy (Raz 1988, 411). Raz asserts that autonomy is valuable because it contributes to well-being, and it contributes to well-being insofar as it allows individuals to choose among the various ways of living a good life. We can interpret Raz as offering a substantive criterion for distinguishing autonomous preferences from nonautonomous ones. Autonomous preferences are those preferences that reflect an agent's own values and are consistent with her flourishing. To use this type of conception of autonomy to define APs, we might say that APs are endorsed or unendorsed preferences that are inconsistent with a person's flourishing.

Like all of the autonomy-based definitions of AP we have discussed so far, this one fails to help us identify APs in a way consistent with our intuitions. A substantive good-centered definition of APs says that all preferences inconsistent with a person's well-being are APs. A person who prefers to compromise her well-being absent limits on her opportunities—like the person with opportunities who chooses to engage routinely in a dangerous sport like bullfighting—does not seem to have APs. This suggests that we need some criteria to describe not only the content of preferences but also something about the processes by which they were formed to come up with an intuitively plausible definition of AP.

Still, a definition of substantive autonomy like Raz's seems more likely to help us identify APs in a way consistent with our intuitions than any of the conceptions of autonomy we have examined so far. This is partly because substantive good autonomy can help us distinguish APs from morally trivial preferences that still seem unchosen. Of course, a substantive good notion of autonomy's capacity to do this depends on the type of theory of the good with which we supplement Raz's conception of autonomy. To distinguish APs from morally trivial preferences that seem unchosen, we need to supplement Raz's theory only with a minimal conception of the good; if we supplement Raz's theory with a maximal theory of the good we end up with an undesirable definition of AP that says that preferences against excellence are adaptive.

What if we defined APs as substantive good autonomy deficits, where well-being was defined by a minimal, vague, and cross-culturally debated conception of the good? We might even add the stipulation that APs are substantively nonautonomous preferences that are arrived at under conditions unconducive to flourishing. We would have a definition of AP not unlike the one I offered in the first chapter. Such a view would likely identify APs in a way consistent with our intuitions; the woman who malnourishes herself to feed her husband would seem to have an AP, where the akratic or unreflective chocolate cake eater would not.

Despite this, I argue against conceiving APs as substantive good autonomy deficits. If we use a minimal, vague, and cross-culturally acceptable conception of well-being and we say APs must be formed under conditions unconducive to flourishing, our modified substantive good autonomy view may seem identical to my perfectionist view. But the difference between calling APs autonomy deficits and calling them reversible deficits in the capacity to lead a flourishing life is not merely linguistic. As I suggested earlier, calling APs autonomy deficits and incorporating a conception of the good into autonomy leads us toward policies that are decidedly illiberal. In political theory, we tend to describe autonomy as the capacity that exempts people from being subject to coercion. A person who can make her own decisions, or knows what matters to her, should not have her decisions overridden, we think. When we say that basic flourishing is identical to autonomy—as the substantive good autonomy-based definition of APs suggests we do—we sound like we are saying that people who have APs cannot make their own decisions. This seems both patently false and morally objectionable. A woman who does not see her husband's decision-making authority over her as unjust may reflectively choose not to defy him and may gain self-esteem from the belief that she is living according to the natural order of things. It is not clear to me why we should want to say that she is necessarily unreflective or incapable of identifying with these desires. Further, because she clearly reasons and makes decisions about what she cares about, it seems that public institutions affront her dignity by coercing her into changing her behavior.

Theorists of substantive autonomy often deny that declaring people substantively nonautonomous justifies coercing them. Raz argues against coercing people who fail to exercise substantive autonomy on the grounds that coercing them would usually have more adverse effects on their well-being than their existing nonautonomous choices do (Raz 1988, 418). He asserts that imprisoning people precludes them from participating in most autonomous pursuits. However true this may be, imprisonment is not the only form of coercion, and Raz's argument is more of an argument against imprisonment than coercion as such. We can imagine forms of coercion that do not prevent people from exercising autonomy in a variety of domains of life. Imagine, for the sake of argument, a policy that refuses vital health care to poor women who undernourish themselves to feed their male relatives. A woman who stops undernourishing herself only in order to retain access to health care has been coerced into changing her behavior, but she certainly does not lose her across-the-board ability to engage in autonomous pursuits as a result. Although I do not want to suggest that coercion of people who deprive themselves is *never* appropriate, it seems that Raz's well-being-based argument against coercion provides insufficient protection against coercion to deprived people.

Other substantive autonomy defenders also claim that we can value substantive autonomy without thereby justifying coercion of people who lack it. They typically make two arguments to this effect. First, they encourage us to think of substantive autonomy as a feature of decisions rather than persons. Autonomous people can make nonautonomous choices, and public institutions should only resort to coercion if a person makes nonautonomous choices consistently. So if the woman who undernourishes herself is only nonautonomous in a single region of her life, public institutions should not regard her as a legitimate object of coercion. But this separation of autonomous agents from autonomous choices does not sufficiently protect people with APs from coercion; if an autonomous agent makes a nonautonomous choice, why not coerce her in the domain of life where she has made the nonautonomous choice while respecting her capacities for choice in other domains of life?

Second, substantive autonomy proponents claim that we can value both substantive and procedural autonomy and use procedural autonomy to be our coercion-limiting concept. Marilyn Friedman advances a position of this sort by claiming that substantive autonomy is a "greater degree of autonomy" than procedural autonomy, not a replacement for it (Friedman 2003, 24). So, on a substantive good autonomy view, we may be able to say that the woman who undernourishes herself to feed her male relatives because of reflective beliefs about femininity is procedurally autonomous and immune from coercion—even if she is substantively nonautonomous. This view may successfully prevent calling APs substantive autonomy deficits from justifying to coercion of people with APs. However, it is not without its problems.

Why Not Call It "Autonomy?"

If we admit, as Friedman suggests we do, that people without substantive autonomy can make meaningful choices, it is not clear what the point of calling

APs "nonautonomous" is. Claiming that APs are characterized by a lack of autonomy—either procedural or substantive—suggests that people with APs have had their capacities to make choices impaired. This is a claim about the *subjective* status of people with APs. We can clearly see the attribution of AP as a judgment about people's subjective capacities in Des Gasper's discussion of APs in his important development ethics textbook. Gasper suggests that we must ask whether people with APs have "the psychological capacity to choose" (Gasper 2004, 214). People with procedural autonomy deficits lack mental capacities to understand or scrutinize their choices; people with substantive autonomy deficits have bad values that render inoperative their capacities to appropriately scrutinize their preferences. Since autonomy is a feature of subjects, defining APs as substantive autonomy deficits encourages condescension toward people with APs. Conceiving of APs as substantive autonomy deficits encourages us to think of people themselves as impediments to their own choosing, and this conception may militate against attempting to seriously understand deprived people's reasoned objections to policies aimed at transforming their preferences.

Furthermore, viewing APs primarily as problems for people's capacities to choose offers a somewhat distorting view of how APs affect the people who have them. At the beginning of this chapter, I suggested that thinking of APs as autonomy deficits was appealing because it helps to make sense of the intuition that APs are somehow imposed on people. But I think our discussion in this chapter asks us to reflect further on that intuition. What does it mean for a preference to be "imposed"? Given our preceding discussion, I think it is implausible to suggest that people with APs exhibit less conscious activity with relation to their preferences than people without APs, or even that APs are less conscious than nonadaptive preferences. Both deprived and nondeprived people make choices based on social values that are internalized. Both deprived and nondeprived people have preferences that are chosen and causally related to social conditions (i.e., that would change under different social conditions). I think that what our foregoing analysis suggests is that APs are not simply imposed preferences; they are preferences imposed *by deprivation*. Once we recognize this, we can see that APs are not characterized exclusively by a subjective stance. *They are characterized by content and a causal relationship to deprivation that is compatible with a variety of subjective stances.*

Calling APs autonomy deficits obscures this fact. It makes it look as though there is a particular attitude of subjects that is the defining feature of APs. It may be strategic or appealing to call APs autonomy deficits, but I believe it is disingenuous. Certainly, calling APs autonomy deficits makes it sound like preference transformation does not involve making judgments about the goodness or badness of people's choices, and this will appeal to liberals. But I hope our discussion in this chapter has shown that however strategic the flight from a theory of the good may seem, it distorts the reality of APs. It may also be appealing to call APs autonomy deficits, because it accounts for our intuition that people with APs have preferences that somehow fail to belong to them. However, I believe that my view of APs as preferences inconsistent with a person's basic flourishing formed under conditions hostile to her flourishing and likely to be reversed under conditions she recognizes as conducive to her flourishing captures our intuition more directly. APs seem imposed because they are causally related to conditions (this is what it means that we think they would be reversed under new conditions), but that is not their only defining feature. They are causally related to conditions that do not allow human beings to realize their potential to flourish.

I hope to have shown in this chapter that conceiving APs as autonomy deficits does not help us get clear about why we view them as unreliable indicators of the well-being of the people who have them. Defining APs as procedural autonomy deficits yields conceptions of APs that are inconsistent with our intuitions or practically inapplicable. Defining APs as substantive autonomy deficits yields conceptions of APs that are at illiberal at worst and potentially obscurantist at best. My perfectionist definition of APs—as reversible preferences inconsistent with human flourishing developed under conditions unconducive to flourishing-helps us get clear about what is morally at stake in identifying them. Admittedly, my perfectionist definition of APs is less obviously compatible with liberalism and respect for moral diversity than the procedural autonomy alternative seemed to be. Those interested in seeing a sustained defense of the compatibility of my perfectionist approach to identifying APs with liberalism can find one in the Chapter 4.

3 ADAPTIVE PREFERENCES AND AGENCY: THE SELECTIVE EFFECTS OF ADAPTIVE PREFERENCE

Many women in South Asia eat less than their male relatives, and this adversely affects their health (Miller 1997; Papanek 1990).[1] Economists Bina Agarwal (1997) and Amartya Sen (1990) have both attempted to make sense of this fact. Why do these women engage in behavior that damages their health? Agarwal and Sen agree that the existence of oppressive social norms that devalue women contribute to this type of unjust intrahousehold food distribution. But they disagree about whether and how much women who deny themselves food *endorse* the oppressive norms that influence their behavior. According to Sen, women who undernourish themselves likely do so because of an inability to see their household contributions as significant that causes them to see themselves as less deserving than men (Sen 1990, 148). Agarwal, in contrast, holds that women undernourish themselves out of self-interest; eating less and worse food helps women curry favor with their male relatives in a context where their survival depends on keeping male relatives happy (Agarwal 1997, 25–26).

Agarwal and Sen's disagreement is partly over an empirical question: assuming there are a range of reasons women malnourish themselves, we can ask how many women malnourish themselves because of diminished self-worth and how many do so out of self-interest. But their disagreement also points to a more general conceptual tension within feminism: how can we theorize about oppressed people as both victims and agents? On one hand, we want to make visible the harms unjust social arrangements inflict on subordinated people, and this means showing that some of the most serious of these harms affect subordinated people's *conceptions of self*. This is what Sen's analysis of women's self-malnourishment as the effect of diminished self-worth helps us to see. On the other hand, we acknowledge that subordinated people make creative and expressive choices within unjust systems, choices that allow them to develop meaningful senses of who they are and what they care about. Agarwal's analysis illuminates the sense in which women who live under patriarchal norms can still "bargain" to improve their lives.

Our desire to portray deprived people as agents is sometimes at odds with our desire to acknowledge the psychological effects of oppression. This potential for conflict is particularly salient in attempts to theorize about adaptive preferences. Many people who have adaptive preferences have limited concepts of self-entitlement (i.e., limited concepts of themselves as deserving) that we would not expect them to have if they lived under conditions conducive to their basic flourishing. Moreover, theorists often discuss adaptive preferences to raise questions about whether oppressed people can be expected to care about their own welfare or know what is good for them. Such discussions of adaptive preference may seem to be at odds with viewing people with adaptive preferences as agents. If unjust social conditions can undermine people's senses of self, how can people living under such conditions make meaningful choices about what matters to them? If their capacities to determine what is good for them have been stunted, how can their projects and goals really be their own? If they fail to recognize what is good for them, why should representatives of public institutions respect or value their desires? To pose the question in the context of intrahousehold food distribution, if a woman in a patriarchal context believes that women deserve to eat less than men, do we have a warrant for viewing her as lacking the capacities to make meaningful judgments about her own good?

If the answer to any of these questions is a straightforward "yes," the deliberative perfectionist approach I advocated in Chapter 1 is in trouble. After all, one sense in which my deliberative perfectionist approach is deliberative is that it encourages development practitioners to deliberate with oppressed and deprived people. It says that people with inappropriately adaptive preferences (IAPs) should guide adaptive preference interventions. In my view, people with adaptive preferences' first-person narratives can provide valuable information about what their preferences mean to them, and people with (IAps) should participate in envisioning more just futures for themselves and their communities. People with IAPs' flourishing-compatible views about what they want for themselves should guide development policy. In sum, the deliberative perfectionist approach recommends engaging deprived people as agents. It also recommends that development interventions aim at cultivating oppressed people's existing agency.

Further, as I argued in Chapter 1, an important advantage of my deliberative perfectionist approach is that it encourages development practitioners to respect and cultivate the agency of people with IAPs. But, in order for this advantage to be clear, people with adaptive preferences must exercise meaningful agency that is available for cultivation. I suggested in Chapter 2 that people with IAPs could be rational agents who make respect-worthy choices about their lives. In this chapter, I expand on that idea. I explain how people with adaptive preferences can retain and develop meaningful agency—that is, how people can have adaptive preferences and simultaneously possess flourishing-compatible senses of who they are and what they care about.

I offer an account of the effects of IAPs on the self that explicates how agency and IAP are compatible. We may think of adaptive preferences and agency as incompatible if we view adaptive preferences as global self-entitlement deficits. My main aim in this chapter is to propose an alternative view of adaptive preferences as *selective* self-entitlement deficits, a view based on acknowledgement of the multiplicity of people's self-concepts and the sometimes-contradictory nature of their preferences. Before I describe my view of IAPs as selective self-entitlement deficits, I enumerate the problems with the alternative view of IAPs as generalized self-entitlement deficits.

The Adaptive Self View of IAPs

I am advocating a deliberative perfectionist approach to IAP transformation. To briefly recapitulate the contents of this approach, I hold that people have a tendency toward basic flourishing. IAPs are preferences inconsistent with basic flourishing that are causally related to conditions where basic flourishing was not available. Because people have a tendency toward basic flourishing, IAPs are likely not their deep preferences. That is, it is likely that people's adaptive preferences would not persist under conditions conducive to their flourishing. IAP transformation should therefore strive to help people live in flourishing ways that they can endorse. A key aspect of my deliberative perfectionism is the view that there are many ways to flourish. My deliberative perfectionist approach prescribes involving oppressed and deprived people in adaptive preference interventions in at least two important ways: (1) the first-person narratives of people with suspect preferences provide crucial information about whether IAPs are present and why people have the preferences they do; and (2) the values of people with adaptive preferences should guide the choice of strategies for preference transformation.

This second way people with IAPs should be involved in IAP interventions is particularly relevant to our present discussion of agency. My deliberative perfectionist approach says that the existing values of people with IAPs should guide attempts at preference transformation. If my recommendation seems perplexing, perhaps it is because we tend to see adaptive preferences as thwarting people's capacities to form authentic values. If people with adaptive preferences cannot form values that are really "their own," it is strange to suggest that their values should influence policies aimed at helping them flourish Before I explicate my view of people with IAPs as capable of possessing flourishing-compatible values, however, I contrast it with the prevailing view of the effects of IAPs on self-entitlement.

This prevailing view sees the state of possessing IAPs as a state of generalized negative self-entitlement. Call this prevailing view the "Adaptive Self View" of IAPs.

Simply put, according to the Adaptive Self View, people with adaptive preferences generally fail to desire what is good for them. We can develop a clearer understanding of the Adaptive Self View through a brief survey of the philosophical writing on adaptive preferences and the feminist writing on autonomy and oppressive socialization. In Chapter 2, we observed a tendency to describe IAPs as autonomy deficits; a second tendency in the literature on IAPs is to describe their effects on the self as affecting almost the entire self. Martha Nussbaum opens her most sustained and influential discussion of adaptive preference with stories about the IAPs of two poor women in India—Vasanti and Jayamma. Vasanti remained in an abusive relationship for several years because she "thought the abuse was painful and bad, but still part of women's lot in life, just something women have to put up with as part of being dependent on men, and entailed by having left her own family to move into a husband's home" (Nussbaum 2001; 112–113). Nussbaum also relates the story of Jayamma, who works in a brick kiln that pays women less than men and does not see a problem with it. According to Nussbaum, both Vasanti and Jayamma lack "concept[s] of [themselves] as person[s] whose rights could be violated" (Nussbaum 2001, 113).

Nussbaum sees Vasanti and Jayamma's acquiescence to injustice as evidence of underlying negative self-concepts. For Nussbaum, Vasanti and Jayamma remain in unjust situations, because they do not think of themselves as deserving better. Nussbaum refers Vasanti and Jayamma's behavior back to beliefs about their *entire* selves.[2] In Nussbaum's view, Vasanti and Jayamma put up with injustice because they hold distorted views about the *types of beings they are*; they do not see themselves as belonging to the class of beings whose rights could be violated. Nussbaum's portrayal of Vasanti and Jayamma as possessed of damaged senses of self-entitlement is part of a larger trend in theoretical literature on IAPs. Some theorists, such as Sophia Moreau, understand adaptive preference as eclipsing people's capacity to criticize their oppression. In Moreau's words, adaptive preference is what happens when an oppressed person "come[s] to fit the image that has been defined for them by the dominant group and lack[s] all motivation for a change of identity" (Moreau 2004, 304). In this locution, it appears that it is the self as a whole, and not just certain preferences, that has adapted to unjust social conditions. Also in line with this trend, Anita Superson describes deformed desires as undermining people's general senses of self-worth (Superson 2005, 117).

Amartya Sen's descriptions of adaptive preference are a bit more difficult to decipher, because they often say very little about the *selves* of oppressed and deprived people. Consider the following passage:

> The hopeless beggar, the precarious landless laborer, the dominated house-wife, the hardened unemployed or the over-exhausted coolie may all take pleasures in small mercies and manage to suppress intense suffering for the necessity of continuing survival, but it would be deeply ethically mistaken to attach a correspondingly small value to their loss of well-being because of their survival strategy. The same problem arises with the other defini-tion of utility: namely, desire-fulfillment, since the hopelessly deprived lack the courage to desire much, and their deprivations are deadened and muted on the scale of desire-fulfillment. (Sen 1988, 45)

The passage contains no explicit discussion of how adaptive preferences affect the self. Yet the passage shares an important feature with the earlier descriptions of adaptive preference by Nussbaum, Moreau, and Superson. Sen, too, seems to see adaptive preferences as reflecting *generalized* negative attitudes. As the theorists of the previous paragraph seem to see adaptive preferences as negative views about the *entire* self, Sen seems to see adaptive preferences as reflecting negative views about well-being *as such*. The hopelessly poor lack the capacity to desire much *at all*—not the capacity to desire large houses or health care or emotional fulfillment. Adaptive preferences do not only affect people in certain spheres of life or contexts; they affect people's general desire for well-being. Anthropologist Arjun Appadurai seems, like Sen, to hold that adaptive preferences diminish peo-ple's overall capacities to want their own goods. Appadurai describes the very poor as lacking "the capacity to aspire" (Appadurai 2004). Without further spec-ification, this term suggests that poor people lack the general desire to improve their lot in life.[3]

Further inspection reveals important similarities between Appadurai's and Sen's views of people with adaptive preferences as bearers of diminished desires for well-being and the Adaptive Self View. Theorists like Nussbaum and Superson portray IAPs as stemming from a concept of the self as unworthy. Sen does not tell us explicitly what views about the self motivate the diminished desire for well-being. Yet people's self-regarding desires are what is at stake in Sen's discussion. Sen does not claim that deprived people stop believing well-being is good *for people* in general. It seems instead that Sen thinks deprived people stop wanting well-being *for themselves*. In David Clark's words, "desiring an object and valuing it are two entirely different things" (Clark 2003, 180). People with adaptive preferences have distorted views about their own access to well-being, not necessarily others' access to it. Why might people stop desiring well-being for themselves without simultaneously believing that well-being was not valuable for anyone? The most plausible answer seems to be that people with adaptive preferences have distorted views of themselves as deserving.

To explicitly connect the views of adaptive preference as diminished desire for well-being and adaptive preference as diminished self-worth, we might characterize all of the foregoing views as versions of the view that adaptive preference adversely affects people's general senses of self-entitlement. My term "self-entitlement" is inspired by Sen's term, "perception of entitlement." Sen's term highlights the subjective dimensions of social and intrafamily distribution of goods; who gets what depends partly on how entitled—that is, deserving—that person perceives herself to be (Sen 1999b, 193). I use the term "self-entitlement" to refer to a person's perception of herself as worthy of flourishing. A person with generalized positive self-entitlement believes she is generally worthy of doing well and thus pursues her flourishing; a person with generalized negative self-entitlement routinely questions whether her flourishing is worth pursuing. Both Sen's portrayal of adaptive preference as diminished desire for well-being and Nussbaum's portrayal of adaptive preference as diminished self-worth can be said to represent adaptive preferences as global self-entitlement deficits. Both the person who does not think she is the type of being whose rights can be violated and the person who "fail[s] to desire much" encounter impediments to desiring goods *for themselves*.

I believe that the Adaptive Self View is a common view of how IAPs affects people's senses of self. In saying this, I do not mean to argue that either Nussbaum or Sen intends to say much about the moral psychology of IAPs. The moral psychology of IAPs is outside the scope of their inquiries, but their work has been highly influential, and the operative definition of IAP in development is drawn from their remarks.[4] Many development theorists and practitioners discuss IAP in ways that suggest it affects people's entire senses of self. For example, Agarwal sees Sen's writing on adaptive preference as entailing the view that "women may not tend to think in terms of self-interest or in favor of their individual well-being" (Agarwal 1997, 22). Deepa Narayan asserts that a woman with IAPs may have a "perception of herself and her world" that is "skewed" (D. Narayan 2005, 34). Naila Kabeer speaks of women with IAPs as "having internalized their status as persons of lesser value" (Kabeer 1999, 440). In an influential article on IAPs, Miriam Teschl and Flavio Comim, describe Sen's descriptions of IAPs as involving a "lack of perception of personal interest" (Teschl and Comim 2005, 234).

Generalized Negative Self-Entitlement as an Impediment to Agency

Positive self-entitlement is a prerequisite for free agency. Let us think of agency as a person's capacity to act in a way that reveals her sense of what matters to her. A person who lacks agency might act, but her actions fail to disclose who she is, and we thus say that her actions are not her own. A person who is an agent identifies with her chosen courses of action rather than regarding them as instances of mere subjection—to another's will or the uncontrollable tides of fortune. She has a sense of what matters to her and attempts to act in a way that reveals this. In order to make choices according to her own sense of what matters, a person must regard her projects as worth pursuing.[5] This is where global negative self-entitlement can preclude free agency.[6] A person who does not have personal desires, or who experiences her desires as not worth pursuing, will not experience her projects and desires as belonging to her. There will be an important sense in which her projects do not reveal her sense of what matters, in which she will experience herself as alienated from them. If a person's lack of self-entitlement is near global, she will be nearly incapable of acting in a way that reveals what matters to her. She will have no sense of what matters to her as distinct from what the social order prescribes, or she will consistently believe that what matters to her is not important.

Many feminist philosophers of autonomy and oppressive socialization portray positive self-entitlement as a prerequisite for agency and understand many oppressed people's psychologies in line with the Adaptive Self View. The feminist conversation on autonomy and oppressive socialization contains diverse strands, but one of these strands focuses on the ways unjust social conditions can damage the oppressed person's experience of herself as a self. Oppressed people may come to feel like they cannot locate their own desires in order to act on them, or they may see themselves as unworthy. Since both a sense of one's true goals and a sense that those goals are worth achieving are prerequisites for authentic action, harm to a person's very sense of self is a deep type of moral damage.

For example, Paul Benson (2000) argues that some women "feel crazy" under unjust conditions; they experience themselves as alienated from their own choices. According to Benson, society encourages women to internalize harmful norms, and the conflict between their desires and those norms produces the sense that they are not worthy of answering for their actions (Benson 2000, 80). Similarly, Susan Babbitt claims that oppression can undermine women's abilities to pursue their own well-being by impeding their sense of their own worthiness (Babbitt 1993). In Babbitt's words, oppressed people can fail to possess "a sense of self that would support a full sense of flourishing" (Babbitt 1993, 248). Superson asserts that many women under patriarchy do not regard themselves as "intrinsically valuable human being[s]" and that this failure "jeopardizes their autonomy and full agency" (Superson 2005, 111). Each of these feminist philosophers of agency holds that people's senses of self can incur broad-scale damage under unjust social conditions, as well as that such damage to the sense of self prevents people from forming and pursuing authentic desires.

The Lack of Agency as a Problem for the Deliberative Perfectionist Approach

If we accept the view that oppressed people cannot form authentic desires, it will prejudice our conclusions about the role oppressed and deprived people should play in overcoming their own IAPs. The Adaptive Self View has an important advantage; it requires us to treat oppression and deprivation as serious and deeply harmful. But it also encourages us to imagine IAP transformation in certain potentially dangerous ways.

We can more clearly see the practical dangers of approaching people with IAPs as victims of the Adaptive Self View by looking at a case. Sarah Castle, Sidy Traore, and Lalla Cisse conducted a participatory study of central Malian women's attitudes toward reproductive health. When asked to define reproductive health, the Malian women repeatedly described it as including bearing healthy children and having a good relationship with one's husband. Castle, Traore, and Cisse concluded from these women's descriptions of reproductive health that reproductive health programs in this community should involve discussions of issues such as gender relations and social taboos, because these issues were important to women in the community (Castle, Traore, et al. 2002, 29).

But we can imagine a development practitioner motivated by the Adaptive Self View reacting to this experience very differently. First, imagine the practitioner believes that most or all of the preferences of people with IAPs are inconsistent with their interests. Such a practitioner may prematurely dismiss *all or most* of these women's claims about what they want. This practitioner might react to the Malian women's reports by refusing to take seriously these women's desires to be faithful to their husbands or raise healthy families. The practitioner may see the women's focus on being faithful to their husbands as *only* indicative of the same general lack of self-worth that contributes the women's being at risk for poor reproductive health. But the women in question may deeply care about marital fidelity and having healthy families—even while they would be willing to adopt healthier contraceptive and childbirth practices. Our practitioner might ignore evidence of the women's deep attachment to marital fidelity on the grounds that one deformed desire implies a whole host of them. She might then design a reproductive health intervention focused on advocating sexual freedom for women. If the practitioner did this, and if the Malian women were deeply attached to marital fidelity in a way that was not causing them harm, the practitioner would be arbitrarily advancing her values at the expense of those of the Malian women. The practitioner could be justified in doing so by the Adaptive Self View. After all, if the women consistently desire against their well-being, is taking seriously their desires for marital fidelity not a way of encouraging them to further deprive themselves?

Second, a development practitioner who thinks that IAPs severely harm people's general senses of self-entitlement may ignore existing resistant, flourishing-compatible desires on the part of people with adaptive preferences. The women in Castle, Traore, and Cisse's study seem to value being faithful to their husbands. Let us presume for a moment that the Malian women do not have a critical relationship to this aspect of their gender role, and that they believe men deserve sexual freedom while women do not. A practitioner who adhered to the Adaptive Self View might assume that this meant that they saw themselves as less entitled and competent than men across most domains of life—and with respect to most social goods. The practitioner would be mistaken here, since the subjects in Castle, Traore, et al.'s study overtly condemn domestic violence and see it as a major problem in their communities (Castle, Traore, et al. 2002, 28). A lack of self-entitlement vis-à-vis sex can coexist with a conception of self-entitlement to freedom from violence. Rather than observing existing opposition to domestic violence and building on it, as the deliberative perfectionist approach would encourage her to do, a practitioner motivated by the Adaptive Self View might misplace the focus of an intervention on teaching women that domestic violence is wrong. Practitioners who endorse the Adaptive Self View will see people with IAPs as generally unreliable sources of judgments about their well-being. In sum, viewing the effects of IAP as generalized can raise the question of why development practitioners should deliberate with deprived people *at all.*

Inappropriately Adaptive Preferences as Selective Self-Entitlement Deficits

I propose that we shift from the Adaptive Self View toward a view of IAPs as *selective* self-entitlement deficits. Before I elaborate this alternative view, I want to qualify my claim about how adaptive preferences affect self-entitlement. I do not hold that *no* adaptive preferences reveal generalized negative self-entitlement. We do sometimes encounter examples of global negative self-entitlement in discussions of how injustice can harm the self. Sawatri Saharso (2000) discusses a case that seems to qualify. Saharso relates the story of a Dutch Hindustani woman who committed suicide by drinking acid. According to Saharso, the woman was in an abusive relationship, and her husband was charged with "deliberately incit[ing] her to commit suicide" (Saharso 2000, 224). Saharso conjectures that the woman's lack of ability to distance herself from the demands of her culture played a causal role in her decision to kill herself, because the woman preferred taking her life over taking advantage of options to exit the relationship—options of which she was likely aware (Saharso 2000, 231). If Saharso is correct about the exit options available to this woman, it seems plausible to conclude that years of abuse—and community acceptance of that abuse—affected this woman's sense of self in a generalized negative way.

Claudia Card's discussion of the situation of the women in Kathleen Barry's 1977 study of prostitutes who had been "'seasoned' for prostitution through torture" lends itself to similar analysis. According to Card, these women come to identify with the pimps who torture them and lack a separate perspective from which to evaluate the pimps' acts; a woman in this situation might find that "her choices [to fulfill the pimp's desires] come to seem normal to her, no longer even morally problematic" (Card 2002, 214). In this case again, it seems plausible to hold that the woman's sense of self-entitlement has been replaced by a conception of herself as an instrument for fulfilling the desires of the pimp.

So, rather than claiming that no IAPs reveal generalized negative self-entitlement, I wish to suggest that this type of generalized negative attitude toward the self is not *typical* of people with IAPs. It may be typical of people who are victims of certain forms of torture and severe, isolating abuse, and I believe that understanding how these forms of abuse function raises important moral and empirical questions for feminists. My deliberative perfectionist approach to responding to IAPs may even be a response ill-suited to people who have been victims of such abuse—whose agency has been deeply deformed or nearly extinguished. However, the deliberative perfectionist approach is useful in responding to IAPs whose impacts on the self are not global. I maintain that most IAPs fall into this latter category. According to the definition of adaptive preference I offered in Chapter 1, both global and selective self-entitlement deficits count as adaptive preferences. I believe that one advantage of deliberating with people with suspect preferences is that it can help development practitioners determine whether generalized or selective self-entitlement is at work in a particular case.

To be sure, my claim that most IAPs are selective self-entitlement deficits is partly an empirical claim that I cannot fully substantiate. Absent empirical data about prevalence rates of different types of IAP, I can only venture that the development literature and other feminist social science is full of discussions of people whose self-harming preferences coexist with manifest positive attitudes toward the self and well-being.[7] If it is the case that IAPs often coexist with positive attitudes toward the self, well-being, and competence, the deliberative perfectionist approach to responding to IAPs will have a particular type of appeal. It can be seen as enabling development practitioners and activists to respond to IAPs in ways that take advantage of and cultivate the very real existing agency of most deprived and oppressed people.

The remaining puzzle is this: how is it possible for people to have desires that run counter to their flourishing without having generally diminished senses of self? How is it possible for people to fail to recognize their own deprivation or report that certain opportunities for flourishing are "not for them" without having the underlying belief that they are unworthy? I think that the answer lies in a view of preferences and self-concepts as multiple and contradictory. If we see people's senses of self and preferences as comprised of varied—and sometimes contradictory—elements we will not be surprised to notice that they may make choices inconsistent with their flourishing and retain partially positive self-concepts.

When I speak of self-concepts and preferences as comprised of multiple and occasionally contradictory elements, I do not intend any sort of strong metaphysical claim. I hope only to make explicit three relatively uncontroversial facts about the world. First, rather than having a single concept of self-entitlement, people have multiple concepts of self-entitlement that operate in different realms of life. Specifically, people's senses of self-entitlement vary interpersonally and contextually. A person may feel highly entitled compared to certain other people and unworthy compared to certain others; similarly, a person may experience herself as deserving of some goods but not others. Second, oppressed people may more or less completely internalize their oppression. Rather than passively internalizing their oppression wholesale, many oppressed people experience some sort of inner struggle over the truth of oppressive beliefs about themselves. Third, preferences can have contradictory impacts on flourishing. A single preference can increase a person's access to flourishing in one domain of life while decreasing it in others, because oppressed and deprived people often confront situations in which successful attempts to advance their objective interests entail some self-harming behaviors.

My notion of multiple and contradictory self-concepts and preferences differs from "postmodern" conceptions of the self as multiple. Many postmodern theorists regard the multiplicity of the self as more metaphysically radical and more worthy of celebration than I do. Some postmodernists argue that people's self-concepts are internally incoherent in ways that make personal identity impossible. These theorists see the fact that people think of themselves differently in different contexts as evidence that the attainment of a coherent self-concept is impossible and undesirable.[8] My view of selves and preferences as multiple and contradictory is not intended as a challenge to the ideal of coherent personal identity. I do not deny that having a somewhat coherent self-concept that allows a person to feel authentically herself is a good thing. My view suggests only that the coherence of a person's self-concept may never be *total* and that oppressed and deprived people may face particular difficulty forming coherent self-concepts.

Self-Entitlement as Context- and Domain-Variant

People's concepts of self-entitlement are context- and domain-variant, which means that high and low self-entitlement can coexist in the same person. People experience themselves as more or less worthy depending on whom they are interacting with and whom they are comparing themselves to. This is what we might call "context variance." People may also experience themselves as more worthy of certain goods than others, or more deserving of flourishing in some domains of life than others. We might call this latter type of variance "domain variance."

We can see how perceptions of self-entitlement vary contextually if we understand concepts of self-entitlement as *comparative* rather than absolute. Rather than viewing themselves as either deserving or undeserving, we view ourselves as more or less deserving than certain other people. Sen and Hannah Papanek's analyses of gender biases in intrahousehold food distribution elucidate the comparative nature of self-entitlement. In his discussion of cooperative conflicts, Sen (1990) considers the puzzle of why women in many "traditional societies" acquiesce to domination by male members of their households. He suggests that these women may accept the domination, because exiting the relationship would subject them to worse forms of domination.[9] That is, the position inside the household is bad, but the "breakdown position" outside of the household is worse. To use a very simple example: to eat less than and after one's husband is bad; to not be able to eat consistently at all because of unreliable access to income outside the relationship is worse.

For our present purposes, Sen's analysis suggests that these women's subservience to their male family members need not reflect a generalized subservience. We know that many women in oppressive family arrangements do perceive the meeting of their needs as less important than the meeting of the needs of their male family members. But does this imply a belief that their own needs are objectively unimportant? Sen's analysis allows us to answer this question in the negative. If the choice to remain in a dominating household secures one's access to flourishing more successfully than leaving it, remaining is a way of advancing one's self-interest. If a woman's conception of self-entitlement were damaged in a generalized fashion, it is not clear what her motivations for choosing to remain in the family might be. A woman in a position like the one Sen describes may have genuinely internalized the belief that her health and well-being are less important than her husband's. But Sen allows us to see that even internalized oppression vis-à-vis one's husband need not obviate her desire to advance her interests, as we know she wants to protect herself from whatever other misfortunes she may encounter outside the relationship.

Further, her IAP to eat insufficiently because her husband supposedly deserves more may reflect more about her attitudes toward her husband than her attitudes toward food. That is, she may prefer to eat less because she sees her interest in food as less important than her husband's, but it does not follow from this that she believes she has no interest in eating. Sen describes intrahousehold conflict as a problem about the distribution of "shares." In real life, decisions about who eats and how much are often decisions about how limited resources should be divided. Dividing these resources is a question of determining the *relative* sizes of people's shares. The question of intrahousehold food distribution is irreducibly a question about how important one's needs are *relative to* those of others.

Importantly, seeing oneself as less worthy than some people does not preclude one from seeing oneself as *more* worthy than other people. Papanek's (1990) discussion of intrahousehold food distribution emphasizes how women learn to see themselves as less worthy than men, and this causes them to accept lesser nourishment. She describes mechanisms of socializing women to believe in their own inferiority that exist across a wide variety of cultures. A striking feature of virtually all her examples of oppressive socialization is that oppression is about the subordination of one's *group* to another group. Women learn that people who belong to their group (women) deserve less than people from another group (men). They hear messages like, " 'a man needs more food than a woman because…' or 'a girl does not have to be as well-educated as a boy because…' " (Papanek 1990, 170). But the belief that women need less than men implies nothing about how much women need vis-à-vis other women. Indeed, women who seem to affirm their inferiority to men can enthusiastically demand more than other women. Papanek herself notes that the same poor South Asian women who deny themselves food may want to have sons so that they can gain the service of daughters-in-law (Papanek 1990, 172). These women will likely sometimes advance their interests at the expense of those of the daughters-in-law.

If we view self-entitlement as a relative rather than absolute concept, we can see how oppressed and deprived people may experience multiple perceptions of self-entitlement. They may experience themselves as less entitled than advantaged others but as entitled as—or more entitled than—other members of their disadvantaged social group. Since oppression and deprivation typically accrue to people because they belong to certain groups, many—perhaps even most—oppressed and deprived people will have groups of peers to whom they consider themselves comparably or superiorly entitled. IAPs and some positive self-entitlement can coexist, because persons circulate in a wide variety of social contexts and compare themselves to different groups of people. A woman's belief that she deserves to eat

less than her husband can coexist with the belief that she needs to eat, even perhaps that she needs to eat more than her daughter-in-law. To put this point more
generally, people's senses of self-entitlement may be context-variant; people's self-
entitlement may vary according to whom they are comparing themselves to. Once
we realize this, we recognize one way in which people may have IAPs and retain
some sense of positive self-worth.

In addition to being context-variant, people's perceptions of self-entitlement are domain-variant. Sabina Alkire's (2007a) work on domain-specific
agency draws attention to the fact that the workings of oppression and deprivation are not identical across all domains. I have just argued that people may feel
more or less entitled depending on the person to whom they are comparing
themselves; people may also feel more or less entitled depending on what goods
are in question. Oppressive systems make some goods particularly off limits for
certain groups of people. For example, women—in both rich and poor countries—are often discouraged from seeking sexual fulfillment or controlling
their reproductive lives. The reasons for this discouragement are inextricably
tied to these women's status as women; "good women" do not seek out sex for
pleasure alone.

I take it to be the case that some oppressed and deprived groups of people
learn that some social goods are not "for them." I also take it to be the case that
social goods are not a single bundle to which people experience themselves as
entitled or not. A flourishing life likely has plural constitutents.[10] The social goods
a person needs in order to flourish likely range from things like opportunities to
use one's cognitive capacities, opportunities to be adequately nourished, opportunities for sexual fulfillment, and freedom from violence.

Much empirical research on gender and development suggests that goods like
these are not only plural but distinct in the following sense: experiencing a high
degree of entitlement to one or some goods does not entail a high degree of entitlement to all of them. Until the 1980s and 1990s it was conventional wisdom in
development that ensuring women greater access to some one good would
increase their abilities to flourish in multiple domains.[11] The most common
"all-purpose" goods were income and education. Sen, for example, argued in his
1990 essay on cooperative conflicts that women who worked outside the home
would gain greater bargaining power within it (Sen 1990, 144–145). More recent
empirical research calls this idea into question. Indeed, women's gains in one
domain are sometimes accompanied by losses or no change in other domains.
According to Alkire, a critique of

> proxy measures, and one that emerges regularly in the literature on wom-
> en's agency, is that the same person may achieve quite different levels of

agency in different spheres of life: the same person can be fully empowered as a wife and mother but excluded from the labor force by social conventions, recently empowered to vote by a grassroots political process, but
not confident to travel alone.... (Alkire 2007a, 11)

If gains in one domain do not necessarily permeate all domains, lacks in one
domain likely do not spread across all domains either. As Alkire's examples suggest, oppressed and deprived people often experience self-entitlement in some
domains and not in others. This will seem less surprising if we acknowledge that
oppressive systems sometimes make self-worth and certain forms of flourishing
accessible *through* preferences that cut off flourishing in some domains. I explain
this idea in more depth in the section on preferences with multiple/ambivalent
effects on flourishing. For now, we can turn to an example from Alkire to illustrate this point. Alkire mentions that a group of poor women in Kerala deeply
value being good wives and mothers (Alkire 2007a, 20). Being good wives and
mothers matters to these women, even while this preference may result in their
taking on extremely burdensome shares of household work and prevent them
from engaging in income-generating activities. This suggests that the women gain
self-worth from engaging in activities that have negative effects on their flourishing in some domains. They enjoy seeing themselves as good wives and mothers,
but being good wives and mothers may require significant sacrifices of income,
leisure time, and bodily health.

We might interpret these women's concepts of self-entitlement as fundamentally muted, but this interpretation would ignore real satisfaction, social recognition, and opportunities to exercise affective and rational capacities they may
gain from fulfilling their socially prescribed roles. I suggest instead that we read
these women's desire to be good wives and mothers as rooted partly in a sense of
self-entitlement to flourishing. Women do not just care about being good wives
and mothers because they desire their own subservience; they care about being
good wives and mothers partly because it gives them social recognition and
opportunities to exercise their rational and affective capacities. They may lack a
sense of self-entitlement to goods like income and participation in public life,
but it does not follow that their behavior expresses no form of self-interest. If we
read these women's acceptance of their roles as directed at securing some objectively valuable goods, we can avoid thinking of these women along the lines of
the Adaptive Self View—as simply lacking a sense of self-entitlement. They possess self-entitlement to self-esteem, love, and recognition but suffer from a deficit of self-entitlement to income, participation in public life, and freedom from
exploitative work. In other words, they have positive self-entitlement in some
domains but not in others.

Internal Resistance to Oppressive Self-Concepts

If self-entitlement is context- and domain-variant, we can see some IAPs as self-entitlement deficits a person confronts only when she compares herself to certain others or attempts to access a specific range of goods. Yet describing adaptive preferences as context- and domain-variant may seem to treat adaptive preferences as insufficiently deep-rooted. To point out that people's concepts of self-entitlement vary based on whom they are encountering and the good in question may seem to ignore the fact that oppression and deprivation can have pervasive-seeming effects. Unjust social conditions often include *systems* of barriers to flourishing for oppressed and deprived people. That is, oppressed people find *most* paths to self-entitlement blocked under unjust social conditions.[12] To describe oppressed and deprived people's concepts of self-entitlement as shifting may seem to deny the fact that oppression marks people as particular types of beings; it shapes people's senses of who they *are*.

We can conceive of IAPs as sometimes affecting people's deep, context-stable sense of who they are without yet seeing their impacts on self-entitlement as global. Some IAPs are probably deeper and more global in their effects than others. The key to explaining how IAPs can affect people's overarching senses of *who they are* and still leave them with some positive self-worth lies in the notion of internal resistance to oppressive self-concepts. People struggle to view themselves positively in the face of adversity, and even under conditions of severely limited access to conditions for flourishing, oppressed and deprived people find spaces and communities in which to develop and express positive views of themselves *as selves*. Where deprivation is particularly systemic or severe, we can expect opportunities for resistance to be rare and expressions of resistance covert, but there is often discernible resistance nonetheless. I speak of *internal* resistance to oppressive self-concepts to emphasize the existence of struggle *within* the psyches of persons with adaptive preferences. The types of resistors I am interested in here have, to some extent, internalized negative views of themselves. People find opportunities for positive self-worth notwithstanding—or perhaps in response to—this fact.

To understand this idea of internal resistance to oppressive self-concepts, it is helpful to understand severely oppressed people as living with fractured self-images. A number of feminist theorists have described self-fracturing as a harm of oppressive socialization.[13] People with fractured self-images cannot maintain consistently positive evaluations of their desires. They live with an internal struggle about the worth of their projects, values, and desires, because they live in a world that does not consistently reward them for seeking their own flourishing. As Catriona Mackenzie argues, self-worth requires social recognition, and oppressed people often receive social recognition for inhibiting their own flourishing (Mackenzie 2000, 142). People with fractured self-concepts negatively evaluate their projects, values, and desires because of implicit or explicit negative beliefs about the types of beings they are—where being a certain type of being means belonging to a certain social group. This is different from negatively evaluating and revising particular goals because of realistic assessments about one's lack of talent in a particular domain, new information, or the realization that a change in goals would better lead to personal fulfillment. Revising one's goals on the basis of new and changing information about one's self and the world is a potential marker of healthy development, whereas frequent self-undermining based on negative beliefs about various aspects of oneself bespeaks a self-image fractured by oppression.

People with fractured self-images identify partly with the negative views about their worth; they judge themselves according to oppressive standards. Yet their identification with these negative views is incomplete. They face difficulty maintaining positive self-images in the absence of consistent social confirmation of the importance of their flourishing. To revisit the example of intrahousehold food distribution, a woman who undernourishes herself because of adaptive preferences likely lives in a world in which she receives positive feedback from others for failing to feed herself (Papanek 1990, 172). She thus faces difficulty maintaining an unequivocally positive attitude toward her nourishment; she may alternately experience her biological desire to eat as an alien urge to be mastered and as a pleasurable incentive to indulgence.

On what grounds might we assert that oppressed and deprived people's identification with negative views about their flourishing is often only partial? There is much anthropological evidence that people living under conditions of severe oppression and deprivation actively seek to defend their flourishing—even when those people *also* actively endorse negative views about themselves. Much feminist ethnographic research focuses on women's—often covert, deeply ambiguous—forms of resistance to oppressive norms. Without claiming that the empirical research on the lives of deprived people conclusively shows that resistance usually accompanies oppression, I do want to suggest that there is ample reason to believe that oppressed and deprived people find opportunities to resist injustice. Let us consider a set of cases of South Asian women's covert resistance to unequal intrahousehold food distributions discussed by Agarwal. Agarwal cites a number of "ingenious strategies" poor South Asian women use to ensure their own nourishment. Among these strategies are "holding clandestine picnics with female friends," "feigning spirit possession to extract food items otherwise denied to them" (Agarwal 1997, 24), and "pleading ill-health, playing off male affines and co-sanguines against each other, threatening to return to the natal home, withdrawing into silence, and withholding sex from husbands" (Agarwal 1997, 18). We can easily imagine women engaging in behaviors like these and endorsing unequal intrahousehold food distributions.[14] A woman who feigns spirit possession to attain food items she would normally not receive may nonetheless feel beset by guilt for doing so.

Perhaps it seems curious that people often fail to completely identify with oppressive social norms when oppression and deprivation are systemic. If oppressed and deprived people often receive negative social messages about attempts to secure their own flourishing, how might they develop competing positive self-images? One reason people comes in the form of the Flourishing Claim I made in Chapter 1. The claim states that people have a natural tendency to pursue their basic well-being. Another reason has to do with the idea that people participate in multiple communities. People probably need some social confirmation of the importance of their flourishing to cultivate meaningful positive self-concepts. The view that people could develop positive self-concepts in the absence of *any* positive social recognition would indeed be mystifying. I suggest instead that oppressive societies do provide (limited) social opportunities for oppressed people to develop and act in accordance with positive self-images. We might think of these opportunities as afforded by "resistant social spaces." Resistant social spaces are groups or modes of expression that allow oppressed people to cultivate self-worth within the larger context of oppressive societies. To hold that resistant spaces exist is not to deny the near-pervasive effects of oppression on some people's self-images; indeed, identifying select social spaces as *resistant* already suggests a backdrop of large-scale injustice.

Resistant social spaces can coexist with oppressive systems, because oppressed people can find ways of communicating desires to flourish that do not cause the destruction of the prevailing social order and because oppressed people often participate in communities with other oppressed people. To briefly explain the former, oppressed people may sometimes communicate their desires for flourishing without destroying the prevailing social order. One clear way they may establish positive self-images is by being involved in movements to challenge the oppressive social order. But oppressed people may also cultivate positive self-concepts without overtly organizing against their oppression; they may find confirmation of their desires for flourishing through modes of expression that do not wholly threaten the established social order. Lila Abu-Lughod, for instance, documents the stories of Bedouin woman who express their dissatisfaction with arranged marriage and polygyny through poems (Abu-Lughod 1986, 215–232).[15] The poems and the traditions surrounding their recitation allow women to express dissatisfaction with marriage norms in the company of others—even if they do not organize to challenge the norms. To the extent that poems are part of a tradition of expressing female sorrow and anger in verse, they provide women access to some social understanding of their dissatisfaction with prevailing gender expectations.

Similarly, recall Agarwal's examples of women who bargain for access to food they would otherwise be discouraged from consuming by feigning illness or spirit possession. Women who feign illness or spirit possession do not overtly challenge social norms that say that women's food needs are less important than men's, but they do ask for—and sometimes receive recognition of—their food needs through these behaviors. Oppressed people can find means of communicating their desires for flourishing that afford them a modicum of social recognition without threatening the established social order as a whole. While these forms of communication certainly afford insufficient opportunities for positive self-image, they may allow for the sustenance of some positive self-image in the face of serious adversity.

Oppressed people may also cultivate positive self-images in the face of injustice by interacting with other members of their oppressed group. This is a possibility suggested by many feminist philosophers of intersectionality and multiple identities.[16] As I claimed earlier, people need positive social recognition of their attempts to flourish in order to sustain positive self-images. Oppressed people's attempts to flourish are often met with negative social recognition from society at large; a woman who wants to eat as much as her male relatives may be regarded as lacking a sense of duty or self-control, and she may come to view herself in this way. However, oppressed people may not only interact with members of dominant groups—or members of subordinate groups who fully accept their oppression. In interactions with other oppressed people, oppressed people may find opportunities to develop positive self-images. Maria Lugones makes this point by discussing how people from marginalized races in the United States develop an alternate perception of the world:

> A sense of home, place, heritage, has been crucial for those who are targets of racism. It has meant the creation and maintenance of an alternative to racist, colonial perception. It has kept one able to practice a double vision: seeing oneself and one's company at once in the racist/resistant construction.... It has kept one cautious of the racist construction, less touched by it, in touch with it so as to handle one's situation with knowledge of the oppressor's delusions of superiority. (Lugones 2003, 156)

If we extend Lugones's logic to the situation of oppressed and deprived people more generally, we can see communities of oppressed people as creating opportunities for collective development of positive self-image. People who are oppressed in similar ways and do not wholly accept that oppression may encourage one another to view themselves positively in spite of—or in response to—the oppression. Abu-Lughod provides a particularly illustrative example of this in her discussion of stories Bedouin women tell one another when they are not in the company of men. Abu-Lughod describes being in the company of a group of women who are trying to explain son preference in their community. One woman says that a little boy "'has a little pisser that dangles'" (Abu-Lughod 1990, 46). Another says, "'You see, the male has no womb. He has nothing but a little penis, just like this finger of mine [laughingly wiggling her figure in a contemptuous gesture]. The male has no compassion. The female is tender and compassionate' [playing on the double meaning of the Arabic root rahama, from which the word womb and the word compassion are derived]" (Abu-Lughod 1990, 46).

Abu-Lughod analyzes the story as an instance of making "the male genitals the sign of a lack—the lack of a womb" (Abu-Lughod 1990, 46). The Bedouin women in Abu-Lughod's example know that prevailing social norms cast them as less valuable than men; they know that having sons is more respectable than having daughters and that lineage passes through men. Yet among themselves they mock men's inflated self-importance and valorize women's ability to bear children over men's capacities as progenitors.[17]

Though Abu-Lughod's example is particularly vivid, we need not consider it an isolated example. Recall that Agarwal states that some poor South Asian women access more food than their socially prescribed role says they should by holding clandestine picnics with female friends. These picnics can be seen as an opportunity for collective affirmation of women's right to nutrition. Women eat together and positively recognize other women's desires to eat more than their socially prescribed shares. Women who participate in these picnics find their desires to eat met with a type of support, and this may help them refuse to simply reject their desires for adequate nutrition. To point out the existence of resistant sub-communities is not to suggest that all interactions among oppressed people are resistant. Such a sanguine view would ignore the role oppressed people can play in socializing other people to oppression; the case of South Asian mothers exploiting their daughters-in-law Papanek describes is just one example.[18]

Through resistant social spaces, oppressed people can cultivate positive self-images and receive positive social recognition for them. These positive self-images exist in opposition to the negative attitudes toward their own flourishing that oppressed people often internalize. To describe some IAPs as taking the form of negative attitudes toward flourishing is to acknowledge that some IAPs have wide-ranging negative effects on deprived people. Does acknowledging that some forms of IAP produce generally negative self-image commit us to a form of the Adaptive Self View—the view of adaptive preferences that I am arguing against? I believe that we can coherently answer this question in the negative. First, the Adaptive Self view is a view about the *essential features* of IAPs, whereas I have claimed only that *some* adaptive preferences affect self-image as such. Self-image-affecting IAPs are just one class of IAPs.

Second, resistant self-images suggest that a person's sense of self does not uniformly adapt to unjust conditions. My view of oppressed people as engaged in internal struggle to retain positive self-image asks us to make salient an aspect of self-image-affecting adaptive preferences that Adaptive Self theorists ignore. Once we emphasize conflicting and resistant self-images, we can see authentic agency operating even in the lives of people with self-image-affecting IAPs. This difference between my view and the Adaptive Self view may be a difference of emphasis, but it is an important one. If we do not make visible the effective agency of people with self-image-affecting IAPs, we may license development practitioners and activists to disregard their flourishing-compatible perspectives and values.

Preferences with Multiple/Ambivalent Effects on Flourishing

It is not only people's selves that may be torn by internal conflict; people's preferences may be internally contradictory as well. A single lower-order preference can reveal a desire to attain one's own well-being and a concomitant desire to thwart it. If we understand this to be the case, we have further reason to question the Adaptive Self View; some forms of IAP actually *entail* positive self-entitlement.

A single preference can embody positive and negative attitudes toward flourishing. We can better understand how this is possible if we contrast the view of preferences as having contradictory effects to the Adaptive Self View. On the Adaptive Self View, any given preference manifests a single attitude toward well-being. IAPs—even lower-order IAPs—reveal underlying negative attitudes about flourishing. Let us briefly return to Nussbaum's example of Jayamma, who accepted the discriminatory wage structure at her brick kiln. Nussbaum sees Jayamma's preference as revealing only a negative attitude about her own well-being. According to Nussbaum, Jayamma did not see the wage discrimination as wrong. There is an inferential structure to Nussbaum's claim that Jayamma lacked a sense of herself as "a being whose rights could be violated" (Nussbaum 2001, 113). It seems as though Nussbaum has *inferred* from Jayamma's lack of protest certain beliefs that Jayamma must hold about herself.[19] For Nussbaum, Jayamma's nonprotest implies that Jayamma does not give sufficient weight to her own well-being.

There are a number of problems with treating expressed preferences as unproblematically revelatory of underlying negative views about the self. I discussed some of these in Chapter 1; people may trade one good away for others, or they may flourish in unfamiliar ways. Oversimplifying the task of preference interpretation obscures these facts. For the purposes of the present discussion, however, I would like to focus on a different problem. It is this: to infer a certain attitude about the self from a preference is to assume that the preference manifests only one attitude about the self. To presuppose that a preference manifests only one attitude about the self is to ignore the fact that multiple beliefs about oneself and the world can influence a single preference. Preferences can, in actuality, be influenced by more than one attitude, and more than one *type* of attitude, about the self.

Let us assume for a moment that Jayamma has higher-order IAPs; the wage discrimination would disappear if she protested, but she does not care very much about changing the wage structure, because she is used to it. Jayamma may well fail to believe that she deserves equal pay for equal work, and this may be one of her reasons for acquiescence to wage discrimination. But she may also believe that protesting is what idle people do, and protesting may not occur to her as an option, because she is not idle; she is a worker. Her positive identity as a worker rather than an idler and her acceptance of sex discrimination are both manifest in her nonprotest. If both of these beliefs motivate her preference not to protest, her lack of protest can reveal contradictory attitudes toward her own flourishing. On one hand, her lack of protest is keeping her from earning sufficient income; on the other, her lack of protest is helping her preserve a sense of herself as superior to others who do not work. Though her need for a subsistence income is probably more urgent than her need to see herself as a non-idler (assuming she has sources of positive social recognition other than being a non-idler), it would be incorrect to say that her preference not to protest reveals no attempt to strive for flourishing. It reveals a simultaneous attempt to retain self-esteem and a lack of interest in earning subsistence income. Jayamma must have some operative concept of self-entitlement if she can be said to actively seek self-esteem.

How is it possible for a person to express positive and negative self-entitlement in the same preference? The answer lies in acknowledging two general facts about preferences. First, a single preference may affect a person's well-being in more than one domain of life. If a single preference affects a person's well-being in two domains, she may simultaneously increase her well-being in one domain and decrease it in another. Second, people's first-order preferences are often directed at achieving higher-order ends. This means that a person's first-order self-harming behavior can function as a means to an end that is consistent with basic flourishing. Let us consider how each of these facts about preferences makes it possible for a given IAP to reveal both positive and negative attitudes toward self-entitlement.

A single preference may have positive effects on well-being in one domain and negative effects on well-being in another. To restate this point, people face decisions with multiple consequences, and the consequences may not be uniformly positive or negative for them. For an example of women faced with choices that positively affect their well-being in some domains and negatively affect it in others, we can turn to Uma Narayan's discussion of the veiling preferences of the Pirzada women of Old Delhi (U. Narayan 2002, 418–422). The Pirzada women of Old Delhi live in *purdah* and veil when they leave their homes. They acknowledge that living in seclusion and wearing the *burqa* (U. Narayan 2002, 420–421) has certain deleterious effects on their flourishing. They complain that veiling and seclusion have limited their access to education and mobility; many of the older women even openly envy younger women who have married into families with less strict *purdah* requirements (U. Narayan 2002, 420). Yet the Pirzada women also speak of benefits they gain by practicing seclusion and veiling; it protects them from discomfort they would feel at having to reveal their bodies to others, it saves them from having to worry too much about what they put on before going out, it helps ensure them good marriage prospects, and it identifies them as superior to other, less affluent Muslim women (U. Narayan 2002, 420).[20]

Narayan introduces the idea that we make decisions among "bundles of elements" to explain the decision the Pirzada women face. The Pirzada women do not face an idealized choice situation where one option gives them access to the goods they care about and the other undermines their access to the goods they care about. Instead, they must choose between two "bundles of elements," each with some positive and negative components. In Narayan's words, decisions like the Pirzada women's "ought to be understood as choice of a 'bundle of elements', some of which they want, and some of which they do not, and where they lack the power to 'undo the bundle' so as to choose only the elements they want" (U. Narayan 2002, 422).

To translate Narayan's point into the language of our discussion of the ambivalent effects of preferences: both positive and negative well-being impacts are entailed in the Pirzada women's decisions to veil. The preference to veil and live in seclusion adversely impacts the women's access to education and mobility but positively impacts their access to social recognition and affiliation. Once we understand this, we can see the Pirzada women's views as manifesting positive and negative views toward self-entitlement; they may downplay the importance of their access to education while valuing their access to social status. It is likely that many IAPs take a form similar to that of the Pirzada women's: positive flourishing impacts in one domain are linked to negative flourishing impacts in another. To make a choice is to opt for increased flourishing in one domain and decreased flourishing in another at the same time. The Pirzada women's choices prioritize social recognition over education, but their choice manifests—at the very least—a positive desire for social recognition. Just as it would be misleading to describe the Pirzada women as not desiring their well-being, it may be misleading to think of most people with IAPs as not desiring their well-being. People with IAPs who prioritize flourishing in one domain above flourishing in another do not have generally negative attitudes toward their well-being as the Adaptive Self View would suggest.

A single preference can be motivated by positive and negative self-entitlement, because a choice may have positive effects on well-being in some domains and negative effects on well-being in others. There is another reason a single preference can reveal both positive and negative self-entitlement: people often express lower-order preferences as means to higher-order goals. If self-depriving behaviors sometimes effectively promote higher-order goals that are consistent with flourishing, people can compromise their opportunities to flourish in certain contexts as part of a flourishing life-plan. Clare Chambers offers an example in the case of Jenna Franklin, a fifteen-year-old English girl who wants to get breast implants (C. Chambers 2007, 192). One of Franklin's stated reasons for wanting breast implants is that she wants to be a television star. If she does not get breast implants, she will not be able to fulfill this goal, since being a female television personality requires having large breasts. Chambers understands Franklin as choosing "to follow a harmful norm," because she believes she "cannot access the desired benefit without following the norm" (C. Chambers 2007, 193). In other words, Franklin prefers to compromise her bodily health[21] in a specific way in order to achieve the higher-order goal of becoming famous. I think there is good reason to suppose that Franklin is correct that breast implants will improve her chances of becoming famous, and I think we can see becoming famous as a flourishing-compatible life-plan. If Franklin is right and becoming famous may be a way of flourishing, we can view Franklin as getting breast implants *in order to flourish*.

The idea of getting breast implants in order to flourish is less paradoxical than it may initially sound. One way oppressive systems work is by linking oppressed people's achievement of higher-order goals to self-depriving lower-order preferences. As Superson claims, people with IAPs believe their self-depriving behaviors are "self-beneficial" (Superson 2005, 110). Where Superson suggests that they are incorrect in believing this, I want to suggest that they are often correct—in that self-depriving behavior often elicits actual rewards. Chambers draws an analogy between Franklin and women who undergo clitoridectemy in order to get married (C. Chambers 2007, 191–193). Even if we are worried about the frequency with which goals like marriage and beauty aggregate to women, neither marriage nor fame is, in itself, a flourishing-incompatible goal. Marriage and fame are capable of helping people access income, food, social recognition, and personal satisfaction—all likely constituents of basic flourishing. In the cases of breast implants and clitoridectemy, there are incentives for women to harm themselves in order to achieve these goals. So the woman who chooses to undergo a clitoridectomy to get married and the woman who chooses to get breast implants to get famous[22] may be seen as simultaneously expressing positive and negative self-entitlement. They want wealth, social status, etc., and they are willing to risk some aspect of their health to get it. Here, too, it seems inappropriate to describe the preference to get breast implants or get one's genitals cut as manifesting only negative self-entitlement. Even if such women's desires for bodily health and sexual functioning are distorted, their desires for income, etc., do not seem to be so distorted.

We have now seen how a single IAP can reveal contradictory attitudes to self-entitlement; a person may harm herself in order to achieve a higher-order, flourishing-compatible goal, or she may harm herself in one domain and increase her well-being in others. An important qualifying remark is in order. I have just suggested that there is a rationality to some forms of IAP; people with IAPs can sometimes improve their flourishing in certain domains or at some higher level by harming themselves. It may seem to follow from this suggestion that the people in question do not have IAPs at all; they are just making the best of a bad situation.

To this I would reply that I have claimed that there is a *self-interested component* to many IAPs. But IAPs can manifest self-interested attitudes without thereby expressing preferences wholly consistent with flourishing; people may live under social conditions where there are few paths to flourishing that do not involve some type of self-deprivation. According to my definition of IAP, people who express preferences inconsistent with their basic flourishing but do so because of a lack of options have IAPs; they are just not higher-order IAPs. The order of people's IAPs certainly makes a difference to the types of interventions that are appropriate (see my discussions of trade-offs and psychologizing the structural in Chapter 1 for more on this). In cases where external constraints alone are the problem, changing social structures seems the appropriate social response. In cases where preferences *and* social structures are at issue, the appropriate public response is likely some combination of preference transformation and structural change.

Further, making a self-interested trade-off is not the same thing as doing the best one can to advance one's interests; people may misperceive their interests. In cases where people misperceive their interests, they can value their well-being and be wrong about how to achieve it. In cases like this, interventions focused on changing people's beliefs and attitudes might be more appropriate. The English girl who wants to get breast implants in order to be famous would probably have a better chance of leading a flourishing life if she adjusted both her higher- and lower-order preferences. Some girls who get their genitals cut cannot get married if they do not cut, but others continue support of the practice even when the social incentives to do so become less strong (imagine, for example, that their mothers who belonged to another generation where cutting *was* necessary have inculcated in them beliefs about marriage that no longer apply).

A person may misperceive her interests and be unaware that she is engaged in any misperceiving. She may simply be wrong about what the world is like. She may give up several forms of objective flourishing in order to pour her energy into an illusory life-plan that will not actually succeed in securing her a high self-esteem (say Jenna Franklin is wrong that entering a profession where she is valued primarily for her large breasts will give her self-esteem). Or, she may undervalue her basic flourishing in some domains and ignore them in order to pursue flourishing in others, but have made an unacceptable and unnecessary flourishing sacrifice in the process (for instance, adolescents who choose clitoridectemy to be accepted by their friends do so based on mistaken beliefs about how clitoridectemy will affect their lives). In these cases, we have women (or girls) who are harming themselves out of self-interest without actually improving their lives. So some people with IAPs express self-interest through preferences that actually decrease both their flourishing and desire-satisfaction because they misperceive their interests. Once we recognize that many IAPs – even ones that do not simply make the best of bad situations—reflect some conception of self-interest, the Adaptive Self View looks much less plausible.

Lessons for IAP Intervention

IAPs need not be thought of as global self-entitlement deficits; I have argued that people can have IAPs and retain positive senses of self-entitlement. People may engage in flourishing-inconsistent behaviors out of (real or perceived) self-interest, they may undermine their projects with relative frequency while maintaining underground resistant self-images, or they may perceive themselves as unworthy only when comparing themselves to certain others or faced with the prospect of having certain goods.

Once we recognize that diminished self-entitlement is often selective, we can begin to make sense of my claim that the deliberative perfectionist approach cultivates the existing agency of people with IAPs. If it seemed before that people with IAPs could not be real agents because they did not direct their projects toward flourishing-compatible ends that were their own, we can now see that people with IAPs can retain and act on positive senses of self-entitlement. Women who undernourish themselves to feed their male relatives can do so and retain the belief that they are objectively deserving of food; women who live in patriarchal societies may sustain positive self-concepts through relationships with other women; and women who harm their bodies in order to get social recognition probably believe in some sense that they are worthy of social recognition. In all of these cases, women have IAPs but those IAPs coexist with desires that are compatible with their flourishing. I hope the foregoing discussion has made clearer how people with IAPs can retain senses of themselves as worthy—as well as the capacity to care about their own interests. We need to see this in order to get a view of people with IAPs that does not end up suggesting that all of their input into development interventions will simply be self-undermining.

What I have not yet explained is how deliberative perfectionist interventions might go about cultivating the existing agency of oppressed and deprived people. It is to this question that I briefly turn. Deliberative processes can improve the capacity of people with IAPs to carry out projects they care about and live according to values they identify with. Through deliberation, people with IAPs may come to a better understanding of the inappropriateness of their own desires. The experiences of some—but certainly not all—participatory IAP interventions bear out this claim. Ann Sutherland and Felicia Sakala (2002) describe a project in Zambia where women were asked to draw pictures of violence in their lives and discuss the pictures. The women often draw pictures that recount experiences of intense suffering. One woman describes her picture by saying, "marriage can be like a torture chamber, closed from outside help and no one to help inside it." At the close of the workshop, participants often say, " 'I have learned that what I used to think of as normal is actually violence against women' " (Sutherland and Sakala 2002, 90). To theorize a bit about what happens in exercises like these, we might posit that group discussions give people—deprived or not—opportunities to interrogate and clarify their desires in light of their deeply held values and the values and desires of others. As Sen puts it, deliberative "processes, are crucial to the formation of values and priorities, and we cannot, in general, take preferences as given independently of public discussion" (Sen 1999a, 11).

The idea that deprived people struggle to retain positive self-entitlement in the face of injustice helps us demystify what is going on in discussions where deprived people come to recognize their own IAPs. According to the Adaptive Self View, it is difficult to see how people with IAPs might identify their own preferences as problematic; if they want nothing for themselves, they are unlikely to be able to perceive the conditions under which they have formed their preferences as *unjust to them*. But if we see people as struggling to maintain positive self-concepts under oppressive conditions, we can see deliberative processes as opportunities for deprived people to voice, explain, and analyze their inchoate dissatisfaction with their deprivation. Gillian Attwood, Jane Castle, and Suzanne Smythe (2005) describe a participatory development project in Lesotho that enabled women to give voice to dissatisfaction they previously struggled to repress. This project was a literacy circle that encouraged participants to question prevalent ideas about "women's work" and gender-unequal labor burdens.

One participant described what she gained from the discussions as follows: "Before, I was afraid to ask these kinds of questions.... Before I thought that if I asked such questions, I would be running away from my responsibility as a woman. I thought I should not bother my husband..." (Attwood, Castle, et al. 2005, 152). The participant's narrative suggests that she had asked herself questions about gender inequality before, yet discussions provided her the opportunity to view her inner questioning and dissatisfaction as legitimate. The discussions did not produce self-entitlement in her for the first time; rather they permitted her to further develop her existing sense of self-entitlement. Lest the distinction between producing and developing self-entitlement seem trivial, we should note that it makes an important difference in practice. The goal of *developing* existing self-entitlement in people with IAPs encourages development practitioners to help deprived people self-identify IAPs, where the goal of *producing* self-entitlement anew encourages practitioners to focus on analyzing deprived people's preferences *for* them. Certainly, positive self-entitlement is closer to the surface and more unambiguous in the lives of some people with IAPs than in others, and practitioners may have to be a bit more leading in deliberative processes with some people with IAPs than with others. Still, the lives of people who recognize their own IAPs and identify with the desire to transform them are more likely to improve than those who are simply told to replace an old set of views about themselves with a new set. Once we see many people with IAPs as possessed of existing conceptions of themselves as worthy of flourishing, it begins to seem more appropriate to prescribe deliberative processes as methods of IAP identification.

My view of IAPs as selective self-entitlement deficits also helps us to see how the existing values of people with IAPs might positively contribute to strategies for improving their flourishing. The Adaptive Self View makes us wonder why the values of people with IAPs should guide policy. If people with IAPs do not value their own goods, will not valorizing their existing beliefs simply retrench their oppression? It seems clear that many people with IAPs hold beliefs that impede their flourishing, and these flourishing-incompatible beliefs should not guide policy. However, my view of IAPs as selective self-entitlement deficits helps us to see that not all existing beliefs held by people with adaptive preferences undermine their well-being.

If we accept that people with IAPs can maintain positive self-entitlement, and that they are most likely to respond to opportunities for flourishing that fit into their existing schemas of value, new imaginative possibilities for IAP intervention open up. Development practitioners and people with IAPs can invent strategies for transformation that draw on existing resources for positive self-entitlement within local practices. We can find one example of drawing on local resources for positive self-entitlement in IAP intervention in the literacy circle in Lesotho discussed in the previous paragraphs. As in many contexts in both rich and poor countries, the women of this community in Lesotho were burdened by gender roles that prescribed them grueling—and often invisible—work. They tended not to see themselves as having much say over their prescribed roles (Attwood, Castle, et al. 2005, 149–150). Yet, the facilitators of some literacy and empowerment circles used familiar, resistant imagery to help participants to see how they could negotiate gender roles. The local proverb, "women are lions in dresses" was used to illustrate the power that women have despite their culturally subordinate role (Attwood, Castle, et al. 2005, 152). The proverb is one example of a belief already familiar to people with IAPs that has potential to support the questioning of IAPs, one that was already functioning to help women sustain positive senses of self-worth in the face of gender oppression. When women reflect on a proverb like this one that widely circulates in their community, they may come to question an oppressive gender distribution of labor. And they engage in this critical reflection in thick, culturally embedded terms—terms they already identify with. If we see people with IAPs as retaining some positive self-entitlement, we can begin to imagine IAP interventions that build on people's existing flourishing-compatible values.

4 THE DELIBERATIVE PERFECTIONIST APPROACH, PATERNALISM, AND CULTURAL DIVERSITY

I have offered a perfectionist approach to identifying and transforming inappropriately adaptive preferences (IAPs). In doing so, I have defined a highly controversial concept with reference to a highly controversial ethical theory. Critics of the notion of adaptive preference typically assert—or suggest—that attributing adaptive preferences to people is somehow disrespectful of them. H.E. Baber sees Nussbaum as objectionably likening the subjective state of poor women with IAPs to that of people who have been brainwashed or manipulated through psychosurgery (2007, 118). A number of philosophers describe adaptive preferences as a version of Marxist "false consciousness" (Deveaux 2002, 517; Jaggar 2005a, 188; 2005b, 58). To liken IAPs to "false consciousness" has the effect of linking the notion of AP to condescension to deprived people—given that the term "false consciousness" has fallen out of favor among feminists. We tend to avoid the term "false consciousness" because it suggests that deprived people are victims of an inability to distinguish between illusion and reality (Kabeer 1999, 441); calling IAPs a version of "false consciousness" rhetorically ties the notion of IAP to the belief that oppressed people are simple dupes of injustice.

Perfectionism, meanwhile, is also the subject of ample philosophical controversy. Critics of perfectionism see allowing a conception of human flourishing to influence public policy as dangerous. Some critics of perfectionism in politics understand perfectionism to justify coercion of people who are not living objectively good lives (Hurka 1993, 147). Other critics of perfectionism in politics, such as Rawls and Nussbaum disavow it on the grounds that it discourages institutions from respecting a variety of conceptions of the good (Nussbaum 2000, 105; Rawls 1996, 188). If public institutions are committed to a vision of a good life and helping people live according it, the argument goes, how can they coherently respect reasonable divergences in people's values? This question is especially urgent in a world where public institutions are increasingly charged with making cross-cultural moral judgments—both within and across national boundaries.

The controversy over public perfectionism and the controversy over IAP I just described are motivated by similar concerns. Critics of both perfectionism and the notion of IAP want to ensure that people are free to live the types of lives that matter to them—and not just the types of lives some external judge believes *should matter* to them. Critics of the notion of IAP worry that questioning people's preferences undermines their authority as choosers of the types of lives they want to lead. Critics of perfectionism worry that public endorsement of a conception of flourishing will vest authority over what type of life a person leads in the hands of public institutions or that it will involve imposition of a culturally specific conception of the good. If these critics are right, endorsing IAP intervention comes at unacceptable cost to our desire to treat moral variation among persons and cultures as reasonable.

To make a persuasive case that my deliberative perfectionist approach to IAP intervention can usefully guide public policy, I respond to these criticisms. For if we need to give up our commitments to choice and moral diversity to support IAP intervention, there are good reasons to give up on promoting the flourishing of people with IAPs. I claim in this chapter that we do not have to choose between supporting intervention in the lives of people with IAPs and respecting moral diversity. My deliberative perfectionist approach offers an approach to IAP identification and transformation that respects people as choosers and valorizes much of the diversity in our "varied moral world."[1] To demonstrate this, I devote this chapter to examining a number of possible objections to the endorsement of a conception of the good in development policy. I claim that none of these objections is decisive against the public policies justified by the deliberative perfectionist approach. The objections to which I respond are divided into two types: objections that claim that public promotion of a conception of the good requires disrespecting *persons'* capacity to form their own conceptions of the good and objections that claim that it requires disrespecting *cultures'* capacities to live according to their own conceptions of the good.

The Deliberative Perfectionist Approach, Perfectionism, and Practice

Many moral diversity objections to the deliberative perfectionist approach are legitimate objections to *some types* of perfectionism, but not the type of perfectionism I advocate here. I thus pause to recapitulate my deliberative perfectionist approach to IAP intervention. The deliberative perfectionist approach begins from a perfectionist conception of what IAPs *are*. IAPs are preferences inconsistent with basic flourishing, formed under conditions nonconducive to flourishing. They are preferences that we expect a person would reverse under conditions conducive to her flourishing that she recognized as such. Underlying this definition is the idea that people have deep preferences for basic flourishing, that people's preferences are likely to become more consistent with flourishing under conditions that promote it.

The deliberative perfectionist approach needs a conception of flourishing for IAP identification to even be possible. Yet the approach does not make light of the task of defining human flourishing or the epistemological difficulties involved in identifying and transforming IAPs in practice. It places specific stipulations on the type of conception of flourishing that should inform IAP interventions—the conception should have been arrived at through a cross-cultural deliberative process and be justificatorily minimal, substantively minimal, and vague. The deliberative perfectionist approach also takes seriously certain facts about the world that make IAP identification and transformation difficult: we do not always know why other people behave in the ways they do, how people's behaviors affect their overall well-being, or how to recognize flourishing in different contexts. For these reasons, my deliberative perfectionist approach recommends that development practitioners deliberate with deprived people to figure out why they have the preferences they do and what (if anything) should be done to change them.

Concretely, we can expect a deliberative perfectionism-motivated interventions to go something like this. Development practitioners notice that the expressed preferences of some person or group of people seem inconsistent with their basic flourishing. In other words, practitioners *suspect* that a set of expressed preferences are inappropriately adaptive. Practitioners then attempt to find out through deliberation whether this initial suspicion is warranted. They deliberate with deprived people to understand *why* they have the preferences they do (Are they trading this basic functioning in order to have access to another? Do they not know what opportunities are available to them? Is this preference important to their religious beliefs?) and *whether* and *how* they are attached to them (Do they want to have the preference they have? What is the role of the preference in their conception of the good life?). If the judgment that people have IAPs seems warranted, the practitioner will engage deprived people in imagining a new future for themselves that is compatible both with objective flourishing and with the deprived peoples' sense of what matters to them.

For an example of something like the deliberative perfectionist approach at work, we can briefly return to the story of PAEM (Programa Educativo de La

Mujer) in rural Honduras, a women's empowerment organization whose story I began to tell in the introduction to this book. PAEM began as a project of Maria Esther Ruiz, a Honduran *campesina* woman who had benefited from more educational opportunities than most other women in her area. Ruiz began her program from the sense that the women of her community lacked a sense of self-worth that would support their flourishing (Rowlands 2008, 92). This lack of self-worth was inhibiting women's capacities for mobility, health, and earning income; many of the community's women lived in extreme poverty, did not frequently leave their houses, and did not frequently engage in discussions with non-family members. However, Ruiz also believed strongly in helping women to identify their own priorities (Rowlands 2008, 69) and therefore initiated the creation of small women's discussion circles where women would identify problems and go about devising solutions to them.

Once it became clear that a lack of self-esteem was impeding the women's flourishing, some early group participants and Ruiz worked together to produce educational materials, notably a pamphlet entitled *Consciendome a Mi Misma* (Getting to Know Myself) (Rowlands 2008, 70). This booklet offered a path to women's empowerment rooted in values and experiences familiar to the community's women—notably Catholic scriptures about the need to love oneself and stories about the sorts of everyday difficulties *campesina* women face (Rowlands 2008, 108). The booklet is not only about self-esteem; it focuses on helping women to identify other deprivations like poverty, isolation, and a lack of education (Rowlands 2008, 109). The booklet was used by over 100 small groups, whose members employed it as a springboard for conversations about their own deprivation. Some groups identified strategies for change they would like to pursue—such as income-generation projects or sexual education projects.

Through these PAEM discussion circles, small groups of women began to realize that their lack of specific types of self-esteem was indeed impeding their access to other parts of flourishing—like income, mobility, and education. Together, they engaged in creating a vision of a more just future and transforming their lives according to it. Some women who participated in PAEM groups demonstrated increased confidence in negotiating with their partners, increased mobility, increased political participation, and increased participation in income-generation activities (Rowlands 2008, 76–85). There is no question that these gains came about through a process that was normatively laden from the outset; the process began from a sense that lacking self-esteem, education, and mobility were deprivations to be worked against. And yet it was the women themselves who analyzed the causes of their deprivation and imagined strategies for transforming it. This participant-driven strategy is consistent with my approach, since a deliberative perfectionist conception of human flourishing *underdetermines* what should happen in any particular situation, and since deliberation itself can enhance people's lives; deprived people should play an important role in determining what strategies for change should be pursued in their communities.

The PAEM story gives us an example of what deliberative perfectionist interventions might look like. However, I have not specified the content of the deliberative perfectionist conception used to identify and respond to IAPs. There are important philosophical reasons for this. First and foremost, I do not believe my intuitions constitute a cross-cultural deliberative process. It would be dishonest and irresponsible for me to present a list I generated on my own as a deliberative perfectionist conception of flourishing. Second, there are a number of existing deliberative conceptions of flourishing that might work—including the list of human rights, Nussbaum's capabilities list (Nussbaum 2001, 78–80), Brooke Ackerly's list of "what human beings should be able to choose" (Ackerly 2000, 114–116), and Sabina Alkire's list of "capability dimensions" (2005). Third, it may be the case that no existing conception of flourishing is sufficiently cross-culturally acceptable and we need new processes to create a cross-culturally acceptable vision of flourishing. I take no stance here on which deliberative conception of flourishing is best.

However, for the purposes of this chapter, it will be helpful to have a conception of flourishing with actual contents so we can get a clearer picture of how deliberative perfectionist interventions might conceptualize their goals. I use Nussbaum's capabilities list as an example of a deliberative perfectionist conception of flourishing. Her list is minimal, vague, and justificatorily bare, so it possesses the structural features of a deliberative perfectionist conception. My point in using Nussbaum's list is not to endorse the list as the right conception of flourishing for the deliberative perfectionist approach. The legitimacy of the process by which Nussbaum arrived at it has been widely questioned,[2] and its contents have been occasionally questioned as well.[3] Still, I believe that we can expect a deliberative perfectionist conception of flourishing to look *something like* Nussbaum's list even if it is not identical to it. Where I need examples of capacities the deliberative perfectionist approach will encourage people with IAPs to cultivate, I refer to capacities on Nussbaum's capabilities list. I reiterate that I use her list only as a heuristic example of a deliberative perfectionist conception.[4] For the contents of Nussbaum's list, see Nussbaum 2001 (78–80).

The Deliberative Approach and the Moral Diversity of Individuals

Deliberative perfectionist interventions are, by definition, motivated by a conception of the good. They will inevitably promote certain types of life-plans over others.[5] They will encourage individuals to choose lives that involve things like "good health," "engaging in critical reflection about the planning of one's life," and "control over one's political environment" over lives that do not. It may seem to follow from this that deliberative perfectionist IAP interventions will thwart individuals' capacities to form and pursue their own conceptions of the good. If this accusation were justified, it would be serious. We might not want public institutions to take IAPs seriously if it meant depriving individuals of the capacity to live by their own lights. Fortunately, it does not. We can see this by looking at how the deliberative perfectionist approach withstands four objections to it motivated by concern for individual freedom. Let us call these objections "the paternalistic coercion objection," "the nonautonomy objection," "the agency objection," and the "conception of the good objection."

In examining these objections and the extent to which they are decisive against the deliberative perfectionist approach, it will be useful for us to keep in mind that the deliberative perfectionist approach does not entail a fully perfectionist theory of politics. A thoroughgoing perfectionist theory of politics would hold that the central goal of public institutions is to promote people's flourishing—at the expense of liberty, if necessary. The deliberative perfectionist approach employs a minimal conception of flourishing and prescribes only a limited role for a conception of human flourishing. The approach commits us to the following perfectionist idea: public institutions should promote people's basic flourishing. But it does not commit us to holding that public institutions should promote excellence or that public institutions should coerce people into flourishing. We can think of the deliberative perfectionist approach as supporting some type of *liberal perfectionist* theory of politics, one that valorizes people's freedom to decide how they want to live as one component of human flourishing.

The Paternalistic Coercion Objection

A common objection against allowing perfectionism to influence public policy is that it justifies forcing persons to live according to a particular conception of the good. Is the deliberative perfectionist approach subject to criticism on these grounds? Because perfectionism "thinks some lives are better than others," we might think, "it favors state coercion to force people into excellence" (Hurka 1993, 147). I have described the deliberative perfectionist approach as a noncoercive approach to IAP intervention. My approach supposes that people have a tendency toward basic flourishing and conceives the best IAP interventions as those that help people flourish *and* help them live lives consistent with what they care deeply about. I have claimed that noncoercive intervention is the type of intervention most likely to achieve both of these goals.

But my assertion that the deliberative perfectionist approach is not coercive has mostly been just that—an assertion. Despite my claim that the deliberative perfectionist approach *does* not support coercing persons with suspect preferences, it may seem that it logically *should*. It may seem to follow from the logic of the deliberative perfectionist conception that people should be coerced into exercising certain functionings. If these functionings are so basic to human life, and we are sure that lives that do not embody these functionings are less flourishing than ones that do embody them, does it not follow that people should not be forced to flourish? Is prohibiting coercion not just a strategic nod to the liberal—one that is not logically consistent with the belief that some types of lives are objectively better than others?

I believe we can honestly answer this question in the negative. There are three reasons we need not think of public promotion of an objectively good form of life as justifying paternalistic coercion. The reasons have differing levels of decisiveness, but I think that they are decisive when taken together. The first reason is pragmatic. In practice, representatives of public institutions can make mistakes. One of Mill's arguments against coercing people into living according to a conception of the good is that general principles "are likely to be misapplied in individual cases" (Mill 2008, 85). Public institutions can affirm that certain basic functionings are necessary for human flourishing without having representatives who always know how to recognize cases of flourishing or how best to make it available. That is, development practitioners may have a general sense of what flourishing is but fail to interpret it accurately in real-world cases. To acknowledge the possibility of this type of error is not a capitulation to moral skepticism. It is only an acknowledgment that applying general principles to individual cases requires a lot of situational knowledge.

We should not expect public institutions' knowledge about particular cases to be infallible. We should especially not expect infallibility when public institutions are working with a vague conception of flourishing. As I suggested in Chapter 1, it is not always evident whether a person's preferences are impeding her flourishing. Development practitioners may mistake preferences that promote people's flourishing for preferences that undermine it. Further, it is also not always evident whether a proposed strategy for preference change will actually increase flourishing. A proposed change may have unintended consequences that a deprived person can foresee with particular acuity, or it may require dangerous trade-offs that third parties are not well positioned to understand. For an example of this, we can imagine, development practitioners in our age of micro-lending who encourage poor women to shift away from subsistence agriculture toward income generation. However, the practitioners' recommendation may be based on an erroneous assumption that cash income is always the best way to secure nutrition. In some cases—say cases where currency is extremely unstable—the shift away from subsistence agriculture may actually reduce food security. Practitioners who forced women to move away from subsistence agriculture could unintentionally decrease those women's flourishing. If we acknowledge that public institutions may err in applying general conceptions to particular cases, and that the stakes are high when persons' basic flourishing is in question, we have a reason to prefer noncoercive intervention.

Yet it may remain troublesome that I have not offered a *principled* objection to coercion that is consistent with perfectionism. The claim that public institutions can make mistakes only prohibits coercion in cases where development practitioners are *not sure* how preference transformation would affect the flourishing of people with IAPs. Furthermore, it may seem that a principled objection to coercion is not forthcoming if we are perfectionists. Perfectionists often argue that overriding people's nonflourishing choices is the best way to respect them. If we believe some life activities are objectively better than others, is refusing to coerce persons into flourishing not just a way of allowing them to destroy their own lives? I believe that the answer is "no." The second and third reasons the deliberative perfectionist approach does not justify coercion will show us how we can use perfectionist premises to oppose the coercion of people with IAPs.

To understand the second reason the deliberative perfectionist approach does not justify coercion, we need to further examine the idea that a functioning is objectively good. It may initially seem that saying that a functioning is necessary for human flourishing requires saying that a life without it is objectively bad. If the conception of human flourishing entails the belief that a life that does not exhibit the functionings constitutive of flourishing is objectively bad, it will be very difficult for the deliberative perfectionist approach to avoid condoning paternalistic coercion. However, I do not think it follows from the claim that certain functionings are necessary to human flourishing that lives that renounce some of them are not good. This may seem paradoxical, but it will seem less so if we recognize a fundamental distinction.

We can distinguish a life that is good *for* a person from a life that is virtuous or admirable. These two types of lives sometimes, but do not always, coincide. They most commonly fail to coincide in cases of self-sacrifice. There are many preferences that involve self-sacrifice that we still think of as virtuous—such as the preference to die for one's principles, to renounce one's possessions to become closer to the divine, or to risk one's life to save the life of another. We can admire these preferences without saying that the persons who exhibit them are flourishing. All we need to acknowledge to allow for this is that flourishing is what is good *for* that person and that persons can make good choices that are not good *for them*. Steven Darwall, who makes a distinction like this one, provides a useful way of thinking about the idea of something being good *for* a person. According to him, we take up the perspective of what is good *for* a person when we are engaged in caring about someone (Darwall 2004). In the terms of his discussion, we might say that persons can live admirable lives without caring very much about themselves.

We may still wonder why the deliberative perfectionist approach—and public attempts to promote well-being more generally—ask public institutions to focus on what is good *for* persons. One reason for this focus on flourishing over virtue is that most life-plans we think of as virtuous also happen to be life-plans that are basically good *for* the persons who live them. Another reason we should focus on flourishing is that we assume that deep preferences for extreme self-sacrifice are rare. Indeed, much of what makes self-sacrificing preferences particularly admirable is the self-discipline they require. The mere fact that they require self-discipline suggests that they go against deep human tendencies. The very moral character of extreme self-sacrifice depends upon a value for flourishing; to be engaged in sacrifice, one must be giving up something we consider to be valuable.

More fundamentally, public institutions that encouraged persons to form extremely self-sacrificing preferences would be harming those persons. If the preferences of a whole group of people were self-sacrificing and their public institutions had deliberately encouraged them to form those preferences, we would decry the extent to which those preferences had been manipulated—not admire them. In cases of admirable self-sacrifice, a person acknowledges the value of the flourishing life he or she is giving up and actively rejects it. This is plausibly the reason we intuitively distinguish between the poor woman who undernourishes herself where patriarchal norms encourage it and Gandhi's choice to go on hunger strike.

As long as we are committed to seeing moral value in some self-sacrificing preferences (of the deep, nonmanipulated kind), we have another reason not to think of the Flourishing Claim as justifying coercion. Public institutions can simultaneously regard some self-sacrificing preferences as admirable and endorse deliberative perfectionist interventions in the lives of people with IAPs. Public institutions that do this will hold open the possibility that some persons have deep preferences for self-sacrifice. The deliberative perfectionist approach understands IAP intervention as an attempt to help people live in accordance with deep preferences—preferences that would persist under conditions conducive to flourishing. If some people's deep preferences are for sacrifice, public institutions motivated by deliberative perfectionism cannot coherently justify forcing those people to flourish.

Even this prohibition on coercion may not seem principled enough to the critic of the deliberative perfectionist approach to IAP intervention. There is a third reason the deliberative perfectionist approach need not justify coercing people with IAPs into flourishing, and a version of this reason supports a fairly thoroughgoing prohibition on coercion. The third reason is this: coercion might impede flourishing. If freedom from coercion is necessary for flourishing, then coercing a person into flourishing looks objectionable on perfectionist terms. There are at least two different ways freedom from coercion can be necessary for flourishing. First, subjective well-being may be a necessary component of flourishing. If this is the case, there will be a point at which coercing a person into exercising other functionings constitutive of flourishing will reduce her subjective well-being so significantly as to generate *a net decrease* in flourishing. Imagine the case of an elderly woman who believes very deeply that women's participation in public life sullies their honor. Even if our deliberative perfectionist conception of flourishing says that mobility and control over one's political life are components of flourishing, it may be possible that forcing this woman to appear in public would cause her to feel a shame so intense that her flourishing would objectively decrease.

Another way we might think of coercion as impeding flourishing is by thinking of some form of freedom or autonomy as necessary for or capable of enhancing flourishing. Suppose we think that, in order to lead a flourishing life, a person must be able to live free of domination. Philip Pettit (2000) develops a theory of freedom as nondomination. For Pettit, an agent is free if and only if others cannot interfere with her projects on an arbitrary basis (Pettit 2000, 55). He argues that freedom requires people's preferences to be "context-independently decisive," or decisive independently of whether some external authority approves of them (Pettit 2001). A person who needs to be coerced into performing certain flourishing functionings likely has higher-order preferences against her exercise of those functionings. To force her into flourishing anyway is to make her self-regarding preferences only decisive when they coincide with the mandates of public institutions. If a person must be able to decide the course of her life without being subjugated by another's will in order to flourish, coercing people into transforming their IAPs does not actually increase her flourishing. Serena Olsaretti (2005) makes a different argument that coercing people into flourishing reduces their well-being. According to Olsaretti, flourishing is improved by endorsement of one's life-projects, and coercion typically impedes people's endorsement of their life-projects. Conceptions of freedom as required for flourishing, like Pettit's and Olsaretti's, can justify strong prohibitions on coercing people with IAPs. Such prohibitions are quite consistent with perfectionism.[6]

The paternalistic coercion objection says that the deliberative perfectionist conception supports coercing people into flourishing because it is a form of perfectionism. We have seen three reasons that the type of perfectionism in my approach need not entail coercing people into flourishing. First, public institutions can make dangerous mistakes in applying the deliberative perfectionist conception, and this means that they should proceed with caution when people resist preference transformation; what seems to development practitioners to be a way of forcing people to improve their lives may objectively decrease the quality of their lives. Second, we believe that some self-sacrificing preferences are objectively valuable, and we can oppose coercing people who seem to have IAPs on the grounds that they may actually be engaging in valuable forms of self-sacrifice. Third, we may define flourishing in such a way that sees coercion as preventing people from flourishing. If we can make freedom from arbitrary coercion a necessary component of flourishing, the very idea of coercing people into flourishing begins to look less plausible.

The Nonautonomy Objection

We have established that the deliberative perfectionist approach does not justify coercion as a means of changing people's suspect preferences. We have not yet established that it does not involve objectionable paternalism. Arguably, part of what is objectionable about public paternalism is that it exhibits condescension toward individuals' abilities to make judgments about what is good for them. Public endorsement of a conception of human flourishing may seem to require treating persons with suspect preferences as though they were somehow morally deficient. Suspecting a person of failing to live in a way that is good for her may seem to mean believing that the moral decisions she makes are not worthy of respect.

Responding to this objection requires us to revisit the relationship between the deliberative perfectionist approach and autonomy. As I claimed in Chapter 2, the role of autonomy in a political philosophy is typically to sort persons whose decisions are worthy of respect from those who are not. The most important thing to note about the deliberative perfectionist approach's relationship to autonomy is that the definition of IAPs on which it is based is *not* a theory of substantive autonomy. My perfectionist definition of IAPs says nothing about who can make worthy moral decisions and who cannot. We can see this more clearly if we compare my perfectionist conception of IAP to a substantive autonomy-based one. If we are inclined to think that my perfectionist definition of IAPs is a theory of substantive autonomy that takes Nussbaum's capability list as its conditions for real choice, we think it thinks of IAPs along these lines:

IAPs are preferences that are not autonomously chosen, because autonomously chosen preferences are consistent with basic flourishing.

This statement differs from the idea that human beings have a tendency to flourish that supports the deliberative perfectionist conception. My perfectionist definition of IAPs divides preferences into the categories deep and not deep based on the likelihood that they will persist and be endorsed under conditions conducive to basic flourishing. This deep/shallow distinction does not clearly map onto the autonomously chosen/unchosen distinction. A theory of substantive autonomy holds that only preferences consistent with flourishing can be chosen. In contrast, I hold that a preference can be chosen, incompatible with flourishing, *and* still not deeply preferred. Imagine a woman who undernourishes herself to feed her male relatives because of patriarchal social norms she has reflectively accepted. On a theory of substantive autonomy, she has not chosen these preferences. On my definition of IAPs, her undernourishing behavior is the result of a choice; the real question for the deliberative perfectionist is whether she would continue to act according to that choice when exposed to the fair value of better options.

It is thus perfectly plausible on my view for a given preference to be shallow (causally related to nonflourishing conditions), inconsistent with flourishing, and still autonomous. A person can coherently be seen as autonomous and lacking a deep commitment to her preferences as long as our conception of autonomy is procedural or normatively thin. But the nonautonomy objection misses the fact that autonomous people can have IAPs, and some IAPs are procedurally autonomous. From the perspective of my perfectionist definition of IAP, a person with shallow, flourishing-incompatible preferences can still be an agent whose preferences are worthy of respect. All she needs is to fulfill the basic (procedural) criteria for autonomy. Let us assume for the purposes of argument that agents who are rational and refer to higher-order preferences in making their decisions are autonomous. On such a definition of autonomy, most persons with flourishing-inconsistent preferences can still be considered autonomous.

Further, my definition of IAPs as selective makes clear how people with IAPs can retain capacities for autonomous agency. If we understand IAPs as affecting people in some domains of life and not others, and if we understand the rational character of many IAPs as my definition of IAP as selective suggests we do, claiming that a person manifests IAPs is no longer a claim about her general capacity to make decisions about her life. My definition of IAPs allows us to hold that people can have IAPs and be capable of making critical decisions about what is good for them.

This is as it should be intuitively. Deprivation does not necessarily make a person irrational or unworthy of being consulted about her good. Many IAPs manifest high levels of rationality. As I suggested in Chapter 2, the poor woman who calculates the amount of nutrition available to her family and makes sure to give herself the least is using deliberative skills. As I claimed in Chapter 3, other types of choices that seem complicit in perpetuating oppression or deprivation need not evince compromised rationality. For one thing, IAPs can evince reflectively endorsed personal values. For instance, many women do notavoid HIV exposure because of fear that their partners—who are the primary sources of income for them and their families—will become violent against them or leave them. This will leave them unable to care for their families, or simply unable to survive.[7] Choices like the choice not to avoid HIV exposure may reflect highly developed (and even flourishing-compatible) conceptions of the good—for instance, the belief it is important to care for one's family. Further, even in cases where a person's reasons for her IAP involve the belief that she does not deserve certain forms of flourishing, it does not follow that her capacities for reflection have been generally compromised. So, even if a woman fails to protect herself from HIV exposure because she believes that good women do not make demands on their husbands, it does not follow that her reflective capacities are compromised—or even that her ability to deliberate about values is completely compromised. This is an important upshot of the view of IAPs as selective that I developed in Chapter 3.

The autonomy of many IAPs is plausible because not all forms of deprivation impede persons' rational capacities. People make meaning from and respond reflectively to their situations—even if those situations are very bad. It is one thing to lack options, knowledge, or even a sense of what is possible for human beings to become, but it is quite another to not to be able to reflect on one's own desires. A person can go to bed hungry every night and still know who she will vote for in the presidential election and why; she can be illiterate and still ask herself what the meaning of life is; she may lack knowledge about contraception but still have thought about how many children she wants to have and why. In short, my perfectionist definition says persons can be rational and have inappropriately adaptive preferences at the same time. It urges representatives of public institutions to recognize this fact and interact with people with IAPs as rational agents.

The Agency Objection

There is yet another way in which deliberative perfectionist interventions might seem to disrespect individuals' capacities to pursue their own conceptions of the good. The deliberative perfectionist approach, since it justifies judging an individual's choices against an objective conception of the good, may seem to rob her of the opportunity to formulate the conception of the good by which her life should be judged. The agency objection states that the ability to actively choose and reflect upon values is a fundamental part of the capacity to pursue one's own conception of the good, and that using an external conception of the good divests individuals of the opportunity to use this ability.

The objection is a bit idiosyncratic, but we will understand it better if we link it to paternalism. Paternalism involves infringing on another's power to make decisions about her own good. Where the paternalistic coercion objection examined earlier suggests that a person is sufficiently free to make decisions about her own good if she is not coerced, the agency objection holds that making decisions about one's own good requires active reflection on values. It holds that the ability to make choices about one's own good requires positive—and not just negative—freedom. The idea behind it seems to be that one of the most important activities in human life is the activity of choosing what to value. We can divide the agency objection into a strong and a weak form, based on how important each holds the activity of choosing what to value to be.

The *strong* form of the agency objection holds that persons need to be engaged maximally—or at least very frequently—in the process of reflecting on and choosing their values in order to count as freely choosing their own conceptions of the good. There are strains in Amartya Sen's work that suggest he thinks something like this. He advances lines of argument that suggest that well-being freedom should be valued for its contribution to agency freedom, that the value of all functionings is derivative of their contribution to a person's ability to make deliberate choices (Sen 1999b, xii), or that making decisions about one's values necessarily increases one's well-being (Sen 1992, 51).[8] From the perspective of the strong form of the agency objection, the problem with the deliberative perfectionist approach is that it removes an opportunity to reflect on and formulate one's values—the opportunity to reflect on the conception of the good according to which one's preferences will be judged.

We can respond to the strong form of the agency objection by contesting its starting point. We should not grant that persons need to be maximally involved in the process of reflecting and choosing their values in order to be regarded as living according to chosen conceptions of the good. The belief that people must engage maximally in moral reflection is inconsistent with our intuitions about what counts as a good life and our intuitions about what types of lives can be reasonably chosen. It is inconsistent with our intuitions about what types of lives can be reasonably chosen, because it disqualifies many lives we think of as plausible objects of choice from being thought of as such. If we believe that persons must be engaged in constant choosing for their life-plans to have a chosen quality, we believe that lives that emphasize things like religious devotion, unfaltering courage, and action out of sympathetic attachment to others are not chosen. This is a very unpalatable conclusion.

Indeed, the notion that having a chosen life-plan requires constant choosing idealizes a type of life most of us would agree is *not* good—a life of incessant reflection.[9] This is how the notion is inconsistent with our intuitions about what counts as a good life. We have no reason to believe that choosing and reflecting always produce economies of scale. There is surely a point at which reflection and choice start to detract from a person's well-being. Most of us would agree that lives in which a person had to reflect on whether to get out of bed every single morning, ask herself whether every purchase she made was consistent with her overall scheme of values, or—to return to an example we have used frequently—make active choices about whether she deserved to eat would be a life full of distress.[10] My point here is not to say that persons should be prevented from living these types of lives. It is rather to show that something has surely gone awry in a view of freedom that asks public institutions to *prescribe* such lives.

The *strong* version of the agency objection—which holds that the deliberative perfectionist approach unacceptably deprives persons of opportunities to choose their values because persons should have maximal opportunities to choose their values—rests on spurious normative assumptions. If we reject the normative assumptions underlying the strong version of the agency objection, it will not strike us as decisive against the deliberative perfectionist approach. However, the *weak* version of the agency objection is based on more plausible normative assumptions. According to it, the problem with the deliberative perfectionist approach is not that it denies persons *an* opportunity to interrogate values; the problem is that it denies persons a particularly *important type* of opportunity to interrogate values. In order to be freely choosing their life-plans, persons should be actively involved in decisions about values that are publicly espoused.

I think that this weaker objection misunderstands the deliberative perfectionist approach. We can be very sympathetic to the spirit behind it without accepting it as reason to reject the deliberative perfectionist approach. It seems fully plausible to say that people are not free to pursue their own conceptions of the good if they are rarely given opportunities to reflect on and publicly discuss values. It also seems correct to say that people are not free to choose their own conceptions of the good if they are not regularly consulted about decisions that affect them. If we think the weak version of the agency objection weighs against the deliberative perfectionist approach, it is because we think deliberative perfectionism justifies unacceptably reducing persons' chances to reflect on values that are publicly espoused or prevents them from being consulted about decisions that affect them.

My approach need not do either, however. Persons can have opportunities to publicly discuss their values and be consulted about decisions that affect their lives without having to have personally participated in forming the most fundamental normative conceptions according to which their lives are judged. Indeed, this is the actual situation of most people who live in thriving contemporary democracies. In thriving democracies, people have opportunities to publicly discuss values and are consulted about courses of action that affect them. But they are not asked to come up with constitutional principles on their own, and we do not think that individuals who have not personally developed the constitutional principles by which they are judged are unfree to pursue their own conceptions of the good.

Nothing about the deliberative perfectionist approach prevents people from engaging in value discussion or being consulted about public decisions that will affect their lives. Rather, the deliberative perfectionist approach encourages interventions that include deliberation with persons with suspect preferences. People with suspect preferences can participate in ascertaining whether or not a preference is actually impeding a basic functioning in their lives and in deciding what should be done about it if it is. The weak version of the agency objection either misconstrues the deliberative perfectionist approach or creates unreasonably demanding criteria for participation in value formation, and the strong version rests on objectionable moral commitments. Thus neither is decisive against deliberative perfectionism-motivated IAP interventions.

The Nonintervention Objection

If we remain unpersuaded that we can value individuals' abilities to choose the types of lives they want and endorse my deliberative perfectionist approach, perhaps it is because my approach is *interventionist*. That is, my approach seems to recommend increased public involvement in the lives of people with IAPs. This aspect of my approach may seem to make it illiberal. Liberals want to respect and promote people's capacities to live the types of lives that matter to them. Some liberals (and most libertarians) think public institutions can best enact this respect by "leaving people's self-regarding preferences alone." Mill's harm principle exemplifies this sentiment. If we think that public institutions should leave people alone because this is the best way to ensure that they can live out their own conceptions of the good, we will have to oppose public intervention in the lives of people with IAPs.

I believe that liberals are right to value people's capacities to live according to their own conceptions of the good. But I do not believe that leaving people alone is the best way for public institutions to help people to exercise this capacity. To assume that public intervention necessarily decreases people's capacities to live according to their conceptions of the good rests on a dubious non-normative assumption: that everything a person is already doing embodies her conception of the good. By "embodies her conception of the good," I mean "is the way of life she deems ideal for herself." A preference can reflect a person's ideal way of life without *embodying* it; she may think that a certain action is the best way she can actualize the values she cares about under her circumstances but also dislike the circumstances. For an example, we might return to the woman who does not avoid HIV exposure only in order to retain access to an income for her children. We can imagine that this woman is able to express values she deeply cares about—like love for her family—by not avoiding HIV exposure. But we can also imagine this woman simultaneously wishing for a life in which she could love her children and protect her own health. If she does retain such a vision, her risky sexual behaviors reflect her conception of the good but do not embody it.

It is odd to assume that the only reason a person expresses the preferences she does is that these preferences embody her ideal way of life. It is particularly odd to assume this when we are discussing the lives of oppressed or deprived people. Deprivation often affects people precisely by making it impossible for people to embody their conceptions of the good. Indeed, many of the participants in Deepa Narayan's famous *Voices of the Poor* study describe knowing what the right thing is but being unable to do it as one of the most devastating aspects of poverty (2000). A deprived person may have her ability to embody her conception of the good undermined by other individuals (the case of a woman who wanted to go to school but whose parents would not let her) or (in)action by public institutions (the case of a woman who wanted to go to school but lived in a rural village with no girls' school for miles). The woman in either of these cases would have her capacity to live according to her conception of the good increased, rather than curtailed, by the type of educational intervention the deliberative perfectionist approach would recommend.

Further, all of a person's preferences do not matter equally to her conception of the good. People have higher- and lower-order preferences, and people are often willing to alter their lower-order preferences in the interests of achieving their higher-order ones. The woman who was never formally educated because her family prevented her may not endorse her persistent preference not to be educated. Rather, she may simply not go to school now, because it is too expensive, because it is a better investment of her limited resources to educate her children, because she needs to earn an income instead, because she is afraid she is not smart enough, and so on. If her reason for not seeking an education now is any of the above, she can be hardly said to subscribe to a conception of the good that does not value her education. In any of these cases, it seems that public intervention aimed changing her lower-order preferences or improving her opportunity set increases her capacity to lead the type of life she wants to lead.

Of course, not all people with IAPs are chafing to live under different conditions; some of them may actually endorse conceptions of the good that are incompatible with their flourishing. These are the tough cases for the deliberative perfectionist approach. They raise legitimate concerns about how public institutions might decrease people's capacities to live the types of lives they want to lead. A woman who is not interested in learning to read because she genuinely opposes women's education will seem to have her capacity to live according to her conception of the good decreased by literacy-promoting interventions. I offer two responses on behalf of the deliberative perfectionist approach here. First, the deliberative perfectionist approach suggests that public institutions should intervene noncoercively and should focus on changing preferences that seem reversible. This means that the deliberative perfectionist approach will not force her to stop living according to an anti-education conception of the good. It also means that public institutions will have to stop attempting her to change her preferences after it becomes evident that the preferences are not reversible. I admit that deliberative perfectionist interventions will interfere to some extent with this woman's capacity to enact her conception of the good. However, once it becomes clear that she deeply prefers illiteracy, her conception of the good will be seen as worthy of non-interference. Whatever interference there is will be noncoercive and temporary.

Second, I think we should move away from a conception of people's conceptions of the good as inflexible and unchanging. Yes, a woman who has grown up with few opportunities for education in a society that devalues female education may endorse the belief that she should not be educated. However, there is a serious ethical question about why public institutions should focus on respecting the conception of the good she had *before* a noncoercive IAP intervention over the conception of the good she has after one. If we see people's conceptions of the good as flexible, it becomes plausible that a deliberative perfectionist intervention—say, consciousness raising—could help her re-evaluate her conception of the good. If this intervention awakens her muted desire to develop her cognitive capacities, she may come to adopt a conception of the good that values her education.

My point is not to claim that all such women who participated in consciousness raising would abandon their anti-education conceptions of the good. Rather, I want to suggest that public institutions may intervene without failing to respect people's capacities to form conceptions of the good, if they engage those people reflectively. To engage a person with a seeming IAP in deliberation is to engage her at the level of her reasons for her behavior—to engage her as the type of being who has a conception of the good worth respecting. Deliberative IAP interventions should be conceived as attempts to help people clarify and evaluate their conceptions of the good rather than as attempts to replace their conceptions of the good with external ones. If we think of IAP interventions as giving people opportunities to clarify their conceptions of the good, deliberative perfectionist interventions need not disrespect people's capacities to live according to their conceptions of the good.

Admittedly, there is a degree of paternalism involved here. Deliberative perfectionist interventions in the lives of people with strong IAPs will involve treating people as though some of their existing values are mistaken. It will involve attempting to persuade people to recognize flourishing-compatible beliefs from among their existing values. But, this degree of paternalism is not necessarily objectionable, since it does not involve an attempt to *substitute* deprived people's conceptions of the good with some other's conception of flourishing. Rather, deliberative interventions encourage people to develop flourishing-compatible conceptions of the good that they see as their own.

Deliberative perfectionist interventions thus do not disrespect people's capacities to live according to their conceptions of the good. In many cases, they actually enhance people's capacities to do so. In other cases, they do encourage people to alter the content of their conceptions of the good, but only by engaging them as choosers and evaluators.

The Deliberative Perfectionist Approach and the Moral Diversity of Cultures

My deliberative perfectionist approach requires public institutions to promote a conception of the good. In the last section, I attempted to demonstrate that the public endorsement of a conception of the good required by my approach does not prevent individual persons from forming and living according to their own conceptions of the good. But it is not only individuals who vary in their conceptions of the good; cultures do also.[11] We know that development policy has not always treated moral variation across cultures as legitimate. In this section, I demonstrate that endorsing the deliberative perfectionist approach does not come at an unacceptable cost to our commitment to valuing cultural diversity. I examine four objections to my approach that are motivated by a desire to respect cultural diversity. I claim that none of them is decisive, because each fails to understand that the deliberative perfectionist approach is supported by a vague and justificatorily minimal conception of human flourishing. Let us call these objections "the universal humanity objection," "the external standards objection," "the homogenizing objection," and "the passive recipients objection."

The Universal Humanity Objection

It may seem that the most fundamental moral commitments of the deliberative perfectionist approach place it at odds with the project of respecting cultural differences in conceptions of the good. I have been candid about the fact that we cannot endorse it without assenting to some basic ideas about the human being.

My central claim—that IAP intervention can be good for deprived people because nonflourishing preferences would not likely be retained by human beings under conditions conducive to their flourishing—assumes that human beings share a nature. This nature is best realized under certain conditions and manifests itself in particular functionings. It may appear that all of this talk of the human condemns deliberative perfectionist interventions to unacceptably reducing difference. We may ask, is it not oxymoronic to think we can promote understanding across difference by starting from the assumption that human beings are, in some very fundamental sense, similar? The universal humanity objection states that, because of its commitment to the idea of humanity, the deliberative perfectionist approach will inhibit cross-cultural understanding.

This type of misgiving about the human is corroborated by a common strand of thinking in contemporary theorizing about the causes of exclusion and oppression. This strand of thinking wants to claim that there is something in the very *logic* of the human (or any universal) that produces the oppression of persons who are different. In contemporary philosophy, it is most familiar to us in theories of liberation influenced by French poststructuralism.[12] In development studies, it manifests itself in what in some strains of what is called "postdevelopment" theory.[13] These theoretical traditions have much to offer contemporary liberation struggles, and I do not mean to minimize this by painting them in broad strokes here. Still, for the purposes of the present argument, we can isolate a particular type of argument about the human that appears in both literatures. This argument type begins from a desire to explain the persistence of harm and oppression to human beings in contexts where ethical theories extolling "universal" features of human beings prevail(ed).

This argument type says that the notion of the human being (or person) in a given context had inappropriate content that caused it to exclude the needs of entire groups of human beings. To take one example from postdevelopment theory, Mitu Hirshman argues that the predominant concept of the human being in development thinks of human flourishing (or thought in the 1980s and 1990s) as requiring only access to material goods. According to her, this view makes the needs of many third-world women not count as needs, because these women value spiritual connection to nature (Hirshman 1995, 43). Some—but not all—postdevelopment and poststructuralist thinkers draw a wide-reaching conclusion from the fact that claims about human nature are susceptible to misuses like this one. They suggest that there is something in the very structure of claims about the human that makes some human beings appear as less than human.

Many arguments of this type advanced by poststructuralist and postdevelopment thinkers accurately identify problems in existing or past conceptions of the human. Even their wide-reaching conclusion is, in some sense, correct. It is unavoidable that using the human as a category of analysis will exclude some beings from the category of the human; drawing boundaries is simply what categories do. However, it does not follow from this that conceptions of the human must exclude beings from humanity in a way that is morally objectionable. It is clearly morally objectionable to define humanity in a way that prevents women, or third worlders, or third-world women from being understood as human. In contrast, I do not think it is morally objectionable to define humanity in a way that excludes trees or chairs or butterflies from being thought of as human beings. We probably do not all agree on the exact limits of who counts as human, because they lie somewhere between these two extremes, and there are important ongoing philosophical conversations—particularly in the philosophies of disability and animal rights—about where these lines should be drawn. I make no attempt here to offer a theory of where the line between human and nonhuman to be drawn. But the general point here is that it is not logically necessary for claims about human to exclude beings in a way that is morally unacceptable.

But, the antihumanist might reply, we know that the conception of the human is dangerous. Would we not do better to just get rid of it? Can we not have understanding across difference without it? My response to the antihumanist is that it is not at all clear that we can. Understanding others as different, or recognizing the differences of others, *requires* reference to some deeper sameness. Susan Babbitt (2005) argues that others' descriptions of their lives and beliefs only appear as *about* difference if we assume a background context of sameness.

Babbitt describes an objection by African feminist philosopher Nkiru Nzegwu to Anthony Appiah's representation of West African women. Nzegwu claims that Western readers need to know that West African women are different from them, that they do not accept subservient roles in the family like Western women do (Babbitt 2005, 9). But, Babbitt points out, in order to know why or how this difference is important, we need to be interested in finding out what is true for women in general (Babbitt 2005, 10). Otherwise her claim that West African women are not subservient is just an anthropological fact. For it to be a fact *about* something, some sense of similarity must be invoked. For instance, if the claim is an anthropological fact, it is about some other sameness—the sameness among human beings. It is not clear that it is possible to understand anything about the lives of others without pointing out fundamental similarities between their lives and our own.

Not only do we need to refer to fundamental similarities to understand the lives of others; it is only by assuming some sort of similarity that we can understand how others are different from us. The assumption that we share certain dispositions with others is what allows us to make sense of differences *as* differences. As Thomas Scanlon puts this point,

Even if [certain] goods...are foreign to us and of no value in our society, we can understand why they are of value to someone else if we can bring the reasons for their desirability under familiar general categories. These reasons might, for example, concern material comfort, status or security; or they might concern health or protection against injury. An alleged benefit which we could not understand as falling under any familiar category, something that somebody just happened to take an interest in, would be totally opaque to us." (Scanlon 2003, 75)

To see a concrete example of this, we can consider the case of minor genital cutting among the Abagusii. Astrid Christoffersen-Deb (2005) found that though most Gusii girls were still undergoing genital cutting, the cutting typically did not involve serious or permanent damage to the genitals. An activist who was not a member of the communities that practiced genital cutting might be genuinely puzzled about why girls were undergoing genital cutting—especially when this cutting was not significantly altering their genitals. However, with a conception of the flourishing that indicates that affiliation is an important functioning in the background, an outsider might come to understand from the stories of young women that this *one* way of becoming accepted by one's community. It may be a way of doing so that it unfamiliar to the practitioner, but the practitioner may think of it as a *different* way of achieving a functioning she also values. Without some frame of similarity, the significance of the practice to the girls undergoing it would simply be unintelligible.

Further, far from undermining the capacity of deprived people to gain respect for the differences they value, the presumption of similarity given by a conception of the human can empower people with suspect preferences to successfully contest judgment that they are deprived. Let us recall the example from Vandana Shiva of the Indian women farmers who were assumed to be deprived because they did not use Western technology (1988, 4). A conception of the good (like Nussbaum's) that includes both the ability to relate to nature and access to income may have provided a framework in which it was possible to persuade outsiders that this was a flourishing way of life. Absent the view that a relationship with nature was an important functioning, and absent discussion about what functionings the traditional ways of life were contributing to, outsiders could not understand why the traditional farming practices mattered to the women who engaged in them.

An appropriately formulated conception of human flourishing actually facilitates understanding of cultural differences. What does it mean for a conception of the human to be "appropriately formulated" for the emergence of difference? At the very least, the conception must be vague. A conception that was highly specific would not allow us to understand different ways of achieving the same functioning as differences and would make it very difficult to understand others as flourishing differently. Non-vague conceptions are the types of conceptions to which many postdevelopment and poststructuralist thinkers object. But since the deliberative perfectionist approach incorporates a vague conception of flourishing, it is less susceptible to these types of objections. This vague conception facilitates understanding across difference rather than obstructing it.

The External Standards Objection

Another objection against the deliberative perfectionist approach is the external standards objection. The external standards objection holds that the deliberative perfectionist approach endorses judging persons in a culture by a conception of the good that is external to it, and that this is a bad thing. We frequently hear criticisms of another deliberative perfectionist conception of flourishing—the existing international human rights regime—that express this conviction. For example, Said Rajaje-Khorassani, the Iranian representative to the United Nations, once said that the Universal Declaration of Human Rights was "a secular understanding of the Judeo-Christian tradition" and thus should not be implemented in his country (Littman 1999). In the late 1990s, the Singaporean Prime Minister, Lee Kwan Yew defended his country's failure to adopt human rights norms on the grounds that "Asian values" provided more appropriate standards by which to judge it (Sen 1997). A more academic version of this view appeared in the American Anthropological Association's 1947 "Statement on Human Rights," whose authors claim that "man is free only when he lives as his society defines freedom" (American Anthropological Association 1947, 43).[14] Let us consider two possible versions of the criticism that persons should not be judged by standards from cultures other than their own—called the "genetic version" and the "understanding version"

The *genetic version* is clearly the less credible of the two. It begins from the belief that persons in cultures should only be judged according to normative conceptions *generated by* those cultures themselves. On a view like this one, the problem with the deliberative perfectionist approach is that it judges persons' levels of flourishing using a normative conception that those cultures did not invent. Mentioning that the deliberative perfectionist conception is based on a cross-culturally acceptable conception of human flourishing will not satisfy this critic. This is because "cross-culturally acceptable" does not mean "endorsed by an 'authentic' representative of every culture on the planet" (this would clearly be an unrealistic ideal). Nor does "cross-culturally acceptable" mean "having independently arisen in every culture on the planet."

If we believe that the deliberative approach is incompatible with the belief that cultures can only be judged by standards generated by them, we are surely right. But, I would suggest, we are wrong if we believe this incompatibility is a bad thing. If we reject the deliberative perfectionist approach because we subscribe to the genetic version of the external standards objection, it is because we are subscribing to a set of beliefs about morality that do not deserve our assent. The arguments against the belief that persons within cultures must be judged only by standards internal to their cultures are very well-rehearsed elsewhere.[15] I only briefly summarize them here.

One basic problem with the view that cultures should only be judged by internal standards is that it is difficult to have a precise sense of *where* an idea— especially a basic moral idea—was generated. This is partly because most cultures do not exist in isolation (and never have); just because an idea appears in a culture does not mean it originated there. But it is also because it is generally difficult to know exactly *where* an idea came from. For example, Uma Narayan responds to those who accuse her feminist ideals of originating outside of India by saying that part of the genesis of those ideals was her witnessing of her mother's pain during her childhood in India (U. Narayan 1997, 7).

Moreover, it is difficult to tell where basic moral conceptions originated, because similar ideas exist in many different cultures. For example, it has been argued that the origins of human rights can only be found in Western cultures, but there seems little reason to credit this argument. Sen (1997) argues that there are strong rights traditions in Asian cultures; Nussbaum argues that there are strong anti-patriarchal traditions in India (2001, 41–48); J.A.I. Bewaji (2006) argues that some of the most fundamental concepts of human rights can be found in pre-colonial Yoruba traditions. It is highly likely that the ideas in any deliberative perfectionist conception will be traceable to multiple different origins—and indeed, that there is some understanding of them within all cultures. I believe that the appearance of similar moral ideas in multiple contexts is part of what should convince us that they are good moral ideals.

A second basic problem with the view that cultures should only be judged by standards internal to them is that it is unclear how to determine what *the* moral standards of a culture actually are. Cultures are not homogenous, and many different strains of thought—both conservative and radical—can exist within any given culture. As Biku Parekh says it, "A culture has no essence. It includes different strands of thought" (Parekh 2000, 175). Along similar lines, Uma Narayan argues that cultures are "idealized constructions" and that attempts to ascertain what the values of a culture are usually involve representing the values of some privileged group as the values of the culture as a whole (U. Narayan 1997, 15). Ironically, it is not even clear that critics of ideas like equality, dignity, and human rights are correct to describe these ideals as *the* standards of Western culture. As Narayan puts it, "One could argue that doctrines of human rights, rather than being pure products of imperialism, were often important products of struggles *against* Western imperialism" (U. Narayan 1998, 97).

Even more problematically, making certain persons' depiction of the standards of a culture the authoritative one runs the risk of legitimizing the most conservative elements in a culture—elements that oppress and dominate other members of that culture. Struggles over the meaning of a culture's norms occur within cultures,[16] and we can easily find examples where claims about a culture's internal norms function to silence members of those cultures who want to reform them. Uma Narayan claims that Hindu fundamentalists in India object to "Westernization" when it seems to manifest itself in the form of feminism, but not when it manifests itself in the form of television watching (1997, 22). We might also argue that it is no coincidence that the claim that conceptions of human rights do not exist in a given culture often comes from defenders of authoritarian regimes. The examples from Lee Kwan Yew and Said Rajaje-Khorassani cited at the beginning of this section are cases in point.

The view that individuals can only be judged by moral standards *generated* within their own cultures is rather widely discredited, and I have described the central reasons for this. However, there is a second version of the external standards objection to the deliberative perfectionist approach that is much more respectable. This is the understanding version. It holds that the real problem with judging persons according to standards that did not originate in their culture is that it means judging them according to standards they cannot understand or in which they do not recognize values of their own. I think that this is what many critiques of human rights as external standards are actually about. For example, Makau Mutua argues that Africans are more familiar with the language of duty than that of rights and that they are thus likely to face some difficulties identifying with the human rights regime (Mutua 1995). Theresa Weynand Tobin cites Maysam Al-Faruqi as claiming that Sunni Muslim women often do not identify with the language of human rights, because they think of themselves in the terms of "Islamic discourse" (Tobin 2007, 157).

Judging persons according to conceptions of the good they cannot understand is, on the whole, a bad thing, and it can have pernicious effects in development practice designed to respond to IAPs. It can produce three types of undesirable consequences. First, it may result in persons leading lives of nonendorsement of the opportunities available to them.[17] Although we should not expect persons to endorse all the standards by which they are judged—contesting bad standards can be a part of a flourishing human life—it does seem that a life in which one has a positive attitude toward one's opportunities for flourishing is better than one that does not. In other words, if we think endorsement is a good, we want persons to identify with the norms that influence their lives. Moreover, endorsement typically increases the success of development projects. Persons are more likely to participate in projects they themselves *recognize* as means of realizing functionings they desire.

Second, judging people according to a conception of the good they do not understand may not only fail to produce endorsement; it may produce active hostility toward public institutions. Persons judged by a conception of flourishing with which they do not identify may see themselves as objects of objectionable paternalism or may come to believe that public institutions are actually interested in harming them (which most certainly *has* been the case in many development projects).

Third, evaluating people's lives with reference to normative conceptions they do not understand can obstruct dialogue between persons with suspect preferences and development practitioners. This is an important concern in projects designed to respond to IAPs. It is easy to imagine cases where practitioners suspect preferences that are genuinely *not* IAPs and the bearers of those preferences do not have the moral vocabulary to respond. This would disempower the bearers of suspect preferences vis-à-vis development practitioners and result in misguided public policy. We may also imagine cases in which practitioners attempt to persuade persons with suspect preferences of the value of some set of opportunities, but the language of the practitioner is totally opaque to them. Lebanese geographer Huda Zurayk offers an example of a conception of flourishing with which persons with suspect preferences may have difficulty identifying because of their cultural background. She says that women in the Middle East may have trouble relating to the idea of consensual sex. "Should every sexual act be consented to?" she asks. "If so, how can that be understood in marriages where the choice of the husband has not been subject to the consent of the woman" (Zurayk 2001, 26)? I do not think that Zurayk's point here is quite that women in the Middle East do not value—or could not come to value—sexual lives that were free of violence. Rather, the idea is that it will be difficult for persons who have never thought of consent as an important value in sexual life to formulate their needs and desires in a vocabulary of consent.

Should we expect interventions justified by the deliberative perfectionist conception to have these types of negative consequences? The only honest answer to this question is to say yes, sometimes. In cases where the rifts between representatives of public institutions and persons with suspect preferences are particularly large, where representatives of public institutions act in bad faith (I discuss practitioner virtues later in this chapter), or where insufficient time and resources are allocated to deliberation, we can expect public responses to suspect preferences to go awry. Moral understanding—especially across cultural difference—is sometimes very difficult, and I do not mean to downplay this. But we also should not assume a priori that moral understanding is impossible. As Benhabib writes about divergent and convergent beliefs, "very often we do not know how deep these divergences are, or how great their overlap may be, until we have engaged in conversation" (Benhabib 2002, 136).

However, the deliberative perfectionist conception of flourishing possesses certain structural features that decrease the likelihood and potential severity of cultural misunderstanding in development practice. Its conception of human flourishing is vague and justificatorily minimal. As we have already seen, the vagueness of the conception promotes deliberation; accurately interpreting it in a given context will typically require taking the first-person perspectives of persons with suspect preferences into account. Done well and in the right circumstances, this type of discussion can foster endorsement of transformation rather than hostility (or neutrality). Persons whose preferences have changed as a result of participatory development programs often report positive attitudes toward the new functionings available to them.

Moreover, these positive attitudes often reveal an integration of new opportunities with previously existing belief systems. For example, Sabina Alkire recounts that some of the participants in the Oxfam-funded rose cultivation project in rural Pakistan cited in Chapter 1 described themselves as valuing rose cultivation because it allowed them to engage in what they thought of as "holy work" (Alkire 2002, 278). Similarly, one participant in a Senegalese Save the Children-funded initiative aimed at changing the nutritional beliefs of elderly women that were detrimental to younger women's maternal health described satisfaction at being able to integrate new knowledge with traditional knowledge. One participant "articulated this feeling: 'the grandmother activities have made us stronger than before. Not only do we have our traditional knowledge and experiences, but we also have the knowledge of the doctors' " (Aubel, Toure, et al. 2001, 67).

We should also remember that the conception of the good used in deliberative perfectionist interventions is justificatorily minimal. This improves the possibility of dialogue between persons with suspect preferences and development practitioners, for one can translate the conception into, and endorse it from, a wide variety of moral languages. Moreover, practitioners can, and should, become familiar with local moral languages to understand how they can be linked to the justificatorily minimal conception. Practitioners can disagree with participants about how they are linked, and participants can disagree with one another.

Some Middle Eastern women may indeed have difficulty relating to the idea of consensual sex as Zurayk claims, but nothing about the functioning of "being secure against sexual assault" requires that discussions of sexual violence be framed in a language of consent. Middle Eastern women who are Muslim, for example, might understand sexual violence as a perversion of the type of love between husbands and wives prescribed in the Koran (Koran 30:21).[18] Or, perhaps actual discussion will reveal that Zurayk is wrong to suppose that most Middle Eastern women do not understand the idea of consensual sex.

Similarly, as Castle, Traore, et al.'s studies of women's conceptions of reproductive health in Mali (2002), discussed in Chapter 3, show, some Malian women may not think of reproductive health in isolation from the idea of interpersonal relationships. Castle, Traore, et al. are quite right to suggest that this need not be seen as catastrophic for public policy motivated by the conception of the good embodied by the post-Cairo definition of reproductive health.[19] Rather, it can be seen as an injunction to justify reproductive-health-related policies in a language that takes interpersonal relationships seriously (Castle, Traore, et al. 2002, 29).

We may have the lingering worry that the possibility of translation and interpretation from one moral language to another only accompanies *certain* deliberative conceptions of the good. It may be correct to say that Nussbaum's list of central human capabilities can function in this way, but it may not seem correct to say that the list of human rights can be seen in this way. After all, most of the examples of the external standards criticism I have cited here are criticisms of the human rights regime. I do not think the conception of flourishing embedded in the human rights regime must be described in the language of rights at the level of actual IAP interventions.

The fact that human rights are *rights* clearly matters at the level of legal interpretation and implementation. However, it is by no means clear that this means development interventions motivated by rights must be formulated in the language of rights. Castle, Traore, et al.'s study of women in Mali studied above is an example of the type of work that can be done to discover the interface between conceptions of human rights and local moral languages. In asking women what they thought reproductive health was, they discovered that this idea was, for them, intertwined with the idea of loving relationships. It is likely that this type of culturally appropriate reframing of a universal conception of the good can be done with any type of justificatorily minimal conception of flourishing.

A justificatorily minimal and vague conception of the good—the type we endorse if we endorse the deliberative perfectionist approach—can be understood by persons from a wide variety of moral perspectives. This means that it is amenable to being understood, interpreted, and manipulated by persons with suspect preferences, and thus indicates that the deliberative perfectionist approach does not justify subjecting persons to normative conceptions they cannot understand. The idea that persons should only be judged by normative conceptions that are generated by their cultures is simply not credible. Neither the genetic version nor the understanding version of the external standards objection is decisive against the deliberative perfectionist approach.

The Homogenizing Objection

Another reason we may not want to authorize public institutions to use a conception of the good to identify and respond to IAPs is that it seems to commit us to a rather frightening grand objective—the project of making everyone in the world the same. Endorsing my deliberative perfectionist approach means saying that preferences consistent with basic flourishing are more worthy of social promotion than preferences that are not. It also means saying that human beings deserve access to conditions conducive to their basic flourishing and expecting many persons' preferences to change when they have access to such conditions. Does wanting all human beings to have access to conditions conducive to their flourishing mean wanting everyone to live under the *same* conditions? Does encouraging persons to change their preferences so that they are adapted to good conditions mean promoting a world in which everyone has the *same* preferences? The homogenizing objection holds that it does. We can distinguish two forms of the homogenizing objection—one we can call the "logical form" and another we can call "the practical form."

The logical form of the homogenizing objection holds that promoting an objective conception of the good logically requires trying to make everyone's expressed preferences the same. Mistrust of objective conceptions of human flourishing in development practice is certainly justified. We know that such conceptions have rationalized many oppressive and totalizing enterprises in past and present development practice. Indeed, this is one of the most important lessons of the postdevelopment tradition I referred to in discussing the universal humanity objection. Translated into philosophical language, we can read many postdevelopment critiques of development as usual as saying something like this: Bad development happens partly because the West thinks it knows what human flourishing is. The development discourse conflates the functionings constitutive of human flourishing with the functionings men in industrial capitalist societies value. Thus, in the name of extending human flourishing, the West engaged (or engages) in a massive project of trying to transform the Rest into the West. Earlier, I offered specific examples of this in my discussions of the purportedly Western assumption that a life that highly values connection to nature cannot be worth living, so I will not repeat them here. What such examples show is that having an objective conception of human flourishing *can* mean having a specific picture of what human life should look like and attempting to uproot everything that does not look like that picture.

If the deliberative perfectionist approach does indeed require a specific picture of flourishing to which everyone ought to conform, public institutions are engaging in a pernicious task when they attempt to identify and transform IAPs. But I do not think deliberative perfectionist interventions strive to make everyone have the same preferences. Before I show how this is so, however, there is a bullet I need to bite. I freely admit that my deliberative perfectionist approach aims at the uprooting of *some* preferences, albeit noncoercively. We cannot endorse deliberative perfectionist interventions and simultaneously believe that difference (whatever this might mean) is an intrinsic good that is more important than the basic flourishing of human beings. Endorsing deliberative perfectionism will mean attempting to change preferences that detract from persons' basic flourishing and were formed under sub-flourishing conditions. We cannot avoid this fact.

However, it does not follow from this that a deliberative perfectionist approach justifies trying to make everyone the same or even similar. Persons have to lead very similar kinds of lives to be recognized as flourishing according to conceptions of flourishing that are very specific and/or not basic. A conception that defines a good human life as one that involves a nine-to-five job, a house in the suburbs, two children, and a minivan does hold that everyone should be pretty much the same. But the deliberative perfectionist approach does not entail a conception of the good like this one. It holds that everyone should have access to conditions conducive to functionings like bodily health and affiliation. But, because it is vague, it says nothing about whether one should be more focused on preventing illness or curing it, or what a family should look like. Moreover, because it is basic, it says nothing about whether it is better to be a vegetarian or a meat eater, or whether marriage should be about love or duty, or not exist at all. Because the conception of flourishing is vague and minimal, it does not bother to morally evaluate many—even most—preference differences.

These features of the conception have an important practical consequence for the deliberative perfectionist approach. My approach is motivated by the belief that people should live under conditions conducive to their basic flourishing and that it is legitimate for public institutions to attempt to change suspect preferences into preferences consistent with basic flourishing. But the deliberative conception of the good radically *underdetermines* what preferences should replace IAPs. In other words, as I have claimed at several points in this book, nothing in the conception of flourishing tells representatives of public institutions what IAPs should be changed *to*. This leaves communities and individuals much latitude to envision new ways of realizing their flourishing—ways that practitioners may never have been able to imagine or predict in advance.

The work of Mandaleo Ya Wanawake, the Kenyan nongovernmental organization (NGO) I discussed in Chapter 1, to stop clitoridectemy and labial removal offers an illuminating case in point. After conducting extensive participatory research, practitioners concluded that something needed to replace the practice of genital cutting if young women and their families were going to stop preferring it. They learned that part of the reason the preference for genital cutting was strong was that it was a coming-of-age ritual that played an important social role in the community. The solution they arrived at kept the coming-of-age ritual—in a new form without the genital cutting. Known as "Circumcision Through Words," this alternative ritual excludes "genital cutting but maintains the other essential components, such as education for the girls on family life and women's roles, exchange of gifts, eating good food, and a public declaration for community recognition" (Chege, Askew, et al. 2001, 3). The transition from an IAP to a better one was not homogenizing in this case. Stopping genital cutting did not have to mean becoming "Western" or even becoming like other Kenyan women from ethnic groups or social classes that did not cut.

Working with a conception of the good that underdetermines human flourishing, as the deliberative perfectionist approach does, allows IAP transformation not to be a simple zero-sum game. It makes possible solutions to IAPs that do not force persons to choose between retaining IAPs that harm their flourishing and abandoning cultural values that are important to them. The girls in the clitoridectemy case end up not having to chose between "having opportunities for sexual satisfaction" and "being able to live with and toward others." In this case, authorizing public institutions to distinguish flourishing from nonflourishing preferences does not mean authorizing them to homogenize cultures.

But this real-world example may seem to be an exception. Even if it is logically possible for a vague and minimal conception of the good to receive a variety of actual instantiations, it may seem that such variety is unlikely to arise in practice. This leads to the second version of the homogenizing objection, the pragmatic version. The pragmatic version holds that actual deliberative processes are unlikely to yield anything but proposals that mirror the practitioner's vision. This is the outcome frequently referred to as "inadvertent ventriloquism"[20] in development; practitioners feed ideas to participants, participants tell practitioners what practitioners want to hear, and the final product looks suspiciously like the one that was always in the practitioner's head. Is it not unrealistic to suggest, as my approach certainly does, that development practitioners can come to distinguish their thick visions of flourishing from other thick visions of flourishing?

This threat of inadvertent ventriloquism is very real, but I believe that participatory development practitioners are already imagining and implementing practices that offset the practitioner tendency to foist her desires onto others. Their suggestions include prescriptions that practitioners should have a deep level of understanding of the cultural contexts in which they are intervening and that they should develop virtues of humility[21] (which I describe in a bit more depth in the upcoming section on the passive recipients objection). They also propose practical strategies that will decrease power inequalities in deliberation[22] and exercises designed to help elicit local values before the practitioner frames the conversation.

Since "inadvertent ventriloquism" is particularly likely to occur in discussions about what should be done, exercises that elicit *values* can militate against it by giving the practitioner a sense of the community's priorities. The practitioner can later check her judgments about what the participants' chosen course of action against their articulation of their values to determine whether she has incorrectly assumed that their chosen course of action and hers coincide. Moreover, these value-eliciting exercises include open-ended questions—questions participants are likely not to know the practitioner's preferred answer to. Alkire (2006) offers a number of examples of such value-eliciting practices. They include asking community members to create timelines of important events in their lives, asking them to reflect on what they know about other cultures and would/would not like their grandchildren to adopt from those cultures, asking individuals to reflect individually on their values before reporting to the group, and asking about how proposed strategies will impact well-being in a variety of broadly specified dimensions (to prevent limiting discussions to only those dimensions of life the practitioner is personally interested in) (2006, 144–148). Without claiming that any of these modifications of development interventions is a magic bullet that will stop homogenization, I do want to suggest that there are ways of conducting development interventions on the ground that decrease the tendency of practitioners to assume community members' thick flourishing-compatible desires are identical to theirs.

The Passive Recipients Objection

A final moral diversity-related objection we may raise against the deliberative perfectionist approach is that it seems to require development practitioners to view persons from cultures that are different from theirs as moral patients. It may seem that suspecting the preferences of another person requires viewing that person as a passive recipient of one's help. The risk of this is exacerbated in practice by the fact that the practitioners doing the suspecting will often come from social groups that are privileged vis-à-vis those of the persons with suspect preferences. Consciously or unconsciously—people from high castes are often habituated to looking down on those from lower ones, educated people often feel superior to uneducated ones, and Northerners often think they know more than Southerners. Anne Ferguson provides an example of the latter sense of superiority.

To summarize a critique by the Southern DAWN collective of the way most Women in Development (WID) projects in the 1990s were conceived by women from the North, Ferguson says that Southern women "are subject to paternalism (or more appropriately 'maternalism')...by projects designed to benefit women seen as Other, as objects of relief rather than subjects who could take place in the planning process themselves" (Ferguson 1998, 100).

Before we can defend the deliberative perfectionist approach from the passive recipients objection, we need to get clearer about what it is an objection *to*. It is an objection to certain types of practitioner attitudes and/or policies whose design suggests that their creators had such attitudes. We can imagine some ways of justifying third-party suspicion of and response to IAPs from which we could reasonably infer that their creators had condescending attitudes. An understanding of IAPs as substantive autonomy deficits, for instance, might be reasonably interpreted as stemming from the belief that the deprived should not be consulted about their own interests. I pointed this out in Chapter 3 and in my discussion of the motivational paternalism objection. Also, we might reasonably interpret the notion that IAPs are simply "bad" preferences as premised upon the belief that deprived people are wicked or stupid. But my perfectionist definition of IAP is neither a conception of substantive autonomy nor a purely content-based account of the apparent authenticity of IAPs. Moreover, as we have seen several times in this chapter, the deliberative perfectionist approach recommends interventions that expressly do *not* treat persons with suspect preferences as moral patients. My approach valorizes the participation of persons with suspect preferences in the interpretation of the vague and justificatorily minimal conception of the good. My approach can coherently oppose IAPs and support the agency of people with IAPs because it does not conceive IAPs as autonomy deficits, and it does not conceive the effects of IAP as destroying people's senses of self-entitlement in a totalizing fashion.

Still, individual practitioners and activists may exhibit arrogant attitudes toward development participants—regardless of whatever anti-paternalist normative commitments they avow. Even those who avow the most radical commitments to empowering beneficiaries can fall into the trap of seeing them as patients. Indeed, we even find conceptions of development beneficiaries as passive recipients in postdevelopment critiques of development! Prominent postdevelopment theorists have portrayed development beneficiaries as having passively internalized the ideas of the dominant development discourse—to the point of comparing them to the recipients of a viral infection (Ziai 2004, 1048). The paternalistic WID practitioners Ferguson criticizes were committed on paper to the idea of empowering women. It is commonly acknowledged in the literature on participatory development that facilitators can and sometimes do use participatory development methods to legitimize achieving "pre-determined objectives more efficiently and effectively" (Groot and Maarleveld 2000, 18).

The deliberative perfectionist approach is not immune to being co-opted by ill-intentioned organizations. Nor is it immune to being used by practitioners who happen to have condescending attitudes toward beneficiaries. It would be unreasonable to expect any normative conception to have such immunity. A project aimed at preference transformation can involve significant amounts of participation and still not respect its intended beneficiaries if the facilitator thinks she has all the answers in advance. We can imagine practitioners who do not know how to—or do not want to—listen to bearers of suspect preferences when they dispute her perception of them as deprived. We can also imagine practitioners who do not know how to take beneficiary suggestions about how preferences might be changed seriously. In short, we can imagine practitioners motivated by the deliberative perfectionist approach manifesting the types of attitudes the passive recipients objection denounces, regardless of what the deliberative perfectionist approach asks them to do.

It should also be clear, however, that the possibility of perverse uses in practice is not unique to the deliberative perfectionist approach. Once participation is incorporated into an approach to IAP intervention, there is not much more that can be done at a theoretical level to prevent such perverse consequences. What can be done is prescribing virtues to practitioners and training them to develop these virtues. Ferguson urges practitioners to engage in "self-interrogation practices" (Ferguson 1998, 104). Ofelia Schutte claims that effectively listening to others across cultural difference means refusing to assume that one immediately understands what they mean. If the statements of the others can be "divided into three categories—readily understandable, difficult to understand, and truly incommensurable—one should never close the communication at the level of the first category, but should make the effort to let understanding reach into the other two domains" (Schutte 2000, 56–57).

Both of these proposals suggest important virtues for practitioners—virtues public institutions should make an effort to inculcate in them and virtues I have elaborated in writings outside this book.[23] Fortunately, training practitioners in such virtues is perfectly consistent with the deliberative perfectionist approach. My approach encourages deliberation by deprived people and thus does not recommend that practitioners see persons with suspect preferences as passive recipients of their benevolence. Indeed, my definition of IAPs as having selective effects that do not destroy the autonomy of people who have them militates against conceiving people with IAPs as moral patients. If deliberative perfectionist interventions are to achieve their goals, they need to be carried out by practitioners who have learned to see deprived people as equals. The passive recipients objection usefully reminds us that those conducting deliberative perfectionist interventions should be attentive to the pitfalls of cross-cultural communication, but it does not give us grounds to reject my approach.

IAP Intervention and Moral Diversity

I have argued that we can value moral diversity *and* endorse deliberative perfectionist interventions in the lives of people with IAPs. Such interventions are not at odds with treating individuals as the ultimate authorities about the kind of lives they want to lead. Such interventions are not coercive, and they promote people's participation in public discussion about the values a community should espouse. Endorsing deliberative perfectionist IAP interventions also does not preclude us from retaining a high degree of respect for people's attachments to culturally particular values. Endorsing deliberative perfectionism does require discouraging some cultural practices[24] and changing certain social conditions—practices and conditions that inhibit the basic flourishing of some people. But discouraging some practices does not mean homogenizing all cultures or objectionably judging cultures by standards external to them. Nor does it mean judging persons by standards they cannot understand or subjecting them to condescending treatment by development practitioners. Instead, it gives people in different cultural contexts much latitude about how to realize flourishing in their particular contexts.

If we recognize that we can respect moral diversity and support deliberative perfectionist interventions, we can adopt a different, more nuanced view of what is at stake in diagnosing and responding to IAPs. This nuanced view allows us to move beyond a dichotomy that asks us to choose between wanting to promote people's flourishing and justifying their coercion. Saying that some peoples' preferences seem inappropriately adaptive need not be a matter of telling individuals or cultures that there is only one "right" way to live. There are a plethora of possible good human lives and a vague and minimal sense of human flourishing allows us to see this. Moving from IAPs to better ones does not have to be about imposing the ideals of some on others. Sometimes it will involve taking strong stances about the acceptability of certain existing behaviors. But improving the flourishing of people with IAPs can be a creative process of imagining how to change preferences *and* preserve values that matter deeply to people and communities.

5 REIMAGINING INTERVENTION: ADAPTIVE PREFERENCES AND THE PARADOXES OF EMPOWERMENT

In this chapter, I elaborate some of the implications of my approach to adaptive preference intervention for contemporary development practice. I argue that the concepts I have developed for identifying and responding to inappropriately adaptive preferences (IAPs) can lend conceptual clarity to discussions of empowerment in development. I demonstrate that ideas from the deliberative perfectionist approach can help us move beyond some of the apparent paradoxes of empowerment identified by feminist development theorists and practitioners. Specifically, I argue that my approach can help us answer two sets of questions that feminist development theorists claim plague women's empowerment projects—questions about the relationship between choice and empowerment and questions about how to identify states of empowerment and disempowerment.

Questioning Empowerment

I begin by describing current feminist conversations in development about the concept of empowerment and its ideological function. To see how these conversations are framed, let us look at a story. The United Nations Development Programme (UNDP) Sri Lanka website tells us about the path to empowerment of one poor woman its programs have helped. The woman is identified as Mrs. K. Ranjani. Before participating in a couple of UNDP projects, she and her family endured harsh conditions and scarce income opportunities. Ranjani says, "When we were living in camps, we lived in a mud hut and were affected by floods and rain. The living conditions were terrible. My husband who is a mason was the sole bread winner [sic] earning only around LKR 1,000 (approx 10 USD) per month. Life was so difficult for us then" (UNDP 2009). Things began to change when Mrs. Ranjani participated in two UNDP interventions. First, she and her husband built a house for themselves through a participatory UNDP project. Second, she joined a UNDP microcredit program and received a small loan to set up her own small grocery store. Her small business has moved her family out of economic precarity. Mrs. Ranjani says of the change, "We now have three meals a day—those days it was a hand-to-mouth existence [sic]. We couldn't send our daughter (7 yrs) [sic] to school, now she attends it regularly" (UNDP 2009). But it is not only her economic life that has changed. Mrs. Ranjani reports an increased sense of self-worth and personal possibilities. "I was not working before. Now I feel empowered as a woman, and my husband and I decide on things together. I see a change in myself—I am a productive member of society and have confidence in myself and this spirit will permeate to my children" (UNDP 2009).

If the story seems familiar, it is because we are inundated with others like it as something called "women's empowerment" becomes integrated into the mainstream development agenda. Stories like Mrs. Ranjani's are increasingly controversial among feminist theorists of development; these theorists have begun to argue that the prevalence of such stories and the vagueness of the term "empowerment" obscure the complex struggles for flourishing real women face. Feminist controversies about empowerment occur against a backdrop of recent mainstream recognition of women's empowerment as a worthy development goal and media celebration of programs that "empower" women. Development agencies increasingly acknowledge that women's empowerment dovetails with other important development goals, such as poverty alleviation and health promotion. The third United Nations Millennium Development Goal stipulates that nations should "promote gender equality and the empowerment of women" (UNDP 2009). Stories like Mrs. Ranjani's make visible the relationship between poverty reduction and women's empowerment in an era where development agencies are trying to present the goals of poverty eradication and women's empowerment as linked. Stories like hers also function to make women's subordinate status in many sociocultural contexts appear as an actionable development problem—to use the words of a publication of the UN Millennium Project, as "a problem with a solution" (Grown, Rao Gupta, et al. 2005).

Some of the feminist controversies sparked by the empowerment discourse concern the ideological function of stories like Mrs. Ranjani's; others concern the lack of conceptual clarity about the term "empowerment" that makes the term susceptible to cooptation by neoliberal development actors and encourages interventions that may not actually transform women's lives. One set of feminist questions about stories like Mrs. Ranjani's is about representation. How accurately do such stories represent the realities of contemporary poor women? Feminists have identified a variety of ways in which the function of such stories may be ideological—that is, that such stories may distort the reality of poor women in ways that serve the interests of the powerful. Some feminist researchers and activists wonder about the extent to which such stories cover over an ambiguous donor stance toward women's empowerment. They wonder whether donor agencies are actually committed to promoting the type of empowerment they advertise. Naila Kabeer, for instance, notes that donor agencies are most likely to take on women's empowerment when it has instrumental value toward the achievement of other development goals (Kabeer 1999, 435). Other feminists ask whether these stories of empowerment function to distract attention from the very real structural impediments to women's flourishing. If helping individual women is repeatedly portrayed as the solution to women's disempowerment, it may seem that women's poverty and subordination can be eradicated without structural change (Poster and Salime 2005). Still other feminist scholars and activists wonder about the extent to which empowerment stories like Mrs. Ranjani's accurately represent the experiences of most women involved in programs designed to empower them. Many women involved in empowerment programs do not experience significant improvements in their lives. Many also experience ambivalent improvements—improvements that undermine their subordination in some areas but retrench it in others.

Another set of feminist questions raised by the empowerment discourse is conceptual. It is to this set of questions that my discussion in this chapter responds. The conceptual questions are about what empowerment is and how to know whether someone is achieving it. Why is it that Mrs. Ranjani's story appears as a success, and how quick should we be to celebrate stories like hers? Whether we celebrate stories like Mrs. Ranjani's will depend partly on how we conceive of empowerment and why we think empowerment is morally desirable. Though donor agencies and academics routinely describe "empowerment" as a development goal, there is limited agreement about what types of life changes constitute empowerment and why such changes are ultimately valuable. This lack of conceptual clarity about empowerment may be seen to have both positive and negative consequences. Some practitioners appreciate the flexibility of an imprecise concept; Kabeer cites a nongovernmental organization (NGO) activist who says, "I like the term 'empowerment' because nobody has defined it clearly yet; so it gives us a space to work it out in action terms before we have to pin ourselves down to what it means" (Kabeer 1999, 436).

On the other hand, there are dangers to using a "fuzzy" definition of empowerment. An unclear concept is particularly susceptible to cooptation by development actors for whom gender is a subsidiary concern. Srilatha Batliwala indicts empowerment as "the most widely used and abused" of development buzzwords, an idea that has been divested of its "cultural specificity, political content, and general[ized] into a set of rituals and steps that simulate its original elements but [lack] the transformative power of the real thing" (Batliwala 2007, 557). In the worst cases the ambiguity of the term may allow neoliberal development actors to surreptitiously define "empowerment" as "increasing people's access to income without structural change" (see for instance, Cornwall 2007b, 42–43). Without a clear definition of empowerment, it is also difficult to distinguish development interventions that are genuinely empowering from those that make only cosmetic changes to the conditions of women's lives. The empirical reality of development is such that programs designed to empower women often have ambivalent effects; even "successful" empowerment programs can increase women's subjection to manipulation by male relatives (say, as in the case of women "forced" by their husbands to participate in microcredit programs)[1] or increase their daily work burdens.[2] A concept of empowerment that is insufficiently nuanced can obscure the ambivalent effects of empowerment interventions and buttress a superficial congratulatory narrative of women's move from states of "disempowerment" to "empowerment." These are just a couple of problems with our lack of conceptual clarity about empowerment, and I do not hope to provide an exhaustive list here. Other dangers feminists have associated with the fuzziness of the term "empowerment" include difficulties in producing qualitative and quantitative indicators of empowerment (Kabeer 1999, 436), the exportation of culturally specific ideals of empowerment, and an inability to counter relativist characterizations of women's oppression and deprivation (Nagar and Raju 2003, 8).

None of this is to suggest that a lack of conceptual clarity is the *sole* or even *primary* cause of ineffective and instrumentalist empowerment interventions. It would be unreasonable to hope for a concept of empowerment that was immune to cooptation, or one that could guarantee effective and ethical development practice. All moral concepts are susceptible to rhetorical cooptation, and all require significant empirical knowledge and goodwill to be appropriately applied in practice. It would also be naïve to ignore the extent to which the setting of the development agenda is a political and politicized process—one that is not only driven by the search for the most reasonable or morally defensible goals. However, I would maintain that a clearer conception of empowerment might be of use to feminist theorists and development practitioners—both analytically and strategically. From a clearer conception of empowerment, practitioners might gain a more reliable sense of what they are looking for when they assess the needs of women who are disempowered and when they evaluate the effects of empowerment interventions. Theorists and practitioners alike may also gain perspective on what is *morally at stake* in empowerment interventions. Feminists may also be able to make more meaningful demands on development agencies that claim to support women's empowerment if they are armed with a more robust conception of it.

My aim here is to contribute to the feminist project of developing a clearer conception of empowerment. I am particularly interested in how the concepts I have developed as part of the deliberative perfectionist approach might help answer two questions about empowering poor women, namely, how are the concepts of empowerment and choice related and how do we identify states of empowerment and disempowerment? In order to illustrate how these conceptual questions arise out of—and matter to—development practice, I draw on examples from two types of interventions: microfinance and income-based interventions and interventions aimed at helping women question and resist established gender hierarchies. My choice of examples from these two areas is deliberate. Microfinance is the area of the women's empowerment agenda that *feminists* most commonly criticize for falling short of feminist goals—for increasing women's susceptibility to male violence and manipulation, for tracking women into traditionally gendered informal sector work, for failing to address women's internalized oppression, and so forth.[3] Conversely, programs aimed at changing women's perceptions of gender hierarchy are those most commonly touted as retaining empowerment's feminist edge.

Empowerment and Adaptive Preferences: A Conceptual Map

In order to explain how the concepts I have developed for identifying and responding to IAPs can clarify the empowerment discourse, I make explicit the relationship between IAPs and empowerment. IAP and empowerment are normative concepts motivated by similar underlying moral assumptions. I have argued that IAP is ultimately a perfectionist concept—that the idea that deprivation-perpetuating preferences are "imposed" on their bearers only makes sense if we assume people have a tendency to choose what is good for them. The notion of empowerment rests on a similar presupposition—that people will tend to pursue their own interests if only they have the power to do so. The concepts of IAP and empowerment derive their meaning from a moral view in which oppression and deprivation prevent people from their acting on behalf of their authentic desires.

I propose a specific relationship between the concepts of empowerment and IAP. Development theorists and practitioners define empowerment in various ways, but underlying most of these definitions is the idea that empowerment is the "process of undoing internalized oppression" (Nagar and Raju 2003, 4). I have defined an IAP as a preference inconsistent with a person's basic flourishing that is causally related to conditions of deprivation; an IAP is a flourish-ing-inconsistent preference that a person would change to a more flourishing-con-sistent one and endorse under conditions conducive to her flourishing. We may understand conditions conducive to flourishing as conditions under which a person has opportunities for flourishing across a number of life-domains and where she understands these opportunities. To link my definition of IAP to the notion of empowerment, I propose that we think of empowerment as the *process of overcoming one or many IAPs through processes that enhance some element of a person's concept of self-entitlement and increase her capacity to pursue her own flourishing.*

Saraswati Raju recounts a real-life story of empowerment that can help us to understand the link between IAP and empowerment I am proposing. Raju describes women in South Asia who live under norms of female seclusion that prohibit interaction with male strangers. According to Raju,

> there are these women who, about five to six years ago, would not even talk face-to-face with male strangers. If they had to respond to any queries from men outside their household and no one else was around, they talked from behind closed doors or remained silent. Sometimes they replied by using a wall as an intermediary: "Bheet, kah do ki Lali ke papa ghar main-nahi hain [wall, tell him that Lali's father is not at home]"!! This denoted reverence towards men, who often did not consider women worth a face-to-face interaction anyway. As a result of interventions by NGOs, along with the central and state governments, the same women now not only talk to male strangers but also offer hospitality and take down mes-sages. (Nagar and Raju 2003, 6)

We may think of these women as having initially possessed IAPs toward their capacities to participate as equals in social or public life. Their transition away from the view that interacting with unknown men is shameful involves the over-coming of these IAPs. Though Raju does not tell us about the processes the NGOs and government used to help these women overcome their shame, we can conjecture that interventions were directed at changing their *consciousness*—at transforming their ideas about women's subordinate status and their conceptions of appropriate behavior for women. If these women's newfound willingness to interact with unknown men came about as a result of interrogating their own self-concepts, we can describe their transition as a process of empowerment. They overcame IAPs toward participation as equals in social life through a process that expanded their perceptions of what they were worthy and capable of.

Not all interventions that help people overcome IAPs are empowering, however, and my view leaves open the possibility of IAP transformation without empowerment. A person may overcome IAPs without any change in self-conception. We can imagine women like those in the foregoing example learning to interact with men through different types of interventions. The NGOs and Indian government might have induced women to change their behavior without changing their consciousness. Imagine an intervention that incentivized interacting with unknown men—say by making health care for one's children dependent on a woman's willingness to invite strange men (health workers, in our case) into her home. We can imagine such an intervention bringing about some changes in women's compliance with norms of seclusion. That is, we can imagine it changing some of their lower-order IAPs. However, we can also imagine the women regarding their recent interaction with male strangers as an enormous sacrifice—as something they have been forced to do as a result of material conditions but that painfully compromises their honor. In a case such as this, the women would overcome an IAP without experiencing empowerment.

The story of women feeling forced to change their behaviors offers one example of IAP change that is not empowering. However, we can also imagine *desirable* IAP interventions that are not empowering. My definition of IAP does not require preferences to be primarily caused by negative self-concepts to count as inappropriately adaptive. People may hold lower-order preferences that are inconsistent with their basic well-being because of simple lacks of knowledge of opportunity; in these cases, IAP transformation may benefit people without necessarily *empowering* them. For instance, we can imagine women who routinely risk disease by serving and eating food off plates that have not been dried and who do so simply because they do not know that this causes disease. An intervention that provides them with knowledge about the spread of bacteria may help them overcome the lower-order IAPs they express in not drying their dishes. The intervention improves their lives but it does not empower them; limited perception of self-worth and agency was not the source of their problem to begin with. Certainly, we can imagine deliberative interventions that teach women about how disease spreads through water that encourage women to cultivate existing agential skills—say by encouraging them to reflect on and publicly discuss how new views about disease might fit into their already existing beliefs about health and disease. My deliberative perfectionist approach recommends such agency-cultivating interventions, but my present point is simply that not all overcoming of IAPs involves empowerment. Only a specific subset of IAPs is susceptible to change by empowerment—IAPs in which people's diminished self-concepts play an important role in inhibiting their flourishing. Also, only specific types of intervention will produce empowerment—interventions that successfully work on people's self-concepts and better enable them to act in their own interests.

A further clarifying remark about how my concept of IAP maps onto the notion of empowerment is in order. I have defended a view of IAPs as *selectively* affecting people's concepts of self-entitlement (see Chapter 3). That is, I do not hold that most IAPs globally undermine people's capacities to act in their own interests. People may pursue their well-being in some domains of life but not others (a woman may vigorously exercise her cognitive capacities by studying at home but still believe that appearing in public would sully her honor). Or, they may rank aspects of their well-being as less important than those of some people and more important than those of others (a woman may believe that her nourishment is less important than her husband's but more important than her daughters'). My idea of IAPs as selectively affecting people's pursuit of their flourishing limits my definition of empowerment in an important way. It discourages us from thinking of people as completely empowered or disempowered. My definition of empowerment does not suggest that a person must overcome all of her IAPs in order to arrive at some end-state called "empowerment." Rather, it suggests that people can be engaged in *processes* of empowerment without thereby having overcome all of their IAPs.

I will now show how the concepts I have developed as part of my deliberative perfectionist approach to IAP intervention can help us answer some pressing analytical questions about empowerment that have arisen in recent development practice. We will have a more precise understanding of what my deliberative perfectionist approach offers if we divide the approach into four discrete parts. First, my deliberative perfectionist approach includes a *selective and perfectionist definition of IAP*. My deliberative perfectionist approach is based on a particular characterization of what IAPs are and what makes them worthy of public concern. As I stated in the previous paragraphs, I see IAPs as (1) preferences that are inconsistent with a person's basic flourishing, (2) preferences that were formed under conditions unconducive to that person's basic flourishing, and (3) preferences that people are likely to reverse and endorse on exposure to better conditions. Perfectionism explains *why* we expect people to ultimately endorse better preferences; people have a tendency toward their basic flourishing. My definition of IAP also stipulates that most IAPs have selective effects—that is, they affect people's well-being in some domains of life or vis-à-vis certain other people.

Second, my approach includes an *acknowledgement of the epistemological difficulties inherent in understanding the preferences of others and recommends deliberation with deprived people in order to help mitigate it*. I insist that third parties cannot usually understand *why* people have the preferences they do simply by observing their behavior. People may act in ways that are inconsistent with their well-being for a whole host of reasons—ranging from straightforward opportunity lacks, to strategies where they trade off one good to obtain another, to deeply ingrained beliefs about their own unworthiness. I argue that responsible judgments about IAP begin by placing deprived people's expressed preferences into the provisional category of *suspect preferences*—preferences that seem inappropriately adaptive but have not been proven to be such. I maintain that the first-person perspectives of deprived people are key to understanding people's preferences and designing appropriate interventions.

Third, I claim that IAP interventions should be guided by a *deliberative perfectionist conception of human flourishing*. This conception of human flourishing should be used to help determine whether people's preferences are consistent with flourishing and to provide a framework for thinking about what people's preferences should be changed *to*. The conception of flourishing should be arrived at through a cross-cultural deliberative process and be *substantively minimal, justificatorily minimal, plural,* and *vague*. This type of conception of human flourishing *underdetermines* what should happen in any particular intervention. It offers a schematic notion of what basic goods human beings should strive to achieve, but it does not offer specific prescriptions for achieving them.

Fourth, I prescribe *that people with IAPs should play a role in deciding what should be done about their IAPs*. Interventions that people have participated in designing are more likely to be effective and produce life changes that people with IAPs can endorse. When people with IAPs participate in envisioning futures for themselves they can begin to imagine paths to flourishing that are compatible with their existing thick values.

The Relationship Between Choice and Empowerment

People who are disempowered encounter barriers to acting in their own interests. The barriers they encounter may be internal ones (like negative concepts of self-entitlement), external ones (like opportunity lacks), or some combination of the two. Most definitions of empowerment converge on these ideas. However, theorists of empowerment struggle to relate the concept of empowerment to other concepts in our existing moral repertoire. One way of linking empowerment to familiar moral concepts is to describe disempowerment as a lack of choice and the process of empowerment as a type of choice enhancement. Kabeer offers one choice-based definition of empowerment. According to her, empowerment is "the process by which those who have been denied the opportunity to make strategic choices acquire such an ability" (Kabeer 1999, 435). Choice-based definitions of empowerment capture some very important things about what the disempowered state is like. By reminding us that the choices faced by disempowered people are few, they illuminate the fact that disempowered people face very limited option sets. Choice-based definitions of empowerment also militate against "blaming" oppressed and deprived people for failures to flourish; such definitions preclude the view that disempowered people fail to act in their own interests because they are simply not trying to achieve well-being.

However, describing empowerment as the process by which people who previously lacked choice come to obtain it has created some puzzles for practitioners. One puzzle is about how to distinguish disempowerment from the genuine desire not to flourish. Do all people who fail to act in their interests do so for reasons that are out of their conscious control? Is it possible to tell the difference between failures to flourish caused by disempowerment and those caused by a deep desire not to flourish? How? Another puzzle concerns the fact that disempowered people do seem to make choices—even if these choices do not challenge the social order that oppresses or deprives them. If choice defines empowerment, are women who choose to collude in their own oppression and deprivation empowered by their choice to collude? Does it follow from this that women who choose not to challenge the established order would not benefit from empowerment interventions? A third puzzle is about the *types* of choices necessary for empowerment. What types of choices should development projects make available to the disempowered? These are the puzzles about the relationship between choice and empowerment that concepts from my deliberative perfectionist approach can help us solve.

Distinguishing Difference from Disempowerment: Is Choice the Solution?

Those trying to develop practical indicators of empowerment struggle to distinguish differences in preferences that seem morally unproblematic from those that manifest disempowerment. We see this in the work of empowerment theorists who take women's household decision-making authority as an indicator of empowerment. They ask whether all women who do not participate—or participate only minimally—in household decision making are disempowered. Is a woman who delegates managing household expenses to her husband so that she will have more time to play soccer just as disempowered as a woman who acquiesces to her husband's management of the household budget because she believes a dutiful wife does not dispute her husband's wishes? Empowerment theorists want to answer this question in the negative. Ruth Alsop and Nina Heinsohn (2005) have attempted to develop an indicator that would allow empowerment practitioners to distinguish the former case from the latter. They suggest that practitioners ask, "If you wished to make decisions with respect to X, could you?" (Alkire 2007a, 14). Presumably, the woman soccer player in the first case above would report that she could make household budgetary decisions if she wanted to where the deferential woman in the latter case would not.

Alsop and Heinsohn's indicator—and others like it—operationalizes a conceptual distinction between disempowerment and simple failure to take an interest in some aspect of one's own flourishing. But what is the conceptual distinction underlying this intuitive case-based distinction? Empowerment theorists typically try to cast the distinction in this way: the former (the soccer player's nonparticipation in household decision making) is caused by choice or preference and the latter (the deferential wife's nonparticipation) is not. According to Kabeer, "we are interested in possible *inequalities* in people's capacity to make choices rather than in *differences* in the choices they make" (Kabeer 1999, 439 emphasis in original). She later writes that we want to "disentangle differentials which reflect differences in *preferences* from those which embody a denial of choice" (Kabeer 1999, 439, emphasis added).

This way of distinguishing between *chosen* or *preferred* flourishing deficits and those caused by inequality may be intuitively appealing, but it does not offer a practical or coherent way of capturing the distinction between difference and disempowerment that empowerment theorists are interested in. For one thing, Kabeer's distinction seems to categorize all differences in flourishing that are chosen or preferred as "just differences." This contradicts much of what we know about IAP. Her use of the word "prefer" in the excerpts above suggests that people cannot prefer disempowerment. To read her charitably, we might think of her as meaning that the difference between preferred difference and disempowerment is that preferred difference manifests higher-order positive attitudes toward one's lower-order behaviors. On this reading, Kabeer might be saying that disempowerment is the state of having disempowering lower-order behaviors absent higher-order endorsements of them. But even this description of chosen or preferred differences as "just differences" is at odds with one of the most basic concerns of Kabeer and other empowerment theorists: a concern with the deeper psychological forms of IAP. Virtually all empowerment theorists acknowledge that disempowerment can function *through* the preferences and desires of oppressed and deprived people. A woman in a patriarchal society may actually believe women should submit to her husband's authority and thus refuse to dispute her husband's choice to spend a significant portion of their income on risky investments.[4] Most empowerment theorists would agree that this woman is disempowered. And yet, this woman clearly has a conception of the good expressed in the preference not to contradict her husband's wishes. The fact that she can prefer disempowering behavior suggests that a distinction between preference and disempowerment does not really get at the distinction between "just difference" and disempowerment that the empowerment theorists are trying to capture.

Kabeer would certainly reply to my criticism by referring to the concept of choice to clarify the distinction between preferred difference and disempowerment. She might say that the deferential woman in my household decision-making example did not choose to prefer to submit to her husband's authority. She states explicitly that preferences based on doxa—that is, prevailing social beliefs—do not reflect real *choices* because people have not imagined alternatives to their doxic beliefs (Kabeer 1999, 441). We will return to the question of whether choices based on doxa are real choices in the following section on self-subordinating choices. But for the moment, let us ask whether we can plausibly hold that preferences against flourishing that have been reflectively chosen are those that reflect unproblematic difference rather than disempowerment.

Even this way of distinguishing difference from disempowerment has its flaws. If we think of choice as a conscious process of deciding and imagining alternatives, it remains fully plausible for a person to *decide* to have preferences against flourishing and be disempowered. The woman who believes women should submit to their husbands may well have thought over this belief and done so with the knowledge that not all women believe this; she may have known that the women in town, or the women of another religion, were more empowered in their households. But if the prevailing custom in her area is female submission, and if her husband expects it, most empowerment theorists would continue to maintain that this woman is disempowered—despite having knowledge about alternatives. It is fully plausible that this woman lives in a social world that penalizes nondeferential women *and* that she consciously reflects about whether she wants to be a deferential woman.

Moreover, it seems practically difficult to determine whether a person made a deliberate choice not to flourish—or not to value her flourishing—at some determinate moment in the past. We develop coherent personalities through some combination of deliberate choice and contingency, but we do not always remember which is which. If we value aspects of our personalities that were thrust upon us by contingency, we may come to endorse them as though they were choices. Conversely, we may disidentify with deliberate choices we made about our characters for a variety of reasons. If it is this difficult to determine whether we made these choices about ourselves, it is likely even more difficult for third parties—like development practitioners—to make them about us.

Further, as I argued in Chapter 2 (in this volume), it is implausible that all unchosen preferences are preferences we would describe as disempowering. For instance, we would be unlikely to say that a woman who accepted doxic beliefs that encouraged her to participate equally in making household decisions was disempowered. This, too, suggests that the identification of disempowerment with the lack of choice does not fully capture the intuitive distinction between disempowerment and unproblematic preference difference.

My perfectionist definition of IAP gives us a more direct and more practical route to distinguishing preferences that are "just different" from those that evince disempowerment. I define IAPs as preferences that are inconsistent with a person's basic flourishing that are causally related to conditions nonconducive to her basic flourishing. In other words, preferences that reveal underlying disempowerment are causally related to lacks of opportunity. When practitioners try to determine whether a person's lack of interest in some aspect of her flourishing is "just difference," I would suggest that they are really trying to determine whether that person has the opportunity to flourish in a given domain and whether she knows that she has it. This is precisely what Alsop and Heinsohn's indicator asks. When practitioners ask a woman whether she could make decisions about how to spend her household budget if she wanted to, they are asking about the presence of opportunities for flourishing—not about the presence or absence of choice.

Does it make a difference whether we speak of the presence or absence of opportunities for flourishing or the presence or absence of choice? We frequently speak of people who lack opportunities as lacking choices, so it may seem that we are dealing with a purely linguistic difference. I would argue, however, that speaking of disempowerment as the absence of choice is misleading because it covers over an important ambiguity within the concept of choice. There is an important difference between *having* a choice and *making* a choice. The rhetoric of disempowerment as lack of choice obscures this difference. To have a choice is to have acceptable options; to make a choice is to go through a particular type of deliberative process. A person needs to *have* some options in order to make a choice, but a person can make choices without having a range of *acceptable* options. To characterize non-flourishing preferences that are "just different" according to their chosen nature may misleadingly suggest that preferences that are disempowering have little or no deliberative content. This is morally problematic for a host of reasons, but one of them is that it discourages us from seeing choices that people make under difficult circumstances as reflective.

Further, the conflation of having and making choices in empowerment discourse may make it seem as though "different" preferences diverge from disempowered ones because of the presence or absence of a certain historical event. It makes it seem as though development practitioners who want to separate unproblematic difference from disempowerment need to find out whether people who are not flourishing made conscious choices at some moment in the past that caused them to have the preferences they currently have. As I mentioned earlier, this path is riddled with epistemological difficulties. But even if it were possible to find out which preferences resulted from deliberate choices and which did not, I would remind us that the results would not track our intuitions about empowerment and disempowerment. People can make deliberate choices against their flourishing under conditions unconducive to flourishing that we should still describe as disempowered. Let us return to the example of the woman who chooses submissiveness while aware of the existence of hypothetical alternatives. She may know that not all women are submissive, but she may also know that submissiveness is her best shot at honor and a nonconflictual marriage in her community. Most empowerment theorists would be compelled to say that she is disempowered *and* that she has made a choice.

My own approach suggests a different path to finding out whether preferences are caused by injustice or just difference. It begins from the assumption that some preferences—preferences inconsistent with basic flourishing—are particularly likely to be causally related to oppression or deprivation. This is what is *perfectionist* in my perfectionist definition of IAP. The idea is that people tend to seek their basic flourishing and that choices inconsistent with basic flourishing are unlikely to persist when people have access to—and an understanding of—objectively better conditions. On my view, finding out whether a preference is the result of "difference" or disempowerment is emphatically *not* a matter of finding out whether it is the result of a choice. Rather, it is a matter of finding out what opportunities were available when the preference was formed and what opportunities are available now. I would maintain that this type of information is much more easily accessible to development practitioners than information about what types of deliberative processes deprived people engaged in the past.

My approach stipulates that practitioners can know something about whether preferences likely reflect disempowerment simply by examining the content of preferences and the conditions under which these preferences were formed/ obtain. If people living under unjust conditions express preferences inconsistent with their flourishing, it is likely not because they are "just different." Most empowerment theorists share this assumption, though they make its moral underpinnings explicit to varying degrees. For instance, Kabeer writes that differences in "basic functioning achievements ... can be taken as evidence of underlying inequalities ..." (Kabeer 1999, 439).[5] There is broad agreement that most choices against flourishing are not "just differences." My approach only adds a more explicit account of the moral presuppositions underlying this agreement. My perfectionist definition of IAP makes clear that we need a normative conception of what human beings tend to desire if we want to claim that people are not deeply attached to their sub-flourishing expressed preferences formed under sub-flourishing conditions.

However, my approach does not hold that *all* preferences inconsistent with basic flourishing formed under poor conditions reflect disempowerment rather than "just difference." My approach leaves much room for epistemic uncertainty. This is why I distinguish between what I call "suspect preferences" and preferences that are genuinely inappropriately adaptive. I argue that non-flourishing preferences formed under poor conditions are likely results of disempowerment. But practitioners cannot know for certain that such preferences result from disempowerment without an actual encounter with people who have suspect preferences. This is why there is an important role for indicators like Alsop and Heinsohn's household decision-making indicator; one way to find out more about the relationship between people's preferences and deprivation is to ask them whether they would choose more flourishing-consistent behaviors if they could.

Empowerment practitioners want to be able to distinguish preferences inconsistent with flourishing that are caused by disempowerment from those that are simply different. My approach suggests a two-tiered approach for making such distinctions in practice. First, it suggests that preferences inconsistent with flourishing formed under poor conditions merit suspicion, and it offers a perfectionist account of why these preferences are particularly worthy of suspicion. Second, it suggests that practitioners need the first-person perspectives of people with suspect preferences to get clearer about the relationship between their preferences and deprivation. However, I do not claim that either of these steps will reveal with absolute certainty whether people's preferences would change under better conditions; deprived people may find that they are more deeply attached to self-deprivation than even they knew, or that what practitioners see as "better conditions" may actually require objective sacrifices from deprived people that practitioners do not understand. Still, my framework offers some theoretical basis for a practical distinction, while resisting the ambiguities inherent in the prevailing conflation of morally unproblematic preference difference with choice.

Is It Possible to Choose Disempowerment?

We have seen one problem with describing disempowerment as the lack of choice; it offers a confusing route for distinguishing flourishing-inconsistent preferences that are caused by disempowerment from those caused by interpersonal difference. A further problem with describing disempowerment as the lack of choice concerns the status of self-subordinating choices. People sometimes behave in ways inconsistent with their basic flourishing as a result of deliberate choices. But if empowerment is the capacity to make deliberate choices, are deliberate choices to engage in behaviors inconsistent with flourishing, by definition, empowering? Kawango Agot (2007) poses this question with reference to a case about female genital cutting in Tanzania in the 1980s. She cites Nypan's study that found that young women recipients of education aimed at empowering them were increasingly choosing to undergo clitoridectomy (Agot 2007, 290). These young women perceived genital cutting as "empowering and giving them some sense of self-worth" (Agot 2007, 290). The reasons these young women would perceive gains from genital cutting are not entirely mysterious; educated women had diffi-culty finding employment and did not have a particularly high social status. In a world where marriage was one of the young women's best economic prospects and genital cutting promised increased marriageability, the choice to undergo clitoridectemy evinced a certain rationality.

It would seem that a purely choice-based conception of empowerment (at least one that considered empowerment as an identifiable "end-state") would stipulate that these young women have become empowered. They are educated, and they have clearly reflected on the costs and benefits of their decision. Indeed, a choice-based definition of empowerment would make it seem that the young women in the above case are *more* empowered than women who do not undergo clitoridectemy simply because it is not popular in their communities. Recall that Kabeer states: "we are interested in possible *inequalities* in people's capacity to make choices rather than in *differences* in the choices they make" (Kabeer 1999, 439 emphasis in original).

But the conclusion that severe female genital cutting is empowering is highly counterintuitive. It seems that the situation of the young women in the case is para-digmatically disempowering; the situation prohibits young women from making choices that will unambiguously advance their interests. They can get financial secu-rity at the expense of their sexual health or vice versa, but they cannot get both. Moreover, the choice to participate in genital cutting perpetuates a social order that subordinates women. We are faced with a puzzle. The empowerment-as-choice discourse assumes that people will pursue their own interests when they have choices about whether to do so. And yet here we have what seems to be a case of women making choices against their interests. Should development practitioners celebrate the success of empowerment programs that result in women choosing to undermine their health, sexual functioning, and status as equals with men?

Concepts from my deliberative perfectionist approach can help us to think beyond this puzzle. I want to suggest that the very appearance of paradox in the foregoing case is based on an imprecise characterization of the choice to have one's genitals cut. My definition of IAP as *selective* can help us locate this impre-cision. The apparent puzzle depicts the choice to have one's genitals cut as a choice not to advance one's interests. But to accept this depiction is to oversimplify the choice the young women are faced with. The women in the case are not choosing genital cutting *for its own sake*. The choice to have one's genitals cut under a particular set of circumstances does not signal a desire to have one's genitals cut under all possible circumstances. It signals a preference for genital cutting over other available options, not over all other possible options.

My definition of IAPs as selective self-entitlement deficits clarifies how the young women's choice is not a choice against flourishing per se. I argued in Chapter 3 (in this volume) that oppressive systems sometimes reward people for self-depriving behavior. There are certain behaviors that are inconsistent with basic flourishing—say, the choice to undernourish oneself, the choice to destroy one's capacity for sexual functioning, or the refusal to develop one's affective capacities. However, bad conditions can transform behaviors inconsistent with basic flourishing into *means for achieving* other functionings constitutive of flourishing. The young women in our case may value genital cutting as a means to feelings of self-worth and stable access to shelter, affective attachment, and nutrition—all functionings that contribute positively to flourishing. Yes, the young women in the case fail to achieve basic flourishing; when we compare their overall states of life to a conception of basic flourishing, we find that they fall short. But it does not follow from this fact that they are not trying to achieve their own flourishing. They are trying to achieve flourishing in some domains, but, in order to do so, they must undermine their flourishing in certain others. Put simply, they may be doing the best they can to advance their interests under circumstances that do not allow them to unambiguously advance those interests.

On my definition of IAP, we can say that the young women express IAPs without saying that they make a deliberate choice not to advance their interests. Rather, they make a deliberate choice given a very limited option set. The young women express preferences inconsistent with basic flourishing in general (and this means that they might benefit from a carefully designed development intervention), but they do not simply fail to value their own basic flourishing. This realization can shed some light on our current puzzle about empowerment. Are the young women who choose clitoridectemy disempowered because they have few options for unambiguously pursuing their flourishing or are they empowered because they have exercised agential capacities by making a choice? My analysis of IAP allows us to say both. The young women are empowered to the extent that they improve their overall well-being, that is—overcome IAPs that they previously had. If the young women exercise agential and deliberative skills that they previously did not exercise, and if effectively secure self-respect and income they could not otherwise secure, they are engaged in an empowering *process*. But they are not straightforwardly empowered. They are disempowered to the extent that choices that would allow them to unambiguously advance their interests are unavailable—to the extent that there remain IAPs for them to overcome. This "both empowered and disempowered" conclusion dovetails with a recent trend in the empowerment literature toward seeking an incremental, less black-and-white, definition of empowerment (Cornwall 2007a, 164–165; Nagar and Raju 2003, 7–9;). I do not intend my "both" conclusion in this case as any sort of apology for clitoridectemy. My point is rather that clitoridectemy may be a self-interested choice under circumstances where it is a route to threshold levels of other goods that there are few other options for attaining.

Notice, however, that my "both" conclusion is possible only if we move away from making choice—or even choice in one's interests—the defining characteristic of empowerment. The young women in the foregoing case make a reflective, self-interested choice. If we wish to maintain that these women have not "arrived" at total empowerment, we need to be able to distinguish between sufficient opportunities for basic flourishing and the option set actually available to an individual.[6] We need an idea of what basic flourishing looks like and the knowledge that circumstances may deprive individuals of sufficient options to achieve it across all domains. A person may engage in behaviors intended to advance her interests without achieving basic flourishing because of a limited option set (or because of a misperception of her interests, but that is another type of case).

Proponents of choice-based conceptions of empowerment offer their own way out of the paradox posed by chosen self-subordination—an account designed to let us maintain that such behaviors evidence disempowerment. Their way out of the paradox is an alternative to my own, but it is highly problematic. Their account stems from the belief I mentioned earlier—that preferences based on doxa reflect disempowerment. Kabeer argues that self-subordinating choices related to gender are not really choices; they are typically motivated by doxa. She reasons that the capacity to choose requires alternatives to choose from; meanwhile, doxic norms—by their very nature—present themselves as without alternatives. For Kabeer, self-subordinating behaviors that accord with doxa are not chosen and thus not empowering.

Both my definition of IAP and Kabeer's notion of doxic preference offer accounts of self-harming choices as disempowering. My account has two important advantages over Kabeer's, however. First, my analysis counts a larger array of cases of self-subordinating behavior as disempowering. Certainly, not all cases of self-subordinating behavior under bad social conditions involve uncritical allegiance to doxa; indeed, the young women in the clitoridectemy case we have been discussing know that it is possible for women to live fulfilling lives without undergoing genital cutting. Many of the young women in Nypan's study had uncut mothers, so it would be false to assert that the girls in the study could not imagine alternatives to clitoridectemy. Second, as I mentioned previously, it is not clear that all behaviors made in accordance with doxa are disempowering. The idea that women should earn their own incomes is part of the doxa of some communities; should we conclude that women from such communities who do not imagine alternatives to earning their own incomes are necessarily disempowered? My conception of IAP as selective allows us to hold that self-subordinating choices can have selective empowering effects under disempowering conditions. But the perfectionism of my conception of IAP allows us to insist that a situation where one cannot seek one's basic flourishing across multiple domains is a tragic one.

Which Choices Matter for Empowerment?

Up to this point, I have treated choice-based definitions of empowerment as though their proponents maintain that empowerment consists in the simple presence or absence of choice. But there is an increasing awareness among empowerment theorists and practitioners that not all types of choices are equally important to women's empowerment. Andrea Cornwall's ethnographic work (2007b) calls development practitioners to think more carefully about the *types* of choices poor women need to improve their lives. In Cornwall's view, contemporary empowerment discourse—particularly the strain of it focused on "giving women choices" through microcredit—confuses two types of choices: strategic and tactical. She illustrates the distinction between tactical and strategic choices with narratives from the lives of Yoruba women traders in Nigeria. One woman's decisions about whether to become a trader and what to trade illustrates the difference between tactical and than strategic choice. Iya Obatta became a trader as a child, because she did not want to return to a school where the prefects would beat her (Cornwall 2007b, 36). Her grandmother did not encourage her to go back to school afterward, because her grandmother appreciated her help with her business as a merchant. After Iya Obatta got married, her husband did not want her to travel as much, so she switched to selling coconut oil and soap in her home village. Then she sustained an injury from making soap, and her soap-making materials had dried up by the time she recovered. So she switched paths again and decided to buy bags and resell them. But when she arrived in Lagos to buy the bags, she discovered the bags were too expensive. She bought shoes instead—mostly because her friend was buying shoes. She has been selling shoes ever since.

Iya Obatta's career has been dictated mostly by what Cornwall, following de Certeau, would call tactics rather than strategies. Tactical choices are choices people make to "scrape by and get on with their lives" (Cornwall 2007b, 42). They are choices by which a person manages and responds to contingency and limited options. Strategic choices, in contrast, are choices that involve long-term goal setting and the deliberate weighing of alternative paths for achieving one's goals. They are choices about the path a person wants her life to take—like the choice of a career. People need alternatives and stability in order to make strategic choices; Iya Obatta did not choose trading as one career among many, and her situation was so precarious that she frequently had to change what she was selling based on factors like her husband's desires and the threat of destitution.

What characterizes the "strategic" choices women like Iya Obatta need in order to be empowered? Cornwall suggests that small-scale choices—like the choice between selling soap or shoes—are insufficient. Small injections of capital of the type favored by microcredit projects, though they may help women make better tactical choices about what to trade, will not give women all the choices they need in order to be empowered. Rather, Cornwall suggests that women like Iya Obatta need opportunities to renegotiate their affective relationships (recall how the wishes of Iya Obatta's husband and grandmother shaped her economic life)[7] and to imagine different career possibilities for themselves.[8]

The shift toward specifying types of choices constitutive of empowerment reveals something very important about empowerment as a moral concept. It is this: empowerment aims at improving people's opportunities for well-being or flourishing, not simply at multiplying their choices. The rhetorical emphasis on choice may sometimes serve the purposes of feminist development advocacy well. However, it is not only choice that feminist proponents of empowerment are concerned with making available. It is a specific type of choice, deemed meaningful or strategic. But what conceptually distinguishes meaningful or strategic choice from other less important types of choice? We know that these more important choices are higher-order choices, but what underlying moral commitments do we need to motivate this focus on higher-order choices? Put differently, on what grounds do we justify an interest in the *types* of choices available to people, rather than their mere number?

A conception of human flourishing like the one that underpins my deliberative perfectionist approach can be of some use here. A conception of flourishing can help us identify realms of life in which choice is particularly important. The notion of strategic life choice seems to rest on an assumption about domains of choice, not simply orders of choice. Empowerment theorists must mean something other than simply "higher-order choices" when they speak of meaningful or strategic choices, for a person can possess a multitude of higher-order choices and still lack strategic choices. For example, we can imagine Iya Obatta having plenty of higher-order choices and engaging in higher-order reflections about what types of objects to trade; she might ask herself whether she should sell brown shoes, whether she wants to want to sell brown shoes, to want and so on. Cornwall would probably not conclude from this that Iya Obatta had sufficient strategic life choices. The reason for this would seem to be that choices about the minutia concerning which objects to sell, regardless of order, do not seem to be critical to determining whether a person's life goes well or whether she has control over that life. It appears that there are some specific domains of life we think it is particularly important to have higher-order choices about—like the choice of a career, a spouse, the use of one's body, etc., I would suggest that we need a conception of human flourishing to know what these domains might be. If we know what types of activities human beings need access to in order for their lives to go well, we can begin to enumerate domains of meaningful or strategic choice.[9]

In order to distinguish strategic choices from other types of choices, development practitioners need a conception of flourishing. A conception of flourishing can offer an account of why choice is particularly important in some domains. But a conception of flourishing has also has another important role to play in facilitating the identification of strategic choices. I would argue that strategic choices are not just characterized by being choices about what to do in certain domains of life. Rather, I would suggest, strategic choice means the presence of opportunities *to flourish* in certain domains of life. To help us to understand this point, we may imagine that a person has a number of choices in a domain of life important to her flourishing, but none of these choices will actually allow her to flourish. Say income is a domain of life in which people need choices. We can imagine a woman who has access to a number of different career choices, but none will give her an adequate income to feed herself. The woman in this case certainly has choices, and they are choices about something important, but I do not think Cornwall would refer to this woman as having *strategic* choices. Having strategic choices means having *acceptable* choices in important domains of life. We need a conception of human flourishing to make sense of the idea of strategic choice—both to identify important life domains and to identify and imagine acceptable options in those domains.

I would further suggest that not just any conception of human flourishing will do for this task. Development practitioners need a sense of what the domains of meaningful choice are, but a very thick, context-specific conception of human flourishing can function to preclude accurate assessment of the presence or absence of strategic choice. We can imagine a list of domains of choice necessary for flourishing that was appropriate for use in one sociocultural context and totally inappropriate for another. For instance, the choice of whether or not to become a petty trader is clearly a strategic choice for Iya Obatta and other women of her community, but it is less clearly a choice that must be available to people where this is not a common profession. A development intervention that focused on teaching women to reflectively weigh the costs and benefits of petty trading in a community where petty trading is neither common nor profitable would be misplaced.

On the other hand, we can imagine a more general way of conceptualizing the domain of life in which Iya Obatta's flourishing could be improved. We might say that people need to be able to make long-term choices about their livelihoods, incomes, or even access to nutrition and shelter. A deliberative conception of flourishing like the one I advocate allows practitioners to identify important domains of choice, but to do so in a way that is attentive to contextual detail. Development practitioners who want to help people become empowered—that is, to overcome IAPs—need a way of distinguishing the trivial choices those people have been denied from the strategic ones. They also need a general sense of what types of opportunities would improve their possibilities for acting in their interests. A vague conception of human flourishing can help development practitioners make such inevitable distinctions without overdetermining the needs of a group of people in any particular situation. Indeed, as I argued in the first chapter, the vagueness of the conception of the good creates an important role for deliberation with the deprived. Such deliberation that can help practitioners and deprived people develop a shared understanding of which concrete forms of strategic choice are particularly likely to improve people's chances at faring well in life.

Identifying States of Empowerment and Disempowerment

We have seen how the concepts I have developed clarify the relationship between empowerment and choice. My perfectionist definition of IAP distinguishes disempowerment from less morally significant forms of interpersonal difference and helps explain why we consider self-subordinating preferences to be (at least partially) disempowering. A deliberative perfectionist conception of human flourishing can also help development practitioners distinguish the strategic choices people need to become empowered from trivial choices.

Another set of conceptual puzzles at the heart of contemporary development practice does not explicitly concern the relationship between empowerment and choice. Rather, it concerns how to identify states of empowerment and disempowerment. Is access to income a sufficient determinant of empowerment, as much of the contemporary microcredit discourse suggests? Can practitioners develop an understanding of the extent of women's empowerment by focusing on objective data alone? That is, what do we make of cases where people's objective well-being seems to decrease but people report increased feelings of empowerment? And to what extent do practitioners need to know what the "finish-line" (to use Agot's term) of empowerment looks like in order to help women improve their lives? Can practitioners help women become empowered without simply molding them according to a pre-established model of empowerment that is familiar to them?

These theoretical questions have arisen mostly in development conversations about how to *measure* empowerment—particularly conversations about how to develop quantitative and qualitative indicators of empowerment for donor agencies.[10] The current conversation on measures of empowerment focuses on developing cross-cultural and contextual indicators of empowerment. Such indicators are necessary for evaluating the success of development projects. However, it is difficult to come up with appropriate indicators without a fairly robust sense of what those indicators are meant to represent. As many development theorists and practitioners note, some of the controversies surrounding the measurement of empowerment arise from deeper theoretical puzzles about well-being. I wish to make clear that I do not intend my discussion of what is philosophically at stake in envisioning empowerment as a substitute for the search for practical measures of empowerment that can guide development planning. I propose only that my concepts from my approach to IAP intervention can illuminate the deep conceptual issues from which many problems with measuring empowerment stem.

Is Income Empowerment?

A survey of mainstream development writing might lead one to conclude that "disempowerment" simply means "asset poverty"—the lack of material goods and entitlements like income.[11] The term "women's empowerment project" is increasingly synonymous with "microcredit project," as though infusions of capital in and of themselves increased power for women. We need only revisit the tale of Mrs. Ranjani, recounted at the outset of this chapter, to see the equation of credit and power in action; UNDP reports that Mrs. Ranjani is empowered because she received a loan and now runs a small shop. Further, the equation of asset poverty with disempowerment is not only rhetorical; it does not only appear in public relations materials aimed at painting a celebratory picture of microcredit.[12] Even some academic studies aimed at measuring empowerment elide asset poverty and disempowerment. Sabina Alkire argues that a serious problem in attempts to measure women's agency is the scholarly use of poverty indicators as proxy measures of women's agency. "Many proxy measures of women's agency are actually *identical* to measures used in traditional poverty analysis, such as years of schooling or employment status or asset ownership or health status" (Alkire 2007a, 10, emphasis in original).

The more sophisticated versions of the claim that poverty reduction produces empowerment are not based on a literal equation of money with power. Rather, they are based on the idea, as Alkire states, that types of asset poverty are "proxy measures" of women's disempowerment. The assumptions motivating a focus on income-generation and other traditional anti-poverty measures as measures of empowerment are double. First, development practitioners widely held, until at least the 1990s, that women with money would have more power to negotiate gender relations within their households (Sen 1990, 144). Second, it was (and continues to be) widely held that women with incomes would automatically pursue their well-being, health, and so on.

We must recognize, however, that both of these assumptions are about empirical facts—and thus subject to questioning on the basis of data. Data increasingly suggest that access to income and other assets can coexist with other deficits in flourishing that feminists identify as disempowering. A famous study by Maria Mies in the 1980s found that women who earned incomes through home-based garment work continued to view their contributions to their households as less important than that of their husbands (Mies 1982, 100–116). Richa Nagar discusses how poor women in the Indian state of Chitakroot involved in empowerment programs, women "who were forging ahead in their literacy and savings programs, their newsletters, their handpump mechanics, masons and caterers were still being beaten, raped, and burned in their own homes" (Nagar 2000, 347). More recently, much has been made of a study by Anne-Marie Goetz and Rina Sen Gupta showing that a significant percentage of women beneficiaries of microcredit programs transferred their loans into their male relatives' names (Goetz and Sen Gupta 1996, 49). This seemed to show that infusions of income need not alter women's submission to men within the household.[13]

Feminist development theorists have drawn upon studies like these, not only to argue for better-targeted empowerment programs, but also to argue for a more nuanced conception of empowerment. They increasingly argue for what are called "multidimensional" measures of poverty and agency. Alkire writes, "agency, like poverty, can lay differently across different spheres of life: a person can be fully empowered as a wife and mother, but excluded from the labor force by social conventions, and recently empowered to vote by political processes" (Alkire 2007b, 171).

My definition of IAPs and my deliberative perfectionist conception of human flourishing help explain what is morally at stake in the search for multidimensional indicators of empowerment. Though we do not know in advance what the contents of a conception of the good that has been cross-culturally deliberated upon will be, we can anticipate that it will suggest that flourishing is plural—that is, that it consists in doing well across a wide variety of different domains. If we acknowledge that flourishing has plural constituents, there is a solid moral basis from which to argue against expecting interventions in any single domain to produce empowerment. To be sure, the boundaries that separate one domain of life from another are somewhat porous. The effects of interventions in one domain may sometimes permeate into others; in many cases, for instance, increased income will translate into improvements in a poor person's bodily health.

However, my notion of IAP helps us to see why we should not always expect interventions in one domain to spill over into others. I argued in Chapter 3 that IAPs are *selective* self-entitlement deficits. One part of my claim there was that people may engage in behaviors that reproduce their deprivation but may do so for self-interested reasons. Under bad circumstances, people may trade away flourishing in one domain to secure it another. Key to this notion was the idea that deprived people often face serious trade-offs where basic flourishing in one domain comes at the cost of basic flourishing in others. What we can see with a notion of well-being trade-offs before us is that interventions in the choice-situations of deprived people may sometimes create new trade-offs. So, for instance, a woman who receives a microcredit loan may have a high level of bodily safety but a low level of income before she receives the loan. After she receives the loan, she may increase her income, but her husband may feel an increased need to control her and thus may begin committing acts of violence against her.[14] To effectively assess such a woman's well-being, development practitioners need not only assess her access to income; they need to assess the effect of access to income on her well-being in other domains.

If practitioners understand decisions about well-being as involving cross-domain trade-offs—as my definition of IAP suggests that they should—there is reason for them to be attentive to how increases in flourishing in one domain may adversely, or unequally, affect flourishing in others. The income-as-empowerment school of development thinking assumes that well-being changes uniformly—where increases in income should translate into concomitant increases in other domains of flourishing. Attention to the types of trade-offs highlighted by my definition of IAP asks instead that practitioners be aware that flourishing does not move uniformly across domains and that sometimes flourishing in one domain may come at the cost of flourishing in others.

My understanding of IAPs as possessed of selective effects also entails the view that people can *mistakenly* believe that harming themselves improves their lives. Not all IAPs involve a person's rationally self-interested attempts to improve her flourishing; a person may have access to opportunities for flourishing across multiple domains but still engage in behaviors that are objectively bad for her. As feminist discourses of empowerment often suggest, oppressed and deprived people's own beliefs and desires can become the primary impediments to their flourishing. If development practitioners take seriously the fact of IAP caused by internalized oppressive beliefs, they have another reason not to expect gains in income to simply spill over into other domains of life; a woman who gains an income but also happens to believe that it is right for her husband to appropriate that income may not experience simultaneous gains in decision-making authority, her capacity to function as an equal in public life, or even her health. My definition of IAP draws our attention to the complexity of people's reasons for making decisions inconsistent with their basic flourishing. If we understand that cross-domain well-being trade-offs often characterize the choice situations of the deprived, and if we understand that people may have deficient conceptions of self-entitlement in some domains and not others, we have reason for pause when considering the idea that income—or any single-domain improvement—is synonymous with women's empowerment.

How Should Subjective Data Figure in Assessments of Empowerment?

Empowerment interventions can differently affect people's flourishing in different domains, and recognizing this fact calls us to develop more nuanced criteria for promoting empowerment and identifying states of disempowerment. A second fact of development practice that complicates attempts to diagnose disempowerment is what we might call "subjective/objective divergence." Cases of subjective/objective divergence occur when the net well-being effects of development interventions appear one way according to objective indicators and another way in the eyes of deprived people. Development participants may feel that an intervention positively affects their well-being while objective indicators seem to show the contrary, or vice versa. Cases of such subjective/objective divergence crop up frequently in qualitative research about women's participation in microcredit programs.

For instance, Kabeer conducted qualitative research that revealed that women microcredit recipients in Bangladesh engaged in more remunerated work than they previously had. However, this economic activity was concentrated in traditionally female sectors and had little effect on most women's desire to live in accordance with *purdah* norms that limited their mobility (Kabeer 2001, 69).[15] Kabeer recognizes that some empowerment theorists would see the microcredit intervention as disempowering, since it increased women's workloads without bringing about changes in their roles (Kabeer 2001, 69–71). Yet, perhaps surprisingly, Kabeer found that most of the women evaluated the intervention positively. The women reported that it gave them increased feelings of self-worth and increased bargaining power in relations with male relatives (Kabeer 2001, 71–73). Many of the women were tired of literally having to beg their husbands to access items they wanted (one participant describes formerly having had to beg her husband for a bandage that cost one taka) and tired of being looked down upon by wealthier members of their community. They believed that the microcredit intervention changed the value other people assigned to them, and that this change was dramatic and important.

Empowerment theorists increasingly acknowledge the need to collect subjective data, but it is not obvious what subjective data are supposed to do in cases of subjective/objective divergences. It may seem that if we believe internalized oppression and other deep psychological forms of IAP are real, subjective data will only obfuscate actual disempowerment. My deliberative perfectionist approach to IAP intervention emphasizes the need for both subjective and objective data in making judgments about whether a person is mistaken about what her flourishing would require. Specifically, it creates a conceptually coherent *role* for subjective data in empowerment interventions; subjective data can provide valuable information about why people have the preferences they have and how their behaviors affect their net flourishing.

My approach asks that we recognize the epistemological difficulties inherent in assessing other people's well-being. I insist that we cannot usually read people's reasons for their behavior—or the effects of their behavior on their flourishing—from their expressed preferences. From observing the types of work the participants in Kabeer's study performed, a development practitioner might conclude that the women had not overcome any of their IAPs that were not income-related. However, this conclusion would offer a dangerously incomplete picture of changes in their flourishing. My approach encourages the use of first-person perspectives of deprived people in assessing their levels of empowerment; it is very difficult for practitioners alone to determine why and whether people are failing to flourish. It recommends that practitioners ask questions of the type Kabeer asked—questions that illuminate seemingly deprived people's perceptions of themselves and their worlds.

Subjective data are particularly useful in helping practitioners see how people's expressed preferences affect their flourishing. In my discussion of the epistemological difficulties entailed in IAP intervention, I claim that some preferences that seem to be IAPs may actually just be ways of flourishing that practitioners do not initially recognize. I also point out that some IAPs involve mistaken higher-order beliefs about flourishing and others do not. A person may manage a limited option set with adaptive lower-order preferences that she would automatically change under better circumstances—that is, impediments to her flourishing are primarily structural rather than psychological. Or, she may have more deeply rooted mistaken beliefs about what her flourishing would require. I also suggest that some people may have preferences inconsistent with basic flourishing but that are so deeply rooted as not to be amenable to change under better conditions; people may want not to flourish without necessarily having IAPs. I argue that deliberation with the deprived is key to differentiating the three above types of preferences.

In short, my approach recommends the use of subjective data, but it does not suggest that subjective data *alone* can explain whether what seems to be disempowerment actually is disempowerment. Rather, I argue that subjective *and* objective data should be used to make *objective determinations* about people's levels of empowerment. My approach rests on an objective conception of the good; that is, I believe that objective judgments about whether a person is flourishing are possible. However, it also holds that the first-person (subjective) evaluations of people who seem to be deprived can contribute usefully to the process of determining whether a person is objectively flourishing. My deliberative perfectionist approach suggests that practitioners and people with suspect preferences can collaboratively arrive at objective determinations about well-being. To return to the example of the women in Kabeer's study, my deliberative perfectionist approach suggests that there is a fact of the matter about whether the women microcredit recipients are flourishing. But it also insists that the first-person perspectives of these women provide valuable information about the fact of the matter.

My approach prescribes deliberation as a way of handling the epistemic uncertainty inherent in making judgments about well-being. In this way, it clarifies the role of subjective data in making sense of the subjective/objective divergences that often appear in empowerment practice. It explains why subjective data are important without compromising the idea that objective judgments about human flourishing are possible. The possibility of objective judgments about flourishing is key to development practice focused on helping people overcome disempowerment; the critical edge of the concepts of empowerment and IAP depends on our willingness to take seriously the fact that oppression and deprivation can cause people to fail to flourish—even if they are not completely aware of their complicity in their own deprivation. However, *that* people *can* be mistaken about what they need does not mean that they *are* actually mistaken whenever they seem to be.

The theoretical challenge posed by subjective/objective divergences in empowerment practice involves acknowledging the need for an objective conception of the good in identifying IAPs without making light of the difficult work involved in understanding the varied and particular struggles for flourishing different people face. My deliberative perfectionist approach begins to answer this challenge by suggesting we view development practitioners and participants as engaged in a collaborative process of making objective determinations about flourishing. Certainly, this collaborative process may be undermined by power inequalities between practitioners and participants. Practical deliberative processes, in order to be successful, must be informed by the large body of work focusing on how to manage power inequalities in deliberation.[16] Still, the vision of first-person data as one part of a collaborative project of making objective determinations about well-being grants importance to subjective data without making the question of whether a person is flourishing into a purely subjective one.

What Does an Empowered Woman Look Like?

In the last two sections, we focused on types of data required to arrive at reliable judgments about empowerment. To know whether a person is moving toward empowerment, we must know how she feels development interventions have affected her life and how she is faring across a number of different domains of life. But it is not only empirical data that development practitioners need in order to tell whether women are moving toward empowerment; they also need a sense of what empowerment is. This is an inescapable logical fact. Practitioners need some vision of empowerment—if only to determine whether changes in the lives of disempowered people embody progress. But does a vision of empowerment always serve to facilitate the normative goals of development? Are there ways in which a picture of the empowered woman might orient development practice away from the focus on improving the lives of deprived people?

Empowerment theorists increasingly suggest that the answer to this last question may be affirmative. They relate stories of practitioners and agencies equipped with specific ideas about the end goals of empowerment—practitioners and agencies that end up misunderstanding the needs of the communities they are supposed to serve because they are doing their best to make real women's lives approximate a specific pre-established image of the empowered woman. One such pre-established image of the empowered woman is what I refer to as the "woman-as-individual" model. This model combines a narrative about the reasons for women's disempowerment with an idealized image of the empowered woman. The narrative about the reasons for disempowerment runs something like this: women in patriarchal societies are disempowered because they depend on men for access to land, income, status, and so on. The accompanying idealization of the empowered woman is one of the successful individual who earns her own income, comes to make demands on her husband, and decreases her dependence on him—in some cases by effecting what Kabeer has called "divorce within marriage" (Kabeer 1999, 460), in others by joining a women's solidarity group or striking out completely on her own.

Cornwall (2007a) and Kabeer (1999) separately argue that this woman-as-individual model shapes contemporary women's empowerment practice. Both caution that this model can guide ineffectual or counterproductive interventions when applied to communities not characterized by this type of patriarchy, communities whose women are unlikely to come to identify with the woman-as-individual picture of empowerment. Cornwall relates how her own earlier beholdenness to the woman-as-individual model caused her to misunderstand— or, to use her word, "misrecognize"—the sources of disempowerment of the Yoruba women who are the subjects of her ethnographic research (2007a). She describes having expected to find Yoruba women empowering themselves to act against men in their women's savings groups; instead, Cornwall learned that women tended to perceive other women as the main obstacle to their empowerment. Cornwall also describes having learned that women's affective relations with men were often sources of, rather than impediments to, women's empowerment (Cornwall 2007b, 43).

The dangers of engaging in empowerment practice according to such a preset model seem to be twofold; one danger is epistemic and the other is ethical. The epistemic danger is this: practitioners who expect women's lives to conform to the wrong preset model will misunderstand the causes of their disempowerment and the possibilities for their empowerment. The ethical danger is about the consequences of such misunderstanding; practitioners may prescribe a sort of homogenizing, one-size-fits-all approach to helping women empower themselves, turning women into "purposive individual agents whose 'empowerment' can be achieved simply by improving their assets and removing institutional barriers" (Cornwall 2007b, 43). Development practitioners need a vision of empowerment, but is it possible to imagine a vision that does not require its adherents to distort the lived experiences of deprived people or shape them according to a single model?

I have argued in this book that a deliberative perfectionist conception of human flourishing should guide development practice. Development practitioners and people with suspect preferences should collaboratively interpret a vague, cross-culturally acceptable, and minimal conception of the good in order to envision strategies for change. I believe that a deliberative perfectionist conception of well-being may offer a vision of empowerment that discourages development practitioners from distorting or homogenizing the realities of disempowered people. To see how this is so, we can begin with the epistemic problem of distortion. A precise vision of empowerment, coupled with practitioner desire to see deprived people become empowered, can cause practitioners to misunderstand the complex realities of people with suspect preferences. The danger here is a specific one; development practitioners can come to see empowerment in behaviors that are not actually empowering in context, because the supposedly empowering behaviors belong to the repertoire of things the "empowered woman" does. As one example of the tendency to view certain behaviors as empowering regardless of their contextual effects, we can take the tendency of microcredit programs to encourage women to start their own businesses—even in cases where working for wages would give them greater access to income (Mahmud 2003, 602). Cornwall's initial desire to see Yoruba women's savings groups as unambiguous sources of women's solidarity against men provides another example of this distorting effect of a specific image of empowerment. Cornwall believed empowered women formed groups to reject men's control over them and thus failed to notice that relationships among women within Yoruba women's collaborative savings groups were often proximate sources of disempowerment.[17]

What is the role of a conception of flourishing in producing this type of error? Certainly, this type of error is partly caused by rigid donor agendas and the personal investment of the practitioner in bringing about a particular type of change. That practitioners' personal investment in bringing about certain types of change can cause them to distort the lived realities of people with suspect preferences suggests that practitioners should be trained to guard against seeing people with suspect preferences as mere mirrors of their preconceived expectations. Though I believe practitioner training is an important step toward preventing practitioners from distorting the experiences of the deprived,[18] I would also argue that dialogue with deprived people can further enable practitioners to recognize mismatches between their expectations and people's actual empowerment needs. Cornwall reports that it is only through extended processes of engagement with and listening to Yoruba women that she came to understand that many Yoruba women experienced their relationships with other women as impediments to their flourishing.

If we accept that a genuine encounter with deprived people can help unsettle development practitioner expectations, we should endorse a conception of the good that promotes dialogue between practitioners and people with suspect preferences. A very specific conception of empowerment can come to function as a checklist of behaviors the empowered woman does or does not engage in. It may thus facilitate practitioner illusion by reducing the task of diagnosing disempowerment to a simple matter of looking around and assessing the presence or absence of certain recognizable behaviors. A more appropriately formulated conception of flourishing will not be a simple checklist of easily recognizable empowering behaviors; it should be a list that presents the task of diagnosing disempowerment as one that cannot be conducted without sophisticated contextual knowledge. I argue that the conception of flourishing practitioners should use to identify IAPs should be vague. A vague conception of flourishing does not list specific behaviors as typical of empowerment but rather asks practitioners to look at specific behaviors and practices to see whether flourishing can be recognized in them. Further, my deliberative perfectionist approach emphasizes the uncertainty involved in judging the well-being effects of the behaviors of unfamiliar others; it prescribes deliberation with the deprived of a way of getting clear about whether and how they are flourishing. I would propose that a vague conception of the good, deliberatively employed, can discourage practitioners from distorting the realities of people with suspect preferences.

Let us turn now from the epistemic to the ethical danger of a specific vision of empowerment—the danger of homogenization. A specific positive vision of flourishing does not only risk functioning as a checklist; it risks functioning as a recipe. If practitioners have a vivid picture of the life of the empowered woman, they may approach deprived people with predetermined strategies for their empowerment. Not only are such strategies likely to be unsuccessful because of contextual misunderstandings and to miss opportunities for cultivating the agential skills of deprived people, they are likely to promote unnecessary cultural homogenization. Any thick picture of flourishing will contain cultural specificities; attempting to mold the world's women according to a precise vision will necessarily involve making disempowered women more like the women of some particular culture. To return to our discussion of the woman-as-individual model, a picture of the empowered woman as one who leads her own household will give development practitioners reason to encourage women to live in the types of small, parent-child households that are common in some areas of the world rather than in others. This seems like an unnecessary type of cultural homogenization.

In pointing out that turning all women into heads of households involves unnecessary cultural homogenization, I do not mean to suggest that forming female-headed households cannot be a good thing for women; the possibility of forming one's own household has transformed the lives of many women in a variety of cultural contexts. Rather, I mean to say that becoming the head of a household consisting of oneself and one's children is not the only way to exercise the capacities constitutive of flourishing. If we do envision the woman who heads her own household as empowered, it is probably because this form of life gives her certain opportunities to live out her human potential; perhaps it allows her to reliably access food and shelter, to be free of violence, to make major decisions about her life, and to live unimpeded by the sense that women are lesser beings.

But there is little reason to believe that this form of household organization is the *only* one that could provide these opportunities, or that women's access to these opportunities could not incrementally improve under different forms of household organization. Cornwall (2007a) and Kabeer (1999, 460) each argue that women who live under conditions where male-headed nuclear families are not the norm may not identify with strategies for empowerment that ask them to simply leave the men in their lives. But their aim is not to claim that such women do not need opportunities for reliable access to food and shelter, freedom from violence, and a decrease in feelings of gender-based shame where those exist. Rather, it is to suggest that the means to achieving these goods may be different in different contexts; Cornwall suggests that women can learn to think of themselves as equals and make their own decisions *within* relationships rather than by exiting them.

The remaining challenge, then, is to avoid overdetermination—to develop a conception of the good that takes a stance about what women need in order to be empowered but that does not preset specific strategies for change or paint a detailed picture of the end-product "empowered woman." One advantage of the type of vague conception of the good I have defended is that it underdetermines what strategies should be chosen in any particular situation. If the conception underdetermines the path to empowerment for any particular woman or group of women, there is little warrant for practitioners to impose a recipe for empowerment on them. Rather, deprived people can participate in imagining flourishing-compatible futures for themselves—ones that may have been unimaginable to development practitioners before the encounter.

Let us think, for a moment, of strategies that might increase the mobility of women whose mobility is significantly restricted by the men in their lives. For instance, the Honduran women of PAEM, described in Chapter 1, have developed a vision of negotiation within husband/wife relationships that differs significantly from the idea that women should simply leave or stop having positive affective relationships with their husbands. The women of PAEM teach and learn skills for representing one's interests to one's husband, for disagreeing, for expressing one's desires to leave the house and the village at will and act upon those desires. Many PAEM participants report that these skills have transformed their relationships with their husbands; others report that the progress toward this goal is incomplete, but they agree on the content of the vision (Rowlands 1997, 82–83). Might such negotiation be one way of increasing women's mobility and decreasing women's gender-based shame that does not require women to take on adversarial relationships with— or simply leave—men? We might think of the PAEM women's vision as an alternative to the "woman-as-individual" model, one that appears to effectively motivate positive change in their communities. By claiming that the PAEM women have come up with a partial solution to their empowerment needs that allows for positive affective relations between men and women, I do not mean to suggest that this is the right model for all communities; in some communities women may genuinely want to leave their husbands or simply tolerate them, and this, too, may be a way of increasing women's access to flourishing. My point is that we need a conception of the flourishing that acknowledges that there are many potential concrete strategies for increasing women's access to mobility—making it possible for women to leave their husbands, making it possible for women to earn incomes in contexts where this will cause men to think twice before restricting their wives' mobility, teaching women how to negotiate with their husbands, and so on. We need a conception of the good that does not decide in advance which of these paths should be chosen. An advantage of a vague conception of the good of the type I advocate is that it discourages practitioners from employing a one-size-fits-all recipe for empowerment. Instead, it promotes deliberation as a means of finding out what strategies might be both flourishing-promoting and culturally desirable, as well as what strategies might be most effective in a particular context.

Conceptualizing Empowerment: Deliberative Perfectionist Clarifications

I have argued that the concepts I have developed in my deliberative perfectionist approach to IAP identification can move us toward more coherent answers to two pressing sets of conceptual questions about empowerment: questions about the relationship between choice and empowerment and questions about how to identify states of empowerment and disempowerment. I have discussed three different puzzles about the relationship between choice and empowerment: how to distinguish morally unproblematic difference from disempowerment, how to make sense of preferences that seem simultaneously disempowering and chosen, and how to separate the types of choices that are necessary for empowerment from those that are not. My approach suggests that we can distinguish disempowering preferences from "just different" ones by asking which preferences are causally related to conditions of deprivation—which ones people would retain if they had a more flourishing-compatible option set. My approach can accommodate the intuition that some preferences are both chosen and disempowering, because it does not take the act of choice to be the distinguishing feature of an empowering preference. It helps us separate choices that are important to empowerment from those that are not by offering a conception of flourishing that can identify domains of life in which access to flourishing is particularly important.

I have also addressed three questions about how to identify states of empowerment and disempowerment: the question of whether income translates into empowerment, the question of how to make sense of subjective/objective divergences in empowerment assessments, and questions about how to envision empowerment in a way that does not distort oppressed and deprived people's realities. I claim, as part of my deliberative perfectionist approach, that flourishing involves plural constituents and that people can have selective deficits in self-entitlement; these claims help explain why income generation need not translate into cross-domain empowerment. My deliberative perfectionist approach also suggests that deprived people's conceptions of their own well-being should be key to well-being evaluations, and my approach helps us to see subjective/objective divergences in well-being assessment as an invitation to further dialogue and investigation of the reasons for these divergences. Finally, my deliberative perfectionist approach includes the idea that IAP interventions should be motivated by a vague, plural, and minimal conception of the good; such a conception of the good prevents empowerment practice from devolving into an attempt to mold the world's women according to a single model.

Feminist conceptions of empowerment have gained some currency in mainstream development discourse. Claims that development projects empower women carry with them enormous rhetoricalforce. But we have sometimes seen this rhetorical force co-opted in the interests of a development agenda that is more interested in increasing women's access to income than improving the overall conditions of their lives, that does not take seriously deprived women's visions of what they want—in short, that takes advantage of ambiguities in the notion of empowerment to cover over the complexities of real women's struggles for flourishing and real women's needs. It is a crucial moment for feminists to work through the difficulties of conceptualizing empowerment and reinvest the concept with meaning. I have offered the deliberative perfectionist approach to this end; part of this feminist project of reinvesting the concept of empowerment with meaning is articulating the moral vision behind it.

NOTES

1. I use the term "flourishing" in an imprecise sense throughout the beginning of this introduction to elicit our intuitions about the El Pital case. I clarify what I mean by this term somewhat nontechnically later in this introduction and spell out my understanding of this concept in Chapter 1 (in this volume).

2. For a discussion of the moral and pragmatic problems associated with public service provision by NGOs, see Nagar and Raju (2003, 2). See also Feldman (2003), Logister (2007), and Malhotra (2000).

3. I am very sympathetic to Amartya Sen's work on the problems with taking a country's wealth as the key indicator of development. See in particular Sen (1999b).

4. Readers interested in the revolutionary origins of the term "third world" should see Isbister (2003, 16).

5. Sen does not use the term "adaptive preference" in this passage, but this passage is widely cited in the literature as one of Sen's early discussions of adaptive preference.

6. I concede that certain discussions of adaptive preference (most notably Elster's) suggest that the person who does not value the objectively excellent has adaptive preferences. In these discussions of adaptive preference, any unconsciously formed preference that devalues an inaccessible good (regardless of the moral urgency of that good) counts as adaptive.

   The fact that some accounts of adaptive preference do not reserve the term "adaptive" for preferences that affect basic well-being may seem to weaken my conceptual analysis of the term "adaptive preferences." I have three responses to this concern. First, I point out that views of adaptive preference that do not discriminate based on preference urgency share the basic perfectionist structure that I argue that all claims about adaptive preferences have. That is, even views of adaptive preference that do not claim that only basic well-being affecting preferences can be adaptive contain presumptions about the content of what people in general prefer. To the extent that proponents of these views claim that people with adaptive preferences inappropriately devalue what human beings prefer, they suggest a connection between what human beings prefer and what is objectively valuable. Second, my aim is to do a conceptual analysis of the term "adaptive preference" as it is used in development ethics, where the notion is often explicitly tied to need—a conception tied to basic well-being rather than excellence. Not only do development ethicists often tie adaptive preference to need; this tying of adaptive preference to need seems to be the implicit justification of public intervention to transform adaptive preferences. So we might say that some of my discussion in this book is only applicable to the types of adaptive preferences that warrant development interventions. Third, and in a related point, we might conceive of the aim of my book as defining those adaptive preferences that merit public intervention. Even if the concept of adaptive preference does not entail a focus on basic flourishing rather than excellence, we can say that only basic flourishing-affecting preferences merit public intervention. One reason we might say this in development ethics is epistemic. We might say that we are less certain about what constitutes excellence than what constitutes basic flourishing, particularly given the fact of cross-cultural divergence on constituent components of excellence. Another reason we might restrict intervention to basic flourishing-affecting preferences is the typical liberal one; we may believe people have a right to choose a non-excellent life even if it causes them to forego the higher levels of well-being.

7. For discussions of how the global economic order causes poverty in the South, see Chossudovsky (2003) and Pogge (2002). For discussions of how the global economic order specifically affects women in the South, see Naples (2002) and UNIFEM (2000). There is some disagreement about the extent to which the global economic order causes poverty; for arguments that the global economic order is not the main cause of poverty in the South, see Risse (2005).

8. The field of global ethics has become more justice-focused since Narayan's piece appeared, and Thomas Pogge (2002) and Alison Jaggar's work (2005b) are major exceptions to the charity-focused trend.

9. Narayan borrows this term from Kandiyoti (1988).

10. Strictly speaking, wearing the *hijab* by choice is unlikely to count as an IAP on my account, because it does not impact basic flourishing.

11. PAEM was founded and run by Ruiz and other Honduran women but received funding from Oxfam.

12. I would tend to favor an analysis like David Crocker's (2004), which suggests that development practitioners should be "insider/outsider hybrids."

NOTES TO CHAPTER 1: A DELIBERATIVE PERFECTIONIST
APPROACH TO ADAPTIVE PREFERENCE INTERVENTION

1. For other mentions of adaptive preference in broader arguments against utilitarianism, see Gasper (2004, 175), Nussbaum (1999, 77, 151; 2001, 135–148), and Sen (1988, 45; 1999a, 53; 2002, 634).

2. See Rawls's (1971, 20–22, 46–53; 1996, 28, 45) discussions of reflective equilibrium for a more detailed account of our pursuit of consistency among our intuitions and normative commitments.

3. The literature on adaptive preferences does contain occasional references to the adaptive preferences of the nondeprived. A couple of cases are Nussbaum's discussion of the adaptive preferences of men who support the exploitation of women (Nussbaum 2001, 165) and the preferences of "lords" (Nussbaum 2001, 141). Though I, like most theorists of adaptive preference, am focused on the adaptive preferences of the deprived here, a perfectionist account may be plausibly extended to describe as deformed the preferences of those who oppress and deprive others.

4. Nussbaum's characterization of preferences based on lack of knowledge about how to flourish as adaptive is slight a shift from her earlier description of such preferences as deformed but not adaptive (Nussbaum 1999, 147–149).

5. John Christman (1991) uses a somewhat similar counterfactual condition to define nonautonomous preferences. For Christman, a preference is autonomous if a person did not resist its development or would not have resisted its development if she had paid attention to the process of its development.

6. Chris Heathwood (2005) attempts to defend utilitarianism from criticisms such as the adaptive preference criticism by claiming that most "defective desires" are "all things considered irrational." Heathwood thinks that utilitarians need not commit to fulfilling defective desires because satisfying most defective desires would frustrate other, future desires that a person has.

7. Of course, the belief that they deserve abuse is not the only reason women remain in relationships with batterers. They may stay because their partners threaten to take their children or further injure them, for instance. See Friedman (2003, 144–148) for a more extended discussion of why U.S. women remain in abusive relationships.

8. I thank Jonathan Warner for suggesting this term to me.

9. The analogy of error in IAP identification to an occupational hazard is imperfect, because the occupational hazards of other practices harm the workers themselves rather than those their work is intended to benefit. In the case of development, however, errors in IAP identification harm prospective development beneficiaries more than they harm practitioners.

10. H.E. Baber (2007) accuses Nussbaum of the same mistake as Ackerly does. Baber describes poor Afghan women who encourage their daughters to get married young and claims that Nussbaum would treat them as bearers of adaptive preferences. Instead, Baber thinks, they are actually just making the best out of the situation where child marriage is a poor girl's best shot at a decent life.

11. Maxine Molyneux (quoted in Kandiyoti 1988, 282) argues that poor women's deprivation-perpetuating behaviors that seem like straightforward false consciousness are often self-interested preferences for incremental over radical social change.

In situations where radical social change would require significant sacrifice of women's social goals, it can be rational for them to prefer incremental change.

12. I thank Uma Narayan for helping me to develop this term.

13. Some readers may wonder why we should call lower-order adaptive preferences "preferences" at all. It may seem more apt to describe them with a word like "behaviors." I retain the language of preferences even in cases of lower-order adaptation, because it helps us to see that even people with very limited options make choices among alternatives on the basis of what they care about. The poor woman who chooses to educate her child over herself under circumstances where she cannot choose both does opt for one alternative over another and does so in a way that reflects something about her values. Readers accustomed to using the word "preference" in regard to higher-order beliefs and attitudes may find it useful to keep in mind that I hold that people can have IAPs without having adjusted their higher-order network of beliefs and attitudes to deprivation.

14. The work of Escobar (1994) and the essays in Apffel-Marglin and Marglin (1996) describe development interventions that they believe mistook difference for deprivation and undertook processes of cultural homogenization.

15. For examples of this view, see Joshua Cohen (2004), Ignatieff (2003), Nussbaum (2000), Sen (1985), and Walzer (1996).

16. This is my understanding of why Nussbaum continually points out that human beings can identify tragedy across times and cultures (1992; 2001, 72–73).

17. Of course, if cross-cultural norms and institutions continue to develop, we can expect convergence on more than basic flourishing in the future. Joshua Cohen makes this point (2004).

18. The Rawls of *Political Liberalism* seems to hold that referring to perfectionist values means referring to a comprehensive conception of the good—a conception of the good that would not be endorsable by people from a variety of different worldviews. This is particularly noticeable in his discussion of the right/good distinction (1996, 173–207). At one point in this discussion, he argues that a politically liberal state can incorporate virtues of classical citizenship as long as those virtues are justified on political rather than perfectionist grounds. The danger of justifying them on perfectionist grounds seems to be that this would mean public endorsement of a comprehensive doctrine. "The crucial point is that admitting these virtues into a political conception does not lead to the perfectionist state of a comprehensive doctrine" (1996, 194).

19. To provide just a few examples, Nigerian legal theorist J.A.I Bewaji (2006) makes a case for human rights based on traditional Yoruba beliefs that evaluate political and economic systems in terms of their contribution the development of human beings; Afkhami (1997) argues that women's human rights can be justified using ideas found in the Koran; S.S. Rama Rao Pappu (2005) argues that the idea of the person in human rights can be justified with reference to Hindu notions of dharma.

20. Crocker discusses the ways in which this intervention may have fallen short of full deliberative participation (2008, 338–375).

21. I do not intend to suggest that illiteracy is never a deprivation but, rather, to suggest that literacy does not always track the exercise of cognitive capacity. Further, even if Khatoum exercises cognitive capacities, it does not follow that she is not deprived by the illiteracy; for instance, illiteracy may render her vulnerable to exploitation. That illiteracy may constitute a vulnerability does not undermine the claim this example is intended to demonstrate; the practitioner who thinks that Khatoum cannot exercise cognitive capacity is wrong about the precise effects of her illiteracy on her flourishing.

22. Street draws the story of Winnie from an unpublished ethnographic paper by C. Kell (2003).

23. Serena Olsaretti argues in a defense of Sen's capability approach that endorsement offers a reason not to coerce deprived people into flourishing (2005).

24. This is the term that the Mandaleo Ya Wanawake activists use.

25. According to Chege, Askew, et al. (2001), Circumcision Through Words later became a preset model that was implemented in communities that did not have a coming-of-age ritual associated with circumcision. This is a cautionary tale of what can happen when interventions that were initially deliberative take on a perfunctory tone.

NOTES TO CHAPTER 2: ADAPTIVE PREFERENCES AND CHOICE: ARE ADAPTIVE PREFERENCES AUTONOMY DEFICITS

* A version of the first part of this chapter appeared as "Adaptive Preferences and Procedural Autonomy" in *The Journal of Human Development* 10(2): 2009, 169–87.

1. Nagar and Raju define empowerment as "the process of undoing internalized oppression" (Nagar and Raju 2003, 4).

2. My portrayal of the "empowerment" discourse in development studies in these last paragraphs is admittedly somewhat reductive. Some theorists, such as Kabeer (1999), freely admit that some type of choice was available to people in their pre-empowered state. Nonetheless, Kabeer, and many of these theorists struggle to describe pre-empowered choice as some type of non-choice. Some empowerment theorists also suggest that empowerment is the capacity to know that other options are available. My argument in this chapter can be read as a response to the empowerment discourse that deploys choice-focused rhetoric to describe empowerment. At its best, I think the vocabulary of choice confuses matters, and at its worst it suggests that deprived people have no agency. I think it is more honest to speak of empowerment as having strong normative goals beyond the provision of choices. I argue this point more fully in Chapter 5.

3. In response to Goetz and Das Gupta's findings, Simeen Mahmud (2003, 583) suggests that official loan control is not a good measure of women's agency over loans.

4. In support of this claim, Chambers cites a description of Sierra Leonean women by Gerry Mackie (2003). It is unclear whether Chamber thinks that *most* women who go through FGM would begin to oppose it upon exposure to information about its health effects.

5. Kalima Rose describes the way in which the women of the Self-Employed Women's Association in India learn a greater sense of what they can do from watching other women engaged in health-promotion or income-generation activities (Rose 1992, 158).

6. Marilyn Friedman (2003) may implicitly appeal to an argument of this sort when she implies that it is appropriate to suspect (or override) the preferences of some third-world women by asking whether they "have been able to develop, earlier in life, the capacities needed to reflect on their situations and make decisions about them."

7. Empirical data about battered women in the United States consistently attest to high levels of domestic violence despite American women's overall high level of educational attainment compared to women in many poor countries. Many studies suggest no correlation between American women's educational level and their risk for domestic violence. Those that do suggest correlations usually show that only very high levels of education (usually a college degree) decrease women's levels of risk for domestic violence (Tjaden and Thoennes 1998). It seems quite likely that confounding variables such as income—and not changes in women's rational capacities—explain the correlation between very high levels of education and decreased risk for domestic violence. More important for our purposes, it seems implausible to claim that only American women with college educations have developed sufficient rational capacity to make reflective decisions.

8. The ideas of APs as preferences inconsistent with people's life-plans is not completely consistent with Meyers' idea of autonomy, since Meyers focuses on what autonomous *people* are like, not what autonomous *preferences* are like.

9. Levey (2005, 133) Nussbaum (2001) both make this point.

NOTES TO CHAPTER 3: ADAPTIVE PREFERENCES AND AGENCY: THE SELECTIVE EFFECTS OF ADAPTIVE PREFERENCE

1. Some recent demographic research calls development agencies to base their claims about the extent of intrahousehold food inequalities on clearer evidence. Though it seems correct that many poor women do undernourish themselves (or their female children) in favor of their male relatives, Marcoux (2002) argues that much of the advocacy conversation about sex bias in nutrition is based on excessively wide generalizations about fairly limited data. Marcoux's analysis shows that many Indian states do have sex biases in nutrition, but many do not. This is a useful caution against assuming that biased intrahousehold food distribution is always the cause of gendered health and mortality differentials.

2. Nussbaum's comments about the effects of IAP on the self do not uniformly suggest that she believes IAPs affect the entire self. In one case, she claims that some parts of the human personality resist social deformation (Nussbaum 2001, 55); this strain in Nussbaum's view is similar to my own view about how IAPs affect the self.

3. Appadurai himself explicitly acknowledges that the relationship of the poor to their poverty involves ambivalence toward it as well as complicity in perpetuating it.

4. As I argued in Chapter 2, I do not believe that Elster's view of adaptive preference is the one animating development discourse. Elster's view is clearly not a version of Adaptive Self View; indeed he seems to view the effects of adaptive preferences as highly selective.

5. To argue that free agents regard their own projects as worth pursuing does not imply that agents must advance their interests at the expense of those of others. Agents can certainly take advancing the interests of others part of their own projects.

6. I think of positive self-entitlement as a necessary but insufficient prerequisite for agency. Young children, for example, may see their interests as worthy of pursuing and yet lack sufficient senses of self to be full-blown agents.

7. For examples, see Abu-Lughod (1986), Agarwal (1997), Luker (1975), Mogobe (2005), Ong (1987), Varghese (1993), and Wells (2003).

8. Patricia Mann (1994) advances a view of this sort.

9. Sen's point in this article (1990) is not simply that women may make some gains by participating in dominating relationships. He seems to hold that the outcome for such women is rational but suboptimal; these women do better in unequal relationships than they might do outside, but that does not mean that they could not improve their well-being through change in the internal dynamics of the relationships.

10. For versions of the claim that a flourishing life has multiple constituents, see Finnis (1980, 95–97), Hurka (1993, 148–149), and Nussbaum (2001, 80).

11. In his essay on cooperative conflicts, Sen seems to think that increasing women's earning power outside the home will increase their empowerment within it (1990), though he does acknowledge an argument from Mies to the contrary (Sen 1990, 144–145). Another famous proponent of the view that increasing women's economic independence would empower them in a more comprehensive way is Esther Boserup (1970).

12. Marilyn Frye (1983) famously uses the metaphor of a bird cage to describe the multiplicity and systematicity of barriers that oppressed people encounter.

13. For feminist views of the oppressed self as fractured, see Babbitt (1993), Brison (1997), Lugones (2003), Mackenzie (2000, 142), and Meyers (2000, 158–159).

14. Agarwal's own stance on the possibility of the coexistence of adaptive preference and resistance is complicated. Her article (1997) warns against jumping to the conclusion that poor South Asian women who do not overtly resist gender

214 • Notes to Pages 124–129

inequality *accept* that inequality. She is thus suspicious of the overapplication of the notion of adaptive preference. However, she does not argue that adaptive preferences do not exist. She notes on a few occasions that women may endorse oppressive norms and agrees with Papanek (1990) that women are more often socialized to intrahousehold altruism than men. I think Agarwal would accept that women can have adaptive preferences and simultaneously engage in covert resistance, though she would caution against quickly jumping to the conclusion that adaptive higher-order desires are an explanation of women's lack of overt resistance. For unambiguous examples of women who endorse social norms and simultaneously rebel covertly against them, see the texts cited in the preceding footnote.

15. Abu-Lughod has since written that her interest in Bedouin women's resistant speech reflected a problematic "tendency to romanticize resistance" (Abu-Lughod 1990, 41–42).

16. See, for instance, Anzaldua (1994), hooks (1994), Lugones (2003), and McClure (1992). Some of these theorists, such as Gloria Anzaldua (1994) and Chandra Talpade Mohanty (1992), also explicitly point out problems faced by oppressed people who rely on resistant community membership for positive sources of identity.

17. Many feminist scholars of societies where women often operate in single-sex environments claim that women who live in these societies have unique opportunities for developing self-esteem that Western women do not have. According to these scholars, women in some sex-segregated societies have an easier time finding positive images of themselves as women, because sex segregation creates women's cultures and makes them less invested in affirmation from men. For instance Leila Ahmed argues that sex-segregated spaces in some Arab societies give women opportunities to develop a positive feminine identity because they participate in a shared culture that does not include men (Ahmed 1982, 528). Similarly, Ifi Amadiume argues that women in sub-Saharan Africa can find resources for claiming power in matriarchal practices and histories (Amadiume 1998).

18. Papanek describes other examples, like women in China who bound their daughters' feet and women in Egypt who perform clitoridectomies on young girls (1990, 176). In Lugones's earlier-cited (2003) discussion about the sense of home people of color may find in antiracist communities, she goes on to argue that people of color who do not pass certain "authenticity tests" may be harmfully excluded by other people of color.

19. It is not clear whether Nussbaum's interpretation of Jayamma's reasons for acquiescence is derived from conversation with Jayamma or speculation. Jaggar (2006, 306) notes that Nussbaum rarely quotes the Indian women on whose stories she draws in *Women and Human Development*. Baber (2007) also argues that Nussbaum gives no evidence that Jayamma has actually changed her desires.

20. Narayan draws the Pirzada women's narratives from an ethnography by Patricia Jeffery (U. Narayan 2002, 420).

21. See Chambers's comparison of female genital cutting and breast implants for a discussion of the healthrisks of breast augmentation (Chambers 2007, 186–88).

22. The term "woman" here may be slightly misleading, since female genital cutting is often undergone by young teenagers, and Chambers's example is about a teenage girl who wants breast implants.

NOTES TO CHAPTER 4: THE DELIBERATIVE PERFECTIONIST APPROACH, PATERNALISM, AND CULTURAL DIVERSITY

1. I borrow this turn of phrase from Bhikhu Parekh (1999).

2. Ackerly (2000, 94–119) and Jaggar (2006) criticize Nussbaum for arriving at her capabilities list through a process that does not require her to filter out her culturally specific ideas about flourishing.

3. Some commentators have criticized the list's contents; Susan Moller Okin criticizes the focus on religion in Nussbaum's list (2003). Interestingly, however, some development practitioners who work directly with the poor, such as Nagar and Raju (2003) and Uyan-Semerci (2007), claim to find Nussbaum's list useful.

4. My choice of this list as an example may be puzzling. It may not be evident that the conception of flourishing embodied in it is actually either deliberative or perfectionist. The list may not seem perfectionist, because Nussbaum proposes the list, at least in its most recent versions, as the subject of a political "overlapping consensus" (Nussbaum 2001, 76, 104; 2000, 132). However, we should not assume that a perfectionist conception—at least a minimal one—cannot itself become the topic of an overlapping consensus. Nussbaum's list is a list of functionings human beings need access to in order to flourish, so it has irreducibly perfectionist content. This is not changed by the fact she refers to it as a list of capabilities; to call them capabilities only means that these are functionings that should not be forced on people by public institutions.

5. One might attempt to defend the Flourishing Claim by saying that policies justified by it do not promote certain sorts of life-plans over others since it does not justify coercive intervention. I do not think we can stop there. Such a line of defense would be disingenuous—despite the popularity of such lines of defense among perfectionists (see Clarke 2006 for an example of such a defense). Providing certain types of opportunities and encouraging individuals to take advantage of them structures individuals' choice situations. It gives them incentives to take advantages of those opportunities rather than others. That is, there is an opportunity cost to providing new opportunities. We cannot escape this fact. The Flourishing Claim does involve promoting certain types of life-plans over others. There remains a moral difference between promoting certain types of life-plans and forcing persons to choose those types of life-plans and the Flourishing Claim justifies the former and not the latter.

6. There are a number of different ways liberal perfectionists have tried to argue that perfectionism does not justify coercive restraints on freedom. See in particular, Raz (1988) and (Hurka 1993, 147–158).

7. A large body of evidence indicates that women's negotiating power in relationships and/or their financial independence affects their rates of condom use. The studies on this have occurred across a wide variety of cultural contexts. See African HIV Policy Network (2006), Greig and Koopman (2003), Pettifor, Measham, et al. (2004), and Tabac (2003).

8. Despite Sen's occasional tendency to valorize choosing in general and choosing one's values in particular, his celebration of choice is not unqualified. "Indeed sometimes more freedom of choice can bemuse and befuddle, and make one's life more wretched" (1992, 52). More recently, he claims that the quality of options matter to whether an increase in options is good. See the discussion of reason to value in Sen (2002, 602).

9. For a discussion of the negative effects of excessive choice on well-being see Schwartz (2004).

10. G.A. Cohen (1993) criticizes Sen in a similar vein. He notes that Sen sometimes speaks as though choosing certain functionings is what gives them their value, when the functionings themselves are the true objects of value.

11. In claiming that there is legitimate moral variation among cultures, I do not mean to imply that cultures are monoliths in which everyone holds the same values. Rather, I mean simply to point out that all of us are motivated by values and beliefs particular to our cultural contexts and that some people want to be able to live according to values they perceive as specific to their cultural contexts. I also do not mean to categorically claim that it is good for people to live according to the values prevalent in their cultural contexts. My position is that there is no warrant for intervening to change the preferences of people who want to live according to culturally specific values that cannot reasonably be said to deprive them. Will Kymlicka (1991) argues that culturally embedded values can help people to flourish.

12. For views in this family, see Derrida (1978) and Irigaray (1994).

13. See Apffel-Marglin and Marglin (1996), Escobar (1994), Rahnema (1997), and Ziai (2004) for postdevelopment critiques of universalism.

14. This is no longer the official position of the American Anthropological Association.

15. Alan Buchanan (2004, 147–175) offers a particularly well-argued and comprehensive response to relativist criticisms of the human rights regime.

16. See Ahmed (1993), Deveaux (2003), Eisenberg (2003), U. Narayan (1997, 1–41), and Okin (1999).

17. I take this to be the worry motivating Qizilbash's (1996, 156) view that using Nussbaum's list of capabilities in practice cannot form a basis for "consensual development."

18. For attempts to elaborate human rights in the framework of Islamic texts and traditions, see Afkhami (1997) and An-Na'Im (2001).

19. The Cairo conference marked a considerable shift in the international community's justification of population policy—from understanding population reduction as necessary for economic development to understanding individuals' reproductive health as an important social entitlement in its own right. See McIntosh and Finkle (1995). Cairo's main effect was to reproductive health a human right.

20. This term comes from R. Chambers (1994).

21. I have written at length elsewhere about virtues that will help practitioners avoid inadvertent ventriloquism. See Khader (2011).

22. For work on how to manage power inequalities in participatory development, see Hickey and Mohan (2004).

23. I have written elsewhere about virtues for development practitioners who wish not to confuse their interests with those of the communities with which they work. See Khader (2011).

24. This does not imply that cultural practices are the only cause of IAPs; it implies only that increasing the flourishing of people with IAPs will sometimes require cultural change.

NOTES TO CHAPTER 5: REIMAGINING INTERVENTION: ADAPTIVE PREFERENCES AND THE PARADOXES OF EMPOWERMENT

1. See Holvoet (2005, 86) for discussion of an actual microcredit program in which most women were "forced" by their husbands to participate.

2. See Poster and Salime (2002) for discussion of microcredit programs that increase women's work burdens.

3. Feminists also frequently criticize microcredit programs for failing in ways less obviously related to gender inequality. For instance, Feiner and Barker (2007, 124–126) criticize microcredit for increasing women's debt burdens. Hazarika and Sarangi (2008) argue that microcredit increases child labor under some circumstances.

4. It is widely held in the microfinance community that women are more risk averse and productive investors than men, but this view has also been criticized as a stereotype (Poster and Salime 2002).

5. Kabeer does not believe that all preferences that evidence disempowerment are preferences against basic flourishing. She worries that preferences to be subordinate may accrue to people whose basic flourishing is not compromised (1999, 439). I would suggest by way of a response that there may be ways of integrating perceptions of entitlement and self-respect into a conception of basic flourishing.

6. Kabeer's apparently choice-based definition of empowerment may be able to accommodate the view that the choice to cut one's genitals is disempowering under

circumstances where income and status are contingent upon genital cutting. Kabeer asserts that the capacity to achieve certain outcomes through one's behavior is a prerequisite for choice, and thus it would be consistent with Kabeer's view to say that a person who has only self-undermining behaviors available lacks choices. However, if we interpret Kabeer's view of empowerment in this way, it becomes clear that she uses the word "choice" somewhat inconsistently and idiosyncratically. As I mentioned in the previous section, she problematically conflates the notions of making and having choices. Moreover, to the extent that Kabeer speaks of the availability of *strategic* choices and outcomes, she has built normative constraints into her conception of choice. Though Kabeer's stated definition of empowerment foregrounds the notion of choice, her analysis of empowerment incorporates moral conceptions other than choice. I make this point more fully in the next section.

7. It is important to distinguish women's need for power to negotiate relationships from the power to *exit* relationships altogether. Part of Cornwall's larger project is to advocate a development policy that recognizes women's affective and social needs as well as their economic ones; interventions that empower women need not always ask them to abandon their existing affective ties.

8. Kabeer is another empowerment theorist who distinguishes the types of choices necessary for empowerment from other choices. Kabeer, for instance, describes a need to focus on "those strategic choices which are critical for people to lead the lives they want (such as the choice of livelihood, whether and who to marry, whether to have children, etc.)" (Kabeer 1999, 437). Kabeer distinguishes these choices from more trivial choices from "lower-order, less consequential choices, which may be important for the quality of one's life but do not constitute its defining parameters" (Kabeer 1999, 437).

9. Alkire (2007a) is developing a notion of domain-specific autonomy based on the idea that people need choices in certain identifiable domains of life in order to be empowered.

10. For an in-depth look at the conversation about how to measure empowerment, consult Alkire (2007a), Alsop and Heinsohn (2005), Kabeer (1999), and Mahmud (2003).

11. A prominent exception to the trend of equating income and power is Sen's capability approach. See Sen (1999b).

12. Readers interested in the debate about whether microcredit empowers women should consult Poster and Salime (2002) and Rahman (2001).

13. Kabeer discusses a body of evidence suggesting that infusions of income do empower women against men, but she cautions that we should not expect infusions of income to empower women against men in societies where woman-headed households are not common or seen as desirable (1999, 460).

14. Kabeer's finding is consistent with a larger body of research that suggests that women microcredit recipients tend to participate in informal sector work that increases their work burdens (Poster and Salime 2002).

15. In her large-scale survey of the empirical data on microcredit, Kabeer argues that increased domestic violence is likely only a temporary effect of microcredit programs (1999). Kabeer's finding is consistent with a larger body of research that suggests that women microcredit recipients tend to participate in informal sector work that increases their work burdens (Poster and Salime 2002).

16. See for example, Ackerly (2000), Alkire (2006), Benhabib (1992), Gujit and Shah (1998), Mosse (1995), and Young (1997, 60–75 and 2002).

17. I use the word "proximate" here, because patriarchal social arrangements are certainly a deep underlying cause of negative relationships among women that Cornwall describes.

18. See Khader 2011.

REFERENCES

Abu-Lughod, Lila. 1990. The romance of resistance: Tracing transformations of power through Bedouin women. *American Ethnologist* 17(1): 41–55.

———. 1986. *Veiled sentiments: Honor and poetry in Bedouin society.* Berkeley: University of California Press.

Ackerly, Brooke. 2000. *Political theory and feminist social criticism.* Cambridge: Cambridge University Press.

Afkhami, Mahnaz. 1997. Claiming our rights: A manual for women's human rights education in Muslim societies. In *Muslim women and the politics of participation,* ed. Afkhami and Friedl, pp. 109–122. Syracuse: Syracuse University Press.

African HIV Policy Network. 2006. Sex: Who calls the shots? *African HIV Policy Network News Clippings, http://www.ahpn.org/news/clippings/index.php?clipping_id=68.*

Agarwal, Bina. 1997. Bargaining and gender relations: Within and beyond the household. *Feminist Economics* 3(1): 1–51.

Agot, Kawango. 2007. Women, culture and HIV/AIDS in sub-Saharan Africa: What does the empowerment discourse leave out. In *Global empowerment of women: responses to globalization and politicized religions,* ed. Carolyn M. Elliott, pp. 287–303. New York: Routledge.

Ahmed, Leila. 1982. Western ethnocentrism and representations of the harem. *Feminist Studies* 8 (Winter): 521–534.

———. 1993. *Women and gender in Islam.* New Haven: Yale University Press.

Al-Hibri, Azizah. 1999. Is Western patriarchal feminism good for third world/minority women? In *Is multiculturalism bad for women,* ed. Susan Moller Okin, pp. 41–47. Princeton, NJ: Princeton University Press.

Alkire, Sabina. 2005. *Valuing freedoms: Sen's capability approach and poverty reduction.* Oxford: Oxford University Press.

———. 2006. Public debate and value construction in Sen's approach. In *Capabilities equality: basic issues and problems,* ed. Kaufman, 133–150. New York: Routledge.

————. 2007a. *Concepts and measures of agency*. Oxford Poverty and Human Development Initiative Working Paper.

————. 2007b. Issues and possibilities in measuring agency. *Indian Journal of Human Development* 1(1): 169–175.

Alsop, Ruth, and Heinsohn, Nina. 2005. Measuring empowerment in practice: Structuring analysis and framing indicators. *World Bank policy research working paper No. 3510*.

American Anthropological Association. 1947. Statement on human rights. *American Anthropologist* 49(4): 539–543.

An-Na'im, Abdullahi. 1999. Promises we should all keep in common. In *Is multiculturalism bad for women*, ed. Susan Moller Okin, pp. 59–65. Princeton, NJ: Princeton University Press.

————. 2001. Human Rights in the Muslim World. In *The philosophy of human rights*, ed. Patrick Hayden, pp. 315–334. St. Paul: Paragon.

Anzaldua, Gloria. 1999. *Borderlands: La frontera*. San Francisco: Aunt Lute Books.

Apffel-Marglin, Frederique and Steven Marglin. 1996. *Decolonizing knowledge: from development to dialogue*. Oxford: Clarendon Press.

Apffel-Marglin, Frederique, and Loyda Sanchez. 2004. Developmentalist feminism and neocolonialism in Andean communities. *Feminist post-development thought: rethinking modernity, postcolonialism and representation*, ed. Kriemild Saunders, pp. 159–179. London: Zed Books.

Appadurai, Arjun. 2004. The capacity to aspire. In *Culture and public action*, eds. V. Rao and M. Walton, pp. 59–84. Palo Alto: Stanford University Press.

Agarwal, Bina. 1997. Bargaining and gender relations: Within the household and beyond. *Feminist Economics* 3(1):1–51.

Archer, David, and Sara Cottingham. 1996. *Action research report on reflect-education*. Research Paper: Overseas Development Administration.

Aristotle. 1998. *Nichomachean ethics*. Trans. J.L. Ackrill. Oxford: Oxford University Press.

Attwood, Gillian, Jane Castle, and Suzanne Smythe. 2005. "Women are lions in dresses": Negotiating gender relations in REFLECT literacy circles in Lesotho. In *Women, literacy, and development*, ed. Anna Robinson-Pant, pp. 35–56. New York: Routledge.

Aubel, Judi, Ibrahima Toure, Mamadou Diagne, Kalala Lazin, Sene El Hadj Alioune, Yirime Faye, and Tandia Mouhamadou. 2001. Strengthening grandmother networks to improve community nutrition: experience from Senegal. *Gender and Development* 9(2): 62–73.

Babbitt, Susan. 1993. Feminism and objective interests: The role of transformation experiences in rational deliberation. In *Feminist epistemologies*, ed. Linda Alcoff and Elizabeth Potter, pp. 245–265. New York: Routledge.

————. 2005. Stories from the South. *Hypatia* 20(3): 1–21.

Baber, H.E. 2007. Adaptive preference. *Social Theory and Practice* 33(1): 105–126.

Barroso, Monica Mazzer. 2002. Reading Freire's words: Are Freire's ideas applicable to Southern NGOs. *Center for Civil Society international working papers*. London: Center for Civil Society.

Batliwala, Srilatha. 2007. Taking the power out of empowerment. *Development in Practice* 17(5): 557–565.

Benhabib, Seyla. 1992. In the shadow of Aristotle and Hegel: communicative ethics and current controversies in practical philosophy. In *Situating the self*, pp. 23–67. New York: Routledge.

———. 2002. *The claims of culture*. Princeton, NJ: Princeton University Press.

Benson, Paul. 1987. Freedom and value. *Journal of Philosophy* 84(9): 465–486.

———. 2000. "Feeling Crazy: Self-Worth and the Social Character of Responsibility," in *Relational Autonomy: Feminist Perspectives on Autonomy, Agency, and the Social Self*, ed. C. Mackenzie and N. Stoljar (Oxford: Oxford University Press, 2000), 72–93.

Bewaji, J.A.I. 2006. Human rights: a philosophical analysis of Yoruba traditions. *Cambrian Law Review* 37: 49–72.

Bhavnani, Kum-Kum, John Foran, and Priya Kuria. 2003. *Feminist futures: Reimagining women, culture and development*. New York: Zed Books.

Boserup, Esther. 1970. *Women's role in economic development*. New York: Saint Martin's Press.

Brison, Susan. 1997. Outliving oneself: trauma, memory and personal identity. *Feminists rethink the self*, ed. Diana T. Meyers, pp. 12–39. Boulder, CO: Westview Press.

Buchanan, Allen. 2004. *Justice, legitimacy, and self-determination*. Oxford: Oxford University Press.

Card, Claudia. 2002. *The atrocity paradigm: A theory of evil*. Oxford: Oxford University Press.

Castle, Sarah, Sidy Traore, and Lalla Cisse. 2002. (Re)defining reproductive health with and for the community: an example of participatory research from Mali. *African Journal of Reproductive Health* 6(1): 20–31.

Chambers, Clare. 2007. *Sex, culture, and justice: The limits of choice*. State College: Penn State University Press.

Chambers, Robert. 1994. All power deceived. *IDS Bulletin*. 25(2): 14–26.

Chege, Jane Njeri, Ian Askew, and Jennifer Liku. 2001. An assessment of the alternative rites approach for encouraging abandonment of female genital mutilation in Kenya. In *Frontiers in reproductive health*. Washington DC: United States Agency for International Development.

Chirkov, Valery. 2007. Differentiating autonomy from individualism and independence: a self-determination theory perspective on internalization of cultural orientations and well-being. *Journal of Personality and Social Psychology* 84(1): 97–110.

Chopra, Priti. 2004. Distorted mirrors: (de)centering images of the illiterate Indian village woman through ethnographic research narratives. In *Women, literacy, and development,* ed. Anna Robinson-Pant, pp. 35–56. New York: Routledge.

Chossudovsky, Michel. 2003. *The globalization of poverty and the new world order.* Ontario: Global Outlook.

Christman, John. 1991. Autonomy and personal history. *Canadian Journal of Philosophy* 21: 1–24.

Christoffersen-Deb, Astrid. 2005. Taming tradition: medicalized female genital practices in western Kenya. Medical Anthropology Quarterly 19: 402–418.

Clark, David A. 2003. Concepts and perceptions of well-being: some evidence from South Africa. *Oxford Development Studies* 31(2): 173—196.

Clarke, Simon. 2006. Debate: state paternalism, neutrality, and perfectionism. *Journal of Political Philosophy* 14(1): 111–121.

COGWO, Nagaad, and WAWA. 2004. Knowledge, Attitudes, Beliefs and Practices of Female Genital Mutilation in Somalia/land: Novib Oxfam Netherlands.

Cohen, G.A. 1993. Equality of what? On welfare, goods, and capabilities. In *The quality of life,* ed. M. Nussbaum and A. G. Jonathan, pp. 9–29. Oxford: Clarendon Press.

Cohen, Joshua. 2004. Minimalism about human rights: the best we can hope for? *Journal of Political Philosophy* 12(2): 190–213.

Cornwall, Andrea. 2007a. Myths to live by? Female solidarity and female autonomy reconsidered. *Development and Change* 38(1): 149–167.

———. 2007b. Of choice, chance, and contingency: "career strategies" and tactics for survival among Yoruba women traders. *Social Anthropology* 15(1): 27–46.

Crocker, David. 2004. Cross-cultural criticism and development ethics. *Philosophy and Public Policy Quarterly* 24(3): 2–9.

———. 2008. *Ethics of global development: agency, capability, and deliberative democracy.* Cambridge: Cambridge University Press.

Darwall, Steven. 2004. *Welfare and rational care.* Princeton, NJ: Princeton University Press.

de Koning, Korrie. 1995. Participatory appraisal and education for empowerment. *PLA Notes* 24: 34–37.

Derrida, Jacques. 1978. Violence and metaphysics: An essay on the thought of Emmanuel Levinas. In *Writing and difference,* pp. 79–154. Chicago: University of Chicago Press.

Deveaux, Monique. 2002. What difference do differences make? *Social Theory and Practice* 23(3): 503–518.

———. 2003. A deliberative approach to conflicts of culture. *Political Theory* 31(6): 780–807.

Dworkin, Gerald. 1988. *The theory and practice of autonomy.* Cambridge: Cambridge University Press.

Eisenberg, Avigail. 2003. Diversity and equality: Three approaches to cultural and sexual difference. *Journal of Political Philosophy* 11(1): 41–64.

Elster, John. 1987. *Sour grapes: Studies in the subversion of rationality.* Cambridge: Cambridge University Press.

Escobar, Arturo. 1994. *Encountering development: the making and unmaking of the third world.* Princeton, NJ: Princeton University Press.

Feiner, Susan F., and Drucilla K. Barker. 2007. *Liberating economics: feminist perspectives on families, work, and globalization.* Ann Arbor: University of Michigan Press.

Feiner, Susan, and Drucilla Barker. 2007. "Microcredit and women's poverty." *The Dominion,* January 17. *http://www.dominionpaper.ca/articles/935.*

Feldman, Shelley. 2003. Paradoxes of institutionalisation: the depoliticization of Bangladeshi NGOs. *Development in Practice* 13(1): 5–26.

Ferguson, Ann. 1998. Resisting the veil of privilege: building bridge identities as an ethico-politics of global feminisms. *Hypatia* 13(3): 95–113.

Fermon, Nicole. 1998. Women on the global market: Irigaray and the democratic state. *Diacritics* 28(1): 120–137.

Ferraro, Kathleen J., and John M. Johnson. 1983. How women experience battering: the process of victimization. *Social Problems* 30(3): 325–329.

Finnis, J. 1980. *Natural law and natural rights.* Oxford: Clarendon Press.

Frankfurt, Harry. 1988. *The Importance of What We Care About.* Cambridge: Cambridge University Press.

Fraser, Nancy. 2008. *Scales of justice: re-imagining space in a globalizing world.* New York: Columbia University Press.

Friedman, Marilyn. 2003. *Autonomy, gender, politics.* New York: Clarendon Press.

Frye, Marilyn. 1983. Oppression. *The politics of reality.* Freedom, CA: The Crossing Press.

Gasper, Des. 2004. *The ethics of development.* Edinburgh: Edinburgh University Press.

Gibson, Christopher, and Michael Woolcock. 2008. Empowerment, deliberative development, and local-level politics in Indonesia: participatory projects as a source of countervailing power. *Studies in Comparative International Development.* 43(2): 151–180.

Goetz, Anne-Marie, and Rina Sen Gupta. 1996. Who takes the credit? Gender, power, and control over loan use in rural credit programs in Bangladesh. *World Development* 24(1): 45–63.

Greig, E.F., and C. Koopman. 2003. Multilevel analysis of women's empowerment and HIV prevention: quantitative survey results from a preliminary study in Botswana. *Aids and Behavior* 7: 195–208.

Groot, Annemarie and Marleen Maarleveld. 2000. Demystifying facilitation in participatory development. *Gatekeeper Series/International Institute for Environment and Development* 89.

Gruenbaum, Ellen. 2006. Sexuality issues in the movement to end female genital cutting in Sudan. *Medical Anthropology Quarterly* 20(1): 121–138.

Grown, Caren, G. Rao Gupta, Aslihan Kes, and Jeffery D. Sachs, eds. 2005. *Taking action: achieving gender equality and empowering women (UN Millennium Project).* London: Earthscan.

Gujit, Irene, and Meera Kaul Shah, eds. 1998. *The myth of community: gender issues in participatory development*. Warwickshire, UK: Practical Action Publishers.

Hadi, Abdulhallel. 2001. Effects of the public role of Bangladeshi women on their reproductive decisions. *Asia-Pacific Population Journal* 16(4): 21–30.

Hazarika, Gautam, and Sudipta Sarangi. 2008. Household access to microcredit and child work in rural Malawi. *World Development* 36(5): 843–859.

Heathwood, Chris. 2005. The problem of defective desires. *Australasian Journal of Philosophy* 83(4): 487–504.

Hickey, Sam, and Giles Mohan. 2004. *Participation: from tyranny to transformation*. London: Zed Books.

Hirshman, Mitu. 1995. Women and development: a critique. In *Feminism, postmodernism, development*, ed. M. Marchand and J. Parpart, pp. 42–55. London: Routledge.

Holvoet, Nathalie. 2005. The impact of microfinance on decision-making agency: evidence from South India. *Development and Change* 36(1): 75–102.

hooks, bell. 1994. Back to black: ending internalized racism. In *Outlaw culture*, pp. 173–183. New York: Routledge.

Hurka, Thomas. 1993. *Perfectionism*. New York: Oxford University Press.

Ibrahim, Solava, and Sabina Alkire. 2007. Agency and empowerment: a proposal for internationally comparable indicators. *Oxford Development Studies* 35(4): 379–403.

Ignatieff, Michael. 2003. *Human rights as politics and idolatry*. Princeton, NJ: Princeton University Press.

Irigaray, Luce. 1994. *Thinking the difference*. New York: Routledge.

Isbister, John. 2003. *Promises not kept: the betrayal of third-world development*. West Hartford, CT: Kumarian Press.

Iyengar, S. S., and Lepper, M. R. 1999. Rethinking the value of choice: a cultural perspective on intrinsic motivation. *Journal of Personality and Social Psychology 76*: 349–366.

Jaggar, Alison. 2002. A feminist critique of the alleged Southern debt. *Hypatia* 17(Fall): 119–142.

———. 2005a. Global responsibility and western feminism. In *Feminist interventions in ethics and politics*, ed. Barbara Andrew, Jean Keller, and Lisa Schwartzman, 185–200. Lanham, MD: Rowman and Littlefield.

———. 2005b. Saving Amina: global justice for women and intercultural dialogue. *Ethics and International Affairs* 19(Fall): 55–75.

———. 2006. Reasoning about well being: Nussbaum's methods of justifying the capabilities approach. *The Journal of Political Philosophy* 14(3): 301–322.

James, Stanlie M. 1998. Shades of othering: Reflections on female circumcision/female genital mutilation. *Signs* 23(2): 1031–1048.

Kabeer, Naila. 2001. Conflicts over credit: re-evaluating the empowerment potential of loans to women in rural Bangladesh. *World Development* 29(1): 63–84.

————. 1999. Resources, agency, achievements: Reflections on the measurement of women's empowerment. *Development and Change* 30(3): 435–464.

Kandiyoti, D. 1988. Bargaining with patriarchy. *Gender and Society* 2(3): 275–290.

Khader, Serene J. 2011. Beyond inadvertent ventriloquism: Caring virtues for participatory development. *Hypatia* 26:4. 1–21.

Kothari, U. 2001. Power, knowledge, and social control in participatory development. In *Participatory development: the new tyranny*, ed. B. Cooke and U. Kothari, pp. 139–152. London: Zed Books.

Kuper, Andrew. 2002. More than charity: Cosmopolitan alternatives to the Singer solution. *Ethics and International Affairs* 16(1): 107–128.

Kymlicka, Will. 1991. *Liberalism, community, and culture*. Oxford: Clarendon Press.

Levey, Ann. 2005. Liberalism, adaptive preferences, and gender inequality. *Hypatia* 20(4): 127–143.

Littman, David. 1999. Universal human rights in Islam. *Midstream* (February): 2–7.

Logister, Louis. 2007. Global governance and civil society: Some reflections on NGO legitimacy. *Journal of Global Ethics* 3(2): 165–179.

Lugones, Maria. 2003. *Pilgrimages/peregrinajes*. Lanham, MD: Rowman and Littlefield.

Luker, Kristen. 1975. *Taking chances: Women, abortion, and the choice not to contracept*. Berkeley: University of California Press.

MacKenzie, Catriona. 2000. Imagining oneself otherwise. In *Relational autonomy*, ed. C. MacKenzie and N. Stoljar, pp. 124–150. Oxford: Oxford University Press.

Mackie, Gerry. 2003. Female genital cutting: a harmless practice? *Medical Anthropology Quarterly* 17(2): 135–158.

Mandaleo Ya Wanawake. 2007. *FGM—Advocacy strategy for the eradication of female genital mutilation in Kenya*. Taver Network Solutions 2000, *http://www.maendeleo-ya-wanawake.org/*.

Mahmood, Saba. 2005. *Politics of piety*. Princeton, NJ: University of Princeton Press.

Mahmud, Simeen. 2003. How empowering is microcredit? *Development and Change* 34(4): 577–605.

Malhotra, Kamal. 2000. NGOs without aid: beyond the global soup kitchen. *Third World Quarterly* 21(4): 655–668.

Mann, Patricia. 1994. *Micropolitics: Agency in a postfeminist era*. Minneapolis: University of Minnesota Press.

Marcoux, Alain. 2002. Sex differentials in undernutrition: a look at survey evidence. *Population and Development Review* 28(2): 275–284.

McClure, Kerstie. 1992. On the subject of rights: pluralism, plurality, and plural identity. *Dimensions of radical democracy*, ed. Chantal Mouffe, pp. 108–127. London: Verso.

McIntosh, C. Allison, and Jason L. Finkle. 1995. The Cairo conference on population and development: a new paradigm? *Population and Development Review* 21(2): 223–260.

Meyers, Diana Tietjens. 1987. Personal autonomy and the paradox of feminine socialization. *The Journal of Philosophy* 84(11): 619–628.

———. 2000. Feminism and women's autonomy: the challenges of female genital cutting. *Metaphilosophy* 31: 469–491.

Mies, Maria. 1982. *Lacemakers in Narsapur: Indian housewives produce for the world market.* London: Zed Books.

Mill, John Stuart. 2002. *The basic writings of John Stuart Mill: On liberty, the subjection of women, and utilitarianism.* New York: Modern Library.

———. 2008. *On liberty and other essays.* Oxford: Oxford University Press.

Miller, Barbara D. 1997. Social class, gender, and intrahousehold food allocations to children in south Asia. *Social Science and Medicine* 44(11): 1685–1695.

Mogobe, Dintle. 2005. Denying and preserving self: Batswana women's experiences of infertility. *African Journal of Reproductive Health* 9(2): 26–37.

Mohanty, Chandra Talpade. 1995. *Feminist encounters: locating the politics of experience. Social postmodernism: Beyond identity politics*, ed. Linda Nicholson and Steven Seidman, pp. 68–86. Cambridge: Cambridge University Press.

———. 2003. "What's home got to do with it?" *Feminism without borders: decolonizing theory, practicing solidarity.* Durham, NC: Duke University Press.

Moreau, Sophia R. 2004. The wrongs of unequal treatment. *University of Toronto Law Journal* 54(3): 291–296.

Mosse, David. 1995. Authority, gender and knowledge: theoretical reflections on participatory rural appraisal. *Economic and Political Weekly* (May).

Mutua, Makau Wa. 1995. The Banjul charter and the African cultural fingerprint. *Virginia Journal of International Law* 35: 339–380.

Nagar, Richa. 2000. Mujhe jawab do! (Answer me!); women's grassroots activism and social spaces in Chitrakoot (India). *Gender, Place and Culture* 7(4): 341–362.

Nagar, Richa, and Saraswati Raju. 2003. Women, NGOs, and the paradoxes of empowerment and disempowerment. *Antipode* 35(1): 1–13.

Naples, Nancy. 2002. Transnational solidarity, women's agency, structural adjustment, and globalization. *Women's activism and globalization: linking local struggles and transnational politics*, ed. Nancy Naples and Manisha Desai, pp. 15–33. New York: Routledge.

Narayan, Deepa. 2000. *Voices of the Poor: Can Anyone Hear Us?* Oxford: Oxford University Press.

———. 2005. Conceptual frameworks and methodological challenges. *Measuring empowerment: Cross-disciplinary perspectives.* New York: World Bank Publications.

Narayan, Uma. 1997. *Dislocating cultures: identities, traditions, and third-world feminism.* New York: Routledge.

———. 1998. Essence of culture and a sense of history: a feminist critique of cultural essentialism. *Hypatia* 13(2): 86–106.

———. 2002. Minds of their own: Choices, autonomy, cultural practices, and other women. *A mind of one's own: Feminist essays on reason and objectivity*, ed. Louise M. Antony and Charlotte E. Witt, pp. 418–432. Boulder, CO: Westview Press.

Nussbaum, Martha C. 1992. Human functioning and social justice: in defense of Aristotelian essentialism. *Political Theory* 20(2): 202–246.

———. 1995. Human capabilities, female human beings. In *Women, culture, and development*, ed. Martha Nussbaum and Jonathan Glover, pp. 61–104. Oxford: Clarendon Press.

———. 1999. *Sex and social justice*. Oxford: Oxford University Press.

———. 2000. Aristotle, politics, and human capabilities: a response to Antony, Arneson, Charlesworth, and Mulgan. *Ethics* 111(1): 102–140.

———. 2001. *Women and human development: The capabilities approach*. Cambridge: Cambridge University Press.

Okin, Susan Moller. 1999. Is multiculturalism bad for women? In *Is multiculturalism bad for women*, ed. Susan Moller Okin, pp. 9–24. Princeton, NJ: Princeton University Press.

———. 2003. Poverty, well being, and gender: what counts and who is heard? *Philosophy & Public Affairs* 31(3): 280–316.

———. 1991. Susan Okin responds. In *Is multiculturalism bad for women?* ed. J. Cohen and M. Howard, pp. 115–132. Princeton, NJ: Princeton University Press.

Ong, Aihwa. 1987. *Spirits of resistance and capitalist discipline: factory women in Malaysia*. Albany: State University of New York Press.

Olsaretti, Serena. 2005. Endorsement and freedom in Amartya Sen's capability approach. *Economics and Philosophy* 21: 89–108.

Papanek, Hannah. 1990. To each less than she needs, from each more than she can do: allocations, entitlement, and value In *Persistent inequalities: women and world development*, ed. I. Tinker, pp. 162–185. Oxford: Oxford University Press.

Parekh, Bhikhu. 1999. A varied moral world. In *Is multiculturalism bad for women*, ed. S.M. Okin, J. Cohen, M. Howard, and M. Nussbaum, pp. 69–75. Princeton, NJ: Princeton University Press.

———. 2000. *Rethinking multiculturalism: cultural diversity and political theory*. Cambridge, MA: Harvard University Press.

Pettifor, Audrey E., Diana Measham, Helen V. Rees, and Nancy S. Padian. 2004. "Sexual power and HIV risk, South Africa." *Emerging Infectious Diseases, http://www.cdc.gov/ncidod/EID/vol10no11/04-0252.htm*.

Pettit, Phillip. 2000. *Republicanism: a theory of freedom and government*. Oxford: Oxford University Press.

———. 2001. Symposium on Amartya Sen's philosophy: 1 capability and freedom: A defence of Sen. *Economics and Philosophy* 17(1): 1–20.

Pogge, Thomas. 2002. *World poverty and human rights: cosmopolitan responsibilities and reforms*. New York: Polity.

Poster, Winifred, and Zakia Salime. 2002. The limits of microcredit: transnational feminism and USAID activities in the United States and Morocco. *Women's activism and globalization*, ed. Jennifer Naples and Manisha Desai, pp. 99–120. New York: Routledge.

Purkayastha, Bandana. 2002. Contesting multiple margins: Asian Indian activism in the early and late twentieth century. *Women's activism and globalization*, ed. Jennifer Naples and Manisha Desai, pp. 189–219. New York: Routledge.

Qizilbash, Mozaffar. 1996. Capabilities, well-being, and human development: a survey. *The Journal of Development Studies* 33(2): 143–162.

Rahman, Aminur. 2001. Women and Microcredit in Rural Bangladesh. Boulder: Westview

Rahnema, Majid. 1997. Development and the people's immune system: the story of another variety of AIDS. In *The post-development reader*, ed. M. Rahnema, pp. 111–134. London: Zed Books.

Rama Rao Pappu, S. 2005. Persons, rights, and dharma. In *India and human rights*, ed. T.S.N. Sastry, pp. 73–81. New Delhi: Concept Press.

Ramachandran, N. (2006) *Women and Food Security in South Asia: Current Issues and Emerging Concerns,* UNU Institute for Development Economics Research, Helsinki.

Rawls, John. 1971. *A theory of justice.* Cambridge, MA: Harvard University Press.

———. 1996. *Political liberalism, the John Dewey essays in philosophy.* New York: Columbia University Press.

Raz, Joseph. 1988. *The morality of freedom.* Oxford: Clarendon Press.

———. 1994. *Ethics in the public domain: essays in the morality of law and politics.* Oxford: Clarendon Press.

Risse, Mathias. 2005. Do we owe the global poor assistance of rectification? *Ethics and International Affairs* (19)1: 9–18.

Rose, Kalima. 1992. *Where women are leaders: the SEWA movement in India.* New Delhi: Vistar Publications.

Rowlands, Jo. 1997. *Questioning empowerment: working with women in Honduras.* Oxford: Oxfam Publications.

Saharso, Sawitri. 2000. Autonomy and the cultural imperative: two hearts beating together. In *Citizenship in diverse societies*, ed. Will Kymlicka and Wayne Norman, pp. 224–244. Oxford: Oxford University Press.

Scanlon, Thomas. 2003. *What we owe to each other.* Cambridge, MA: Harvard University Press.

Schutte, Ofelia. 2000. Cultural alterity: cross-cultural communication and feminist theory in North-South praxis. In *Decentering the center*, eds. Sandra Harding and Uma Narayan, pp. 47–67. Bloomington: Indiana University Press.

Schwartz, Barry. 2004. *The paradox of choice.* New York: Harper Perennial.

Sen, Amartya. 1984. *Resources, values and development.* Oxford: Basil Blackwell.

———. 1985. Well being, agency, and freedom: the Dewey lectures. *The Journal of Philosophy* 82: 169–221.

———. 1988. *On ethics and economics.* Malden, MA: Blackwell.

———. 1990. Gender and cooperative conflicts. *Persistent inequalities: women and world development*, ed. by I. Tinker, pp. 123–149. Oxford: Oxford University Press.

———. 1992. *Inequality re-examined*. Cambridge, MA: Harvard University Press.

———. 1997. "Human Rights and Asian Values". *The New Republic* July 14-July 21.

———. 1999a. Democracy as a universal value. *Journal of Democracy* 10(3): 3–17.

———. 1999b. *Development as freedom*. New York: Knopf.

———. 2002. *Rationality and freedom*. Cambridge, MA: Belknap Press.

Shiva, Vandana. 1988. *Staying alive: women, ecology, and development*. London: Zed Books.

Shaffer, Paul. 1998. "Gender and Deprivation: Evidence from the Republic of Guinea." World Development 26:12. 2119–2135.

Silberschmidt, Margarethe. 1992. Have men become the weaker sex? Changing life situations in Kisii District, Kenya. *The Journal of Modern African Studies* 30(2): 237–253.

Stoljar, Natalie. 2000. Autonomy and the feminist intuition. In *Relational autonomy: feminist perspectives on autonomy, agency, and the social self*, ed. C. Mackenzie and N. Stoljar, pp. 94–111. Oxford: Oxford University Press.

Street, Brian. 2005. Implications of the new literacy studies for researching women's literacy programs. In *Women, literacy, and development: alternative perspectives*. ed., Anna Robinson-Pant, pp. 57–67. New York: Routledge.

Sunstein, Cass. 1991. Preferences and politics. *Philosophy and Public Affairs* 20(1): 3–34.

———. 1995. Incompletely theorized agreements. *Harvard Law Review* 108(7): 1733–1772.

Superson, Anita. 2005. Deformed desires and informed desire tests. *Hypatia* 20(4): 109–126.

Sutherland, Ann, and Felicia Sakala. 2002. Using visual techniques to initiate discussions on gender violence in Zambia. In *Realizing rights: transforming approaches to sexual and reproductive well-being*. London: Zed Books.

Tabac, Lara. 2003. "Diary: A weeklong electronic journal with Lara Tabac." *Slate*, *http://www.slate.com/id/2088748/entry/2088987/*.

Tamir, Yael. 1999. Siding with the underdogs? In *Is multiculturalism bad for women*, ed. Susan Moller Okin, pp. 47–53. Princeton, NJ: Princeton University Press.

Teschl, M. and Comim, F. (2005) 'Adaptive preferences and capabilities: some preliminary conceptual explorations', *Review of Social Economy*, LXIII(2), pp. 230–246.

Tjaden, Patricia, and Nancy Thoennes. 1998. *Extent, nature, and consequences of intimate partner violence*. Centers for Disease Control and Prevention and National Institute for Justice.

Tobin, Theresa Weynand. 2007. On their own ground: strategies of resistance for Sunni Muslim women. *Hypatia* 22(3): 152–174.

UNIFEM, Progress of the World's Women 2000 (NewYork: UNIFEM, 2000), p. 31; available at www.unifem.org/attachments/products/153_chap1.pdf.

———. 2005. "Investing in women: Solving the poverty puzzle" http://www.women-fightpoverty.org/docs/WorldPovertyDay2007_FactsAndFigures.pdf

United Nations Development Program. 2009. *Millennium development goals: Goal 3: Promote gender equality and empower women,* *http://www.undp.org/mdg/goal3.shtml.*

Uyan-Semerci, Pinar. 2007. A relational account of Nussbaum's list of capabilities. *Journal of Human Development* 8(2): 203–221.

Varghese, Shiney. 1993. Women, resistance, and development. *Development in Practice* 3(1): 3–15.

Walzer, Michael. 1996. *Thick and thin: morality at home and abroad.* Notre Dame: University of Notre Dame Press.

Wells, Julia C. 2003. The sabotage of patriarchy in colonial Rhodesia: rural African women's living legacy to their daughters. *Feminist Review* 75: 101–117.

Young, Iris M. 1997. *Intersecting voices: dilemmas of gender, political philosophy and policy.* Princeton, NJ: Princeton University Press.

———. 2002. *Inclusion and democracy.* Oxford: Oxford University Press.

Yount, Katharyn M. 2002. Like mother like daughter: female genital cutting in Minia, Egypt. *Journal of Health and Social Behavior* 43(3): 336–358.

Ziai, Aram. 2004. The ambivalence of post-development: between reactionary populism and radical democracy. *Third World Quarterly* 25(6): 1045–1060.

Zurayk, Huda. 2001. The meaning of reproductive health for developing countries: the case of the Middle East. *Gender and Development* 9(2): 22–27.

INDEX

Printed in Great Britain
by Amazon